SKY BLUE REVOLUTION
Jimmy Hill at Coventry City
1961

Best wishes
Jim Brown

Best wishes
Ron Farmer

To Hugh
Best wishes
Dietmar Bruck

Best wishes
Mick Kearns

Best Wishes Hugh
Bob Wesson

JIM BROWN'S HISTORIES OF COVENTRY CITY BY DESERT ISLAND BOOKS

	ISBN
Coventry City: The Elite Era 1967-2001	978-1-874287-83-4
Coventry City: An Illustrated History	978-1-874287-59-9
Coventry City at Highfield Road	978-1-905328-53-6
Coventry City: The Seven-Year Itch 2001-2008	978-1-905328-44-4
Sky Blue Revolution: Jimmy Hill at Coventry City	978-1-905328-95-6

SKY BLUE REVOLUTION

JIMMY HILL AT COVENTRY CITY 1961-1967

Series editor: Clive Leatherdale

Jim Brown

DESERT ISLAND BOOKS

First published in 2011
by
DESERT ISLAND BOOKS LIMITED
32 Lascelles Gardens, Ashingdon, Rochford, Essex SS4 3BP
United Kingdom
www.desertislandbooks.com

© 2011 Jim Brown

The right of Jim Brown to be identified as author of this work has been asserted under The Copyright Designs and Patents Act 1988

British Library Cataloguing-in-Publication Data
A catalogue record for this book is available from the British Library

ISBN 978-1-905328-95-6

All rights reserved. No part of this book may be reproduced or utilised in any form or by any means, electronic or mechanical, including photocopying, recording or by any information storage and retrieval system, without prior permission in writing from the Publisher

Printed and bound in Great Britain by
4edge Ltd, Hockley. www.4edge.co.uk

Contents

		PAGE
	Acknowledgements	6
	Introduction	8
1	Prelude	10
2	1960-61: Robins in Charge	13
3	1961-62 (Part 1) The Gathering Storm	17
4	1961-62 (Part 2) Jimmy Hill Rides into Town	24
5	1962-63 (Part 1) A New Forward Line	37
6	1962-63 (Part 2) The Revolution Takes Off	49
7	1963-64 (Part 1) Counting Bantams	61
8	1963-64 (Part 2) Let's All Sing Together	69
9	1964-65 (Part 1) The Wheels are Wobbling (I)	79
10	1964-65 (Part 2) Time to Catch Breath	89
11	1965-66 (Part 1) The Sky Blue Special Pulls Out	96
12	1965-66 (Part 2) Hudson's Shock Departure	122
13	1966-67 (Part 1) The Wheels are Wobbling (II)	131
14	1966-67 (Part 2) We are the Champions	139
15	1967-68 The Top Division: JH Decides to Go	156
16	Post-Hill	165
	Appendix: Players Bought and Sold by Jimmy Hill	168
	Guide to Seasonal Summaries	169
	List of Subscribers	208

Acknowledgements

Just as I was completing this book I heard that Derek Henderson, the *Coventry Telegraph* football writer throughout the JH era had passed away. It was Derek who inspired me as a teenager to study the club's history and his match reports from the 1960s are a constant source of pleasure and an invaluable resource in chronicling the *Sky Blue Revolution*. 'Nemo,' which was his by-line for many years, kept City fans abreast of the news from Highfield Road in the era before multi-media and mass coverage of the sport. For most of his time reporting on the club he was the only source of news for supporters. In those days Derek travelled to away games on the team bus and had virtually unlimited access to the manager and players. He never abused that privilege and was always the soul of discretion. As far back as 1968 Derek allowed me access to his scrapbooks and the *Coventry Telegraph* archives, whch started my love affair with the club's history. I hope my version of the story meets his approval.

A word of thanks to Rod Dean, for his wonderful memories and his great friendship over the last 40-odd years. Barely a day has gone by in that time without contact of some kind, with news of the Sky Blues always top of the agenda.

Thanks, too, to numerous others who have given me assistance with the book, including, in no specific order: Ron Farmer, Dietmar Bruck, Bob Wesson, Bob Allen, Mick Dixon, Marshall Stewart, David Instone, Mike Young, Alan Ludford, Paul O'Connor, Nick Cook, Frank Pritchard, Tom Dentith, Kevin Monks, David Brassington, Don Chalk, Lionel Bird, Ian Nannestad, Joe Elliott, Peter Lea, Trevor Lloyd, Alan Poole (*Coventry Evening Telegraph*), Carl Newell and Nick Connell (Coventry City). I am sure there were others and if I have not mentioned you I apologise.

The majority of pictures used in the book were obtained from some of the above, and special thanks are due to Marshall Stewart, the author of *Miracle in Sky Blue*. Marshall, who worked on now-defunct Coventry newspapers in the 1950s and 60s, offered me some wonderful pictures from his collection. The holders of copyright on the remaining photographs are difficult to identify.

I have used many books in the course of my research but the following have been the most important:

Gary Imlach, *My father and Other Working-Class Football Heroes* (2005).
Marshall Stewart, *Miracle in Sky Blue* (1967).

Derek Henderson, *The Sky Blues: the Story of Coventry City FC* (1968).
David Brassington, Rod Dean, Don Chalk, *Singers to Sky Blues* (1985).
Jimmy Hill, *The Jimmy Hill Story* (1998).
Bobby Gould, *24 Carat Gould* (2010).
John Tudor, *King For A Day* (2010).
Jimmy Hill, *Striking for Soccer* (1961).

Thanks to my editor and publisher Clive Leatherdale of *Desert Island Books*. Clive's consistent support of football club histories and their authors remains as strong as ever, despite a book industry struggling to survive in the digital age. Many publishers specialising in this field have fallen by the wayside in recent years, but *Desert Island Books* continue to flourish, mainly, I believe, through Clive's professional approach, his attention to detail, and his passion for the subject. But for Clive's support it is highly unlikely that the history of Coventry City would have been as well-represented as it has.

Last but not least, thanks to my wonderfully supportive wife Doreen who has been loyal and patient with my obsession for too many years to mention.

Introduction

Fifty years ago Jimmy Hill changed my life. His arrival at Coventry in 1961 coincided with my growing interest in football and the need every young schoolboy has to support a team. From my first visit to Highfield Road in May 1962 for an end of season friendly with Burnley I was hooked. Jimmy Hill was the Pied Piper and the schoolboys of Coventry danced to his tune. To us he could do no wrong and even though some adult fans were occasionally critical, we boys trusted him implicitly. He revolutionised the club and took the city of Coventry with him on a magical mystery tour from the lower reaches of Division Three to the top level of English football for the first time ever.

Many years later I had the pleasure of meeting JH, donning my historian's hat quizzing him about his controversial decisions. Even though he was into his 80th decade, he charmed me with his charisma and made me realise why so many footballers played the best football of their careers under him. Whilst writing this book I have spoken to a large number of those players and have never heard a negative word spoken about him. Even players given a tough time, like Hudson and Gibson, are full of praise for the man and his motivational ability.

JH was the blueprint for modern managers – he was the first to be savvy with the media, ensuring his team were in the news all the time, something fans take for granted these days. His innovations at Coventry, and later in television, were groundbreaking and legendary.

Above all, though, he transformed Coventry City by building a football team that shot to the nation's notice with an exciting Cup run in 1963, and then won two promotions in four years. Hill did not suffer prima donnas. His was a team of honest, hard-working professionals whose motto could have been 'one for all and all for one'. The question that will never be answered is what might have happened had he stayed in 1967, instead of moving into the media. I am convinced that, given time, he would have consolidated the club's position in Division One and then achieved more success than did his successors. One former player told me: 'JH had the Midas touch – everything he touched turned to gold.' I am convinced his touch would have made Coventry a top-six side challenging for top honours in the 1970s.

As I write this introduction, a statue to the great man is being unveiled outside the Ricoh Arena in recognition of his huge achievements. The recognition is well deserved because Jimmy Hill will always be remembered as the greatest manager the club ever had.

JIM BROWN
July 2011

Chapter One

Prelude

In 1961 most Coventry City fans over the age of 40 could wax lyrically about the club's golden period before the Second World War. The old saying went 'but for the war'; in City's terms that meant that if the war had not intervened the club would have reached the First Division with the outstanding side assembled by manager Harry Storer.

The facts are compelling. Storer's team won the Third Division South in 1936 with a solid defence marshalled by captain George Mason, described by some as the best English uncapped centre-half of the era, and an old-fashioned attack with lively wingers, two outstanding inside-forwards, Les Jones and Jock Lauderdale, and the most prolific goalscorer in the club's history, Clarrie Bourton. Goals flowed and the crowd's shout of 'Come on the Old Five' stemmed from the regularity of the side scoring five or more goals in a game, especially at Highfield Road.

After a season of consolidation in the higher division in 1936-37, when the team finished eighth, promotion should have been achieved the following year. After a fifteen-game unbeaten start, the team eventually finished fourth, one point short of their dream, let down for once by a lack of a prolific goalscorer, the ageing Bourton having faded in the higher division.

In 1938-39 the team again finished fourth, but it was a fitful season with attendances slipping as supporters' expectations were not fulfilled. Many thought the chance of First Division football had gone. On reflection, the club had made massive strides during the 1930s and given their followers some great moments. But ever-upward progress had stalled and fans had taken the club's success for granted.

In 1945, as the war drew to a close, the architect of the 1930s' success, Harry Storer, decided his ambitions could be achieved better down the A45 at St Andrews, and in the first post-war league season, 1946-47, he took the Blues into Division One.

At Highfield Road the club was grappling with the effects of the 1940 blitz, an ageing team, and serious financial difficulties. The first two seasons were disappointing. In 1948-49 a poor start set alarm bells ringing and manager Billy Frith was sacked after only eighteen months in charge – replaced by Harry Storer, the prodigal son returned from Birmingham.

Storer was regarded as the saviour when he lifted the team clear of relegation, and after a season of reconstruction he made a serious assault on promotion in 1950-51. Playing exciting, attacking football once again, City topped the table at Christmas and promotion talk filled the air. Sadly it was a false dawn. A disastrous slump cost them a promotion place and they finished a disappointing seventh. The slump continued into 1951-52 and Storer's ageing team (five of the side had made their debuts before the war) was relegated to Division Three after nine seasons in the higher division.

For the next six years the Bantams promised much but achieved little and floundered in Division Three South. Storer laboured on as manager for another eighteen months, forced to sell some of his best players to balance the books, but after his departure in November 1953 the management roundabout saw six further managers in five years. Boardroom politics dominated the scene, with stormy shareholders' meetings and mass resignations of directors. There was a brief period of excitement in 1955 when new chairman Erle Shanks pulled off a coup by persuading AS Roma's English coach, Jesse Carver, to become manager. The smartly dressed, tanned Carver arrived in a blaze of publicity, promising to play attacking football, but found the hard grind of Division Three too much and within six months was lured back to Italy's Serie 'A'.

In 1956-57 Coventry finished sixteenth, their lowest placing since 1928, and new manager Harry Warren struggled to raise performance levels. Once again the club's star man, this time England international goalkeeper Reg Matthews, was sold to reduce the debts and a watershed season loomed.

Rod Dean sums up what it was like to be a young Coventry fan in those depressing days: 'A decade of no real hope, certainly no hope of promotion back to the Second Division and constant taunts from school chums. However, it was a steep learning curve for a ten-year-old who was certain he was supporting a great football team, and at the start of every season believed chairman Erle Shanks when he was quoted as stating "Promotion this season is our aim!" When I moved up to Leamington College in 1957 I seriously hoped that at last I would meet up with hordes of City fans with whom I would be able to spend hours talking up City's prospects – what a shock I received when after a couple of years or so I counted about half a dozen other supporters in a school of 570 boys. Sadly we were totally swamped by those of the "Big Four"; Villa, Blues, Albion and Wolves, who were fixtures in the First Division and easy to get to by train or coach from Leamington.'

In 1958 the Football League voted to scrap the regionalised Third Division: the bottom halves of the old divisions would now form a new Fourth Division. The Bantams did not wish to be 'relegated' to the new division, but a poor start made it an uphill struggle to pull out of what became known as the 'disaster half'. The board acted, sacking Warren and re-engaging Billy Frith, ten years after he had been sacked.

Frith was unable to avoid 'relegation' but built an exciting cut-price team and twelve months later pulled the club out of Division Four at the first time of asking. Frith's team was a mixture of experienced campaigners, like Ray Straw, Roy Kirk and Paddy Ryan, and promising youngsters, like George Curtis, Mick Kearns and Brian Hill. The key signings in mid-season of Ron Farmer and Arthur Lightening strengthened the team and both of them, and the aforementioned youngsters, would go on to play under Jimmy Hill.

Frith was determined to make it two promotions in a row and regain a Second Division place. With an enviable home record, the team stayed in touch until Easter 1960, when three defeats cost them dearly and they finished fifth.

The promotion near-miss had been a gamble that failed. In March, Frith had persuaded the directors that inside-forward Ron Hewitt would be the man to boost the promotion push. However, with no money in the coffers, chairman Walter Brandish and his fellow directors clubbed together to find the £4,000 to pay for Hewitt.

With another season in Division Three, and attendances plummeting at Highfield Road, and to be fair, around the country generally, the club was on the brink once again.

Chapter 2

1960-61: Robins in Charge

The Sky Blue revolution can be traced back to 18 October 1960. Then, sixteen games into the season, with Coventry City languishing in eighteenth place in Division Three with only four wins from sixteen matches, chairman Walter Brandish Jnr stepped down and was replaced by Derrick Robins. Forty-eight hours earlier, Brandish, whose father, also Walter Brandish, had been chairman in the 1930s and whose family ran the profitable Vauxhall dealership in the city, had admitted to a local journalist that he was 'worried sick about the financial position'.

The club had suffered losses of around £10,000 in the previous two seasons, gaining promotion from Division Four in 1958-59 and having a good stab at a second promotion in 1959-60, and Brandish wasn't prepared to bankroll the club any more. The directors had pinned their hopes on a share offer earlier in the year which had intended to raise £21,000, but disappointingly less than £10,000 was subscribed, and Brandish had probably run out of financial ideas.

Attendances had also dropped dramatically in the autumn of 1960 from the previous season's average of over 16,000. The most recent home game, versus Southend, had attracted only 7,422, compared to the 28,000 who had watched the vital promotion game with Norwich the previous April, and the 18,000 present at the opening league game the following August. The Southend gate had prompted Brandish's comments, and the opportunistic Robins saw his chance of power.

The Kent-born Robins had served as a major in the Army during the war. After being demobbed he had taken a job as a cake salesman before establishing a successful building firm, Portable Concrete Buildings, specialising in prefabricated garages and sheds, which later became Banbury Buildings. Robins was truly a self-made man.

Cricket, however, was his first sport. Although not good enough to make a career of the game he did, after two outings for Warwickshire in 1947, become a prominent cricketer in local circles during the 1950s, playing for Coventry and North Warwickshire as a wicket-keeper. Later he helped organise the Eastbourne cricket festival and had his own team – the DH Robins XI, which played prestigious games against the touring test teams in the 1960s.

Robins' football pedigree was less impressive – he supposedly played in the Kent Amateur Leagues before the war, and during it played in goal for South-Eastern Command against the Navy. He had joined the Coventry City board in 1954 following an invitation from chairman Erle Shanks, a Coventry timber merchant with whom Derrick had business connections at that time.

In his six years on the board, Robins had kept a low profile but now, with his business booming, he could see a way to improve his profile and, although it was not apparent at the time, earn his company lucrative contracts for the Highfield Road rebuilding project.

The club statement read: 'In view of the difficult time through which the club is passing, the board of directors has to give serious consideration to new financial plans. As part of the reorganisation Mr Derrick H Robins, who is prepared to help in this respect, has been appointed chairman. Mr Walter Brandish, the retiring chairman, will of course, continue as a director and becomes vice-chairman. Two additional directors have been elected. They are Mr G H Smart and Mr J W Stevenson.'

Unlike the reticent Brandish, Robins was a master at public relations, ever ready to speak to the press, knowing that publicity was a sure way to win back fans and keep Coventry City's name in the spotlight. On the day of his promotion he gave an exclusive interview to the *Coventry Evening Telegraph*'s 'Nemo' (Derek Henderson) in which he outlined the options for the club to escape from its predicament.

'There are only three ways out – to sell players, borrow money, or boost the pool. We cannot take the first two, so the third [option] is the logical answer. While I can bridge the gap, it is essential that the weekly pool is revitalised. By imagination and drive we can put an entirely new complexion on it.' By talking of bridging the gap, he presumably meant lending the club money or guaranteeing an overdraft.

The weekly pool referred to was a money-raising venture pioneered by Warwickshire Cricket Club and tried at Coventry City with little success. 'Punters' were encouraged to 'play the pools' with the cricket club rather than the traditional pools companies like Littlewoods and Vernons. Local commission rewarded agents, who would collect weekly monies from punters, and the profits from the pool would go to the cricket club rather than to the privately-run pools companies.

Prizes were attractive and contestants had the added bonus of their cricket club (or their football club) enjoying the benefits. Robins had witnessed the benefits of the pool at Edgbaston in Birmingham, in the shape of building projects to cement the ground's status as a Test match venue, and he saw the pool idea as Coventry City's salvation, especially as the football club arguably had more potential supporters than Warwickshire CCC.

2. 1960-61 ROBINS IN CHARGE

In the same interview Robins talked about Billy Frith, describing him as 'among the best six managers in the country. I am sure we can cooperate very well. There is a lot of hard work ahead but we can do it. If Bill decides he wants the side strengthened, the money will be found.' After finishing fifth the previous season, Frith had been awarded a four-year contract.

Two days later Frith and Robins travelled to Chester to sign Scottish international winger Stewart Imlach. Imlach, who had represented his country at the 1958 World Cup and starred for Nottingham Forest in the 1959 FA Cup final, had left Forest in the summer to join Luton, but things were not working out and a move back to the Midlands suited him and his family. City paid Luton £8,000 and Imlach debuted against another of his former clubs, Bury, the following day. City lost their unbeaten home record to the league leaders, 1-2, but better times were around the corner for Frith's team.

Following the Bury defeat, City went eighteen games through to early March losing only twice. The run included 30 goals in eight home wins out of nine. The team's finest moment probably came in a third round FA Cup-tie at Anfield when the team pulled level from 0-2 down, only to have a lucrative replay snatched away by a third Liverpool goal.

Weeks after Robins' elevation, the supporters' club handbook was published. Robins used it to outline his ambitious, but still vague, plans for improvement. He mentioned 'many things we have to do, the chief of which is to improve the accommodation for the spectators, level the playing pitch, which could well include underground heating, cover the Spion Kop and, indeed, more cover generally'. He observed that the old stand (built in 1910) would not last for ever, but prefixed the whole piece with the 'fundamental' aim, which was to put the club's finances on a sounder basis 'than has been the case in the past'.

Robins stressed that the club was losing £250 per week, which had the effect of putting all the pipedreams for the ground, not to mention team strengthening, into perspective. He put meat on the bones of the pool plans, announcing a Bantams Fighting Fund to generate extra income for the club. The retiring club captain Paddy Ryan would run the scheme.

The club's winter form in 1960-61 was possibly helped by the poor state of the Highfield Road pitch after the wettest autumn since the war. In his match report for the Tranmere game in November, 'Nemo' describes a surface 'more suited to a hippopotamus' and questioned the sense in playing: 'Spectators pay to see football, not 22 grown men floundering like helpless ducks in a farmyard morass.' Another key factor was the return from injury of Ron Hewitt. The former Welsh international might not have been the fastest player at the club, but he had skill and could strike the ball with power. Ron was badly missed in the autumn.

In January 1961 Jimmy Hill appeared on Robins' radar for probably the first time when the Professional Footballers Association (PFA), of which Hill was chairman, threatened strike action over wages and freedom of contract. Robins was vehemently against a strike, describing the PFA's threats as 'crass stupidity'. After players with southern clubs voted for a strike, which would have forced postponements, he tried to stop the midland vote going the same way.

Whilst not naming Hill, there was no doubt who Robins referred to when he said: 'I gather the impression that the majority of the players at yesterday's meeting didn't want to strike but were swayed by one man. It may suit that one man to have a strike but the vast majority of footballers know that a strike is not in the best interests of themselves or their clubs.' The bulk of the Coventry first team, addressed by Ron Hewitt, the PFA representative, affirmed its support for Hill's cause, but strike action was averted at the eleventh hour and many demands of the players were met, including the removal of the weekly £20 maximum wage. Less than a year later Robins would appoint 'that man' as his manager.

After the excellent winter form the season petered out, with just three wins from the last fourteen games. The club finished fifteenth, having touched eighth in February. Gates dwindled and there were under 8,000 for the final home game against Swindon. Another season of hope, ambition and disappointment had gone, and when the season ended the only conclusion to be reached was that the team had gone backwards. No further signings had been made and Frith's best team was virtually the same that had started the campaign, with the half-back line of Kearns-Curtis-Farmer virtually ever-present, as they would be over the next six eventful years. In that Swindon game Dietmar Bruck, aged seventeen years and nine days, became the third youngest player to appear for the club, evidence of Frith's insistence on a strong youth policy.

During the 1961 close season Robins set about improving the Highfield Road ground. Years later he was quoted as saying: 'It had a terrible entrance to it and the whole place seemed to cry out "Don't come in". I felt we needed a smart entrance to make people feel welcome, plus a decent manager's office and boardroom. So I told the other directors "You put in what you can afford and I'll make up the rest". From then on we were pulling together. I also said that no director must charge a farthing to the club.' A new façade was built for the main stand, incorporating a new directors' entrance and modern air-ventilated offices, including a dedicated office for the pools team.

Chapter 3. 1961-62 (Part 1)

The Gathering Storm

Finances dominated boardroom discussions at Highfield Road in the summer of 1961. After reasonably successful experiments with a handful of Friday night home games in 1960-61, the club took the radical decision to stage nine Friday night games in 1961-62. Chairman Robins believed that the club could get bigger crowds on a Friday night. Likewise, all reserve-team games would be played on midweek evenings instead of the traditional Saturday afternoons.

Early reports from the money-raising pools was positive; weekly profit had increased from £180 to £700 during the season, and in addition the supporters' club (a valuable source of funds for ground improvements since the 1920s) handed over a cheque for £7,000 in August to be used for further ground improvements. The newer pool, the Bantam Fighting Fund, made an unspecified donation directly to the club.

Three signings were made by Frith in the summer – 30-year-old winger Mike Grice arrived from West Ham for £6,000, and two players were signed from Luton. Young inside-forward Albert McCann joined for a 'four-figure sum' and 23-year-old centre-forward Mike Dixon came on a free transfer. The blond Grice had played in West Ham's Second Division promotion team in 1958 and was described as 'a fast winger with a strong shot'.

Two City players were in dispute over their contracts. Mick Kearns, halfway through his two-year National Service in the Army, was only being paid £1 per week and £6 appearance money – in line with Football League regulations. However, when the club learned of the removal of the cap on appearance money, the situation was resolved to Kearns' benefit. The other player in dispute was long-serving defender Frank Austin, the only remaining player from the legendary Modern Machines football team (City's youth team in all but name) from the late 1940s. Austin refused City's terms when they refused to allow him to play part-time, and he took a job in a Leamington factory. After discussions with Frith, Austin signed his contract for another year.

Austin's reluctance to sign had given Frith a potential headache, as his other left-back was Don Bennett, one of the last of a breed who played first-class football and cricket. Bennett was a key man for Middlesex in the summer game, but unless Middlesex were involved in the county cricket championship race he would be expected to be available to play for City from the start of the season. That summer, Middlesex, boasting a strong first XI that included England test players Peter Parfitt, John Murray and Freddie Titmus, were in contention for the title and it was already clear that Bennett would not be available to play for City until mid-September.

Two weeks before the start of the season City dropped a bombshell by selling leading scorer Ray Straw to Mansfield. Frith had talked up Straw's importance to his plans, and one has to wonder whether Frith was involved in the decision to sell the player. The proceeds, according to the *Coventry Evening Telegraph* would go towards paying for Grice. The previous season Straw had gone through a bad patch and been dropped, but bounced back and scored twenty goals from 37 games. Added to his 65 goals in the previous three seasons, this meant he was the club's leading post-war goalscorer and would be difficult to replace.

On the eve of the season City's board was expanded with the addition of former journalist and Leamington travel agent John Camkin. His role at the club would be press liaison officer, and after his appointment he commented: 'I have seen developments in the big clubs abroad which may be of some use to Coventry in the future.' Camkin's influence at the club over the next few years would be immense.

In his preview of the season on 12 August 'Nemo' described City's team as 'one of the strongest, on paper, in the division' and was confident of City's chances: 'if City can gather in the points on their travels I think they will be in at the kill next April. If not … well draw your own conclusions.'

City opened the season at Reading's Elm Park with an embarrassing 0-4 defeat, Frith afterwards ordering the players in for Sunday morning training. Two days later the first home game, against Swindon, attracted a pitiful crowd of 13,761, well below the supposed 'break-even' figure of 16,000 and the lowest 'opening' crowd since 1953. Swindon were beaten 2-1 but it was unconvincing. Four nights later a Grice brace helped City to a comfortable win over Newport, with debut boy Mike Dixon thrilling the fans with an all-action display. A 3-3 draw at Swindon and a 3-1 home win over Halifax put a gloss on what had been an inauspicious start.

When the club's accounts were published early in the season they disclosed a loss of £11,500. That figure would have been worse but for a £5,000 donation from the supporters' club. The accounts also showed an increased overdraft to £8,000, partly guaranteed by a director, presumably Robins, and interest-free loans of £5,800 from directors.

Robins repeated his determination to run the club on a firm financial basis. It was announced that Walter Brandish Jnr had resigned from the board after 26 years as a director, less than a year after relinquishing the chairmanship. Brandish was made president of the club, a vacant position since Lord Kenilworth relinquished the role earlier in the year.

On 13 September the team suffered an embarrassing 0-3 League Cup exit at Fourth Division Workington. 'Nemo' described City's players as 'complacent', 'sluggish' and 'half-paced'. The League Cup may have been a new, Cinderella competition, but victory could have earned a lucrative tie with a First or Second Division club. In his book *The Sky Blues* Derek Henderson suggests that this result was the catalyst for Robins to start the search for a new manager.

Days later, for the trip to Shrewsbury, Frith reacted by dropping five players – Kletzenbauer, Austin, Nicholas, Hewitt and Myerscough – and handing debuts to seventeen-year-old full-back Bill Tedds and new man McCann. For Tedds it completed a meteoric rise, as he had been a regular for the 'A' team the previous season and impressed in the first three reserve games of the season. The revamped side got a plucky point at Gay Meadow but lost to bottom club Brentford in midweek. The unbeaten home record went next, to newly promoted Peterborough. Posh's noisy fans boosted the crowd to almost 20,000, the biggest for almost eighteen months, and although George Curtis stopped the prolific Terry Bly from scoring, Bly's team-mates clinically ripped City apart and fully deserved their 3-1 victory.

Two days later the home crowd was down to 10,000 as Brentford were dispatched 2-0, and a mini-run of five games without defeat earned seven points to keep City in mid-table. The fans, though, were voting with their feet and there were under 7,500 to see Bradford on Tuesday night, the smallest crowd since 1958, and barely 8,000 turned up for the next home game, Barnsley, on a Friday night. From time to time City's so-called 'stars' did turn on the style, finally winning at Lincoln and thumping a mediocre Bradford 3-0, but the form was inconsistent and the rare gems did not fool the fans.

At the AGM in late September, Robins reported a club debt to the tune of £62,000, but spoke of the promising results from the pools business and reiterated his desire to put the club on a firmer financial footing. He told shareholders that he had informed Frith that there was no money for new players (a volte-face from a year earlier) and that the manager would have to work with the players he had, many of whom he still believed were among the best in the division. Shareholders criticised the club's coaching, and Alan Higgs (father of future club director Derek Higgs) warned that Frith had been appointed almost four years ago to the day, but Second Division football was as far away as it ever had been.

It wasn't only the first team suffering. In the first week in October, City's youth team were eliminated from the FA Youth Cup by Aston Villa at Highfield Road. Few expected a City win but Villa's margin of victory, 9-1, was humiliating. Villa's centre-forward, Ralph Brown, led the annihilation with seven goals for a team which featured young George Graham, ex-Coventry schoolboy Graham Parker, and four players who had already appeared in the First Division. City's team, including future stars Dietmar Bruck, Ronnie Rees and fifteen-year old Bobby Gould, were totally out of their depth.

In early November, whilst attending the Lord's Taverners Ball at the Grosvenor Hotel in London, as a guest of former England cricketer Jim Laker, Derrick Robins had a chance meeting with Jimmy Hill. England team manager Walter Winterbottom, a friend of Hill's, introduced them and they hit it off immediately, chatting at length about football and Robins' other passion, cricket. By the end of the evening Robins was convinced he had met the man who could put his new ideas for a football club into practice.

At Highfield Road team morale was low but the FA Cup seemed to offer a lifeline to a season rapidly going downhill, not to mention a financial boost. After a first round win over Gillingham, Frith greeted the home pairing against Southern League King's Lynn with confidence: 'It looks as though our luck with the draw has changed. While no cup-tie is easy, it looks as though we have a reasonable chance of getting through.' His confidence was misplaced.

A week later, Cup defeat by King's Lynn brought an end to Frith's second spell in charge. 'Nemo' described it as Black Saturday and 'probably the most grim page in City's modern history'. Only captain George Curtis was exempted from scathing criticism: 'City's strolling attitude to this whole tie was not just dangerously complacent, it was sheer folly.'

Despite City taking the lead through an own-goal, the Linnets quickly bounced back with two goals. 'Wait until the second half, class will tell,' was the cry at half-time. But City's pathetic efforts proved fruitless and King's Lynn, bottom of the Southern League with only three league wins all season, progressed to the third round. Lynn manager Len Richley was serious when he said: 'It wasn't as hard a fight as we expected.' At the final whistle the ground was virtually empty; only about 1,000 hardy souls stayed to the bitter end. Afterwards Frith and Alf Wood were spotted by 'Nemo' in the corridor outside the dressing room: 'They were standing together, both looking at the floor – stunned and speechless.'

On the Monday, Robins tried to put a brave face on things: 'It was an utterly disastrous result but let's not get it out of proportion. It is a game and these things happen.' A sanguine Frith ruled out an inquest: 'What's the point in holding one when we know what happened?'

Robins had, in fact, decided to sack Frith before the King's Lynn debacle, but poor Frith set off the following afternoon with the reserves for an evening game at Brighton, 130 miles away. In those largely pre-motorway days it would have taken a good three or four hours to get home from the Goldstone Ground. The reserves won 2-1, which would have cheered Frith up, but he was probably a little jaded when he arrived at Highfield Road on Wednesday morning to check the status of his injured players and saw Robins' Rolls Royce parked outside. Robins had come to carry out the culling of Frith and his backroom staff.

Dietmar Bruck played at Brighton and remembers the events well: 'Billy Frith didn't come home with us on the coach; he had his car. It was a dreadful foggy night and Peter Hill was in charge of us and we wanted to stop in a hotel for the night but he said the club couldn't afford it. We crawled home and stopped at a motorway service station until the fog cleared. We didn't get home until 10 o'clock in the morning. I was in bed when my next-door neighbour woke me to say I had to report to Highfield Road at 2.30 that afternoon. I caught the bus to the ground and at 2.30 we all filed into the dressing room and in walked the chairman, Derrick Robins, and Jimmy Hill. He introduced himself and said we weren't to call him Mr Hill, nor Boss, nor Gaffer, but JH. He told us to get our training gear on and get on the pitch and he stripped off and we had a practice match.'

This was big news and an official press statement was flashed to radio, television and the national and local newspapers. Jimmy Hill had been appointed with immediate effect. Forty-nine-year-old Frith was sacked, along with his chief scout Arthur Jepson, the former Stoke and Port Vale goalkeeper, Nottinghamshire cricketer and Test match umpire; so were the club's trainers Alf Wood and Ted Roberts, both of whom were former City playing colleagues of Frith under Harry Storer.

A shell-shocked Frith emerged to meet the press and was as ever the true gentleman. He said: 'You become cynical with the way football is run these days, and I have become a fatalist. It looks as if football is finished with me. This is the second time Coventry have sacked me – and this time I don't feel bitter.' He went on to say: 'I've got to have all my papers and things out of here by noon, and I must tell my wife before she reads it in the papers.' His contract, which ran until 1964, was honoured in full.

Long-serving Alf Wood had been a brave goalkeeper who had made his Coventry debut before the Second World War. Towards the end of the war he contracted spinal meningitis and it was feared he would never play again. He recovered, however, and went on to make 260 consecutive appearances over the next six seasons. In 1952, aged 36, he was considered to be past his best. He moved to Northampton and was a regular at the County Ground for four years until he returned to City as assistant trainer. In 1958, at the age of 43, following injuries, Alf was recalled to play twelve first-team games, of which City only lost two. On being sacked, a bitter Wood gave the press a tactless but powerful quote: 'We're the victims of results. We have been trying to teach cart-horses to be footballers.' When asked if he would be going to the game on Saturday he said he would probably go, but only because it was against his old club Northampton and added: 'Frankly I feel rather bitter about Coventry City after this, and I wouldn't go near the place for any other reason.'

In a press conference later that day, Robins praised the four sacked men, describing them as 'great servants' and saying the decision to sack them was one of the hardest decisions he had ever made.

A club statement from secretary Bernard Hitchiner revealed that Robins had approached Hill the previous Wednesday. Hill had been at the King's Lynn game. Describing the events of that time in his autobiography, Hill says:

'I was invited to Derrick Robins' house in Leamington alongside the cricket ground ... and [over lunch] the subjects varied from the potential of a football club in the city of Coventry to Derrick's enthusiasm for the game of cricket, and not least his intention to turn Coventry City Football Club into something worthwhile. The question was put, might I like to become manager?

'At the end of the afternoon, I promised to think it over during the coming week and was invited to their home match ... against ... King's Lynn. For a number of reasons it was thought prudent to keep my intended visit to Highfield Road a secret. A ticket for the far stand arrived in the post, not the stand in which the directors' box was situated. I sneaked into my seat, tucked my collar up around my ears and pulled a trilby hat well down over my forehead in the hopes that few people would notice me ... not easy with a nationally known chin, and here and there came acknowledgements, and stifled gasps of surprise that I should be at Highfield Road, the reason not easy for them to detect.'

In the modern day of Facebook and Twitter, a celebrity like Hill's presence at a game would have been communicated to all and sundry by Saturday evening, but it is clear that Frith had no inkling of what was coming.

On the day following the King's Lynn defeat, Hill telephoned Robins to tell him he had decided to accept his offer. Robins had assumed that the appalling performance would have dissuaded Hill from taking the job. Hill, who later said he had been courted by several clubs prior to Coventry's approach, insisted that he be given the power to appoint his own coaching staff. Thus began a partnership that would take Coventry City from Third Division strugglers to the First Division in five exciting seasons.

Hill, it was announced, would give up his role as chairman of the Professional Footballers Association and resign from a job he had taken only weeks before with Harvey Bagenal, the London-based sports agent. A disappointed Bagenal was mollified by winning Hill as a client, a relationship which lasted many years.

The Sky Blue revolution was under way.

Chapter 4. 1961-62 (Part 2)

Jimmy Hill Rides into Town

Jimmy Hill's roots were in Balham, South London, not so far from Kent, where Derrick Robins hailed from. The two men appeared to share similar values. Hill had been a bright child and had attended a grammar school after passing the eleven-plus exam. Like most other players of his era, Jimmy had begun his working life in a 'real' job, but whilst most of his contemporaries would have either been apprenticed to a trade or have worked in heavy industry before reaching the age of seventeen and turning professional, Hill had worked as a stockbroker's clerk in the City of London, and later for an insurance company. This background set him apart from other players of his era and perhaps helped explain how he was able to rise to become chairman of the PFA, a role he still held when appointed as the Coventry manager.

Fresh from his successful battle in defeating the maximum wage, Hill was already thinking about the future of the game and the direction he wished it to take. In his book *Striking for Soccer*, published in 1961, he devoted a chapter to what he saw as the way forward. His vision of the future included a 'Super League', floodlit football, a winter break, improved spectator facilities, modernisation of training methods, coaching of players, and a live televised match to be shown every Friday evening. Fifty years later, with the exception of the winter break, these ideas have all become accepted and are an integral part of the game.

As a player, despite being rejected by Reading after a spell on their books just after the war, Hill was not disheartened and earned a contract at Brentford. Tom Dentith, a long-time City fan, remembers seeing Hill in Brentford colours at Highfield Road in the late 1940s: 'I remember Jimmy playing because they had a big away contingent who stood by us on the Kop and they didn't have a good word to say about him. It was the first time I had heard a player being barracked by his own fans.'

For most of his playing days Hill was the butt of the crowd, but after his move to Fulham in the early 1950s the admirers began to outnumber the barrackers. He was known for his boundless energy on the pitch – no player ran as far in a match as Jimmy – an attribute demanded after his playing days were over. Nicknamed 'the Rabbi' by Fulham fans, he built up a great understanding with Johnny Haynes, a future England captain, and helped Fulham to promotion to the First Division for the first time in 1959. One of his greatest claims to fame was scoring five goals in an away match at Doncaster. Ron Farmer recalls Hill's reminiscences: 'whenever the City team coach passed Doncaster's ground Jimmy would remind us how he scored five there. We got so used to it, that almost as soon as the ground came into view, we would all groan as he began his trip down memory lane.'

A bad knee injury ended Hill's playing career prematurely and enabled him to concentrate his efforts on his role as chairman of the PFA. His efforts for the players' union resulted in the abolition of the maximum wage, but only after the threat of strikes and considerable brinksmanship. The protracted negotiations won him many friends amongst the players but also many enemies amongst football club directors. His many appearances on radio and television during the dispute also brought him to the attention of every football fan in the country and did his reputation no harm at all.

Having sacked his entire City coaching staff on day one, Jimmy Hill had to rely on Arthur Cox, a former youth-team player who was a part-time trainer, to help prepare his team for his first game in charge, at home to Northampton.

Hill himself donned a tracksuit on his first afternoon to conduct a practice match on the Highfield Road pitch, and then, at 5pm, he stepped into his first press conference alongside Robins.

Facing the press, Hill was asked what he thought of City's performance against King's Lynn: he replied that it was fairly obvious that there was a lack of the right mental approach. He confirmed that a specialist had confirmed that he, Hill, must not play again, quashing any thoughts that he might be a player-manager. He announced, in a style that would become Hill's trademark, that the club wanted to foster stronger ties with local junior sides and he would be making this a priority.

The press corps was informed that Hill had been given a five-year contract. One journalist asked Hill what he would like to see at the end of that time. Hill replied in a flash, almost prophetically as it turned out: 'A new ten-year contract.'

Many of the Midlands press men had seen and heard it all before at Highfield Road. One hard-bitten hack said afterwards: 'Hill will need a miracle to get this club off the floor.'

Rod Dean recalls: 'As a disgruntled fifth-former sitting on the X57 Midland red bus waiting at 16.15 on a dark, dank November evening at Leamington Bus Station, and with no means of hearing such news until I got home to read the *Evening Telegraph*, I was surprised when my Napton friend held up an exercise book with "Frith has gone, Jimmy Hill manager" written in large letters. Then someone else on the bus confirmed the news – it was true. I got home and my father, always mistrustful of Londoners and other Flash Harrys, said, "Jimmy Hill, what good will he do!" In spite of this, on the following Saturday we were in our seats in New Wing Stand B as usual to see an exciting, gutsy display and a fortunate 1-0 win against local rivals Northampton. The rest of the season after that was an anticlimax – attendances withered away to 5-6,000 by the end of the season but as always at Highfield Road there were great plans a-foot.'

Alan Ludford was similarly underwhelmed by Hill's arrival: 'I was at the King's Lynn game and remember talking to schoolmates the following week about Billy Frith and his staff being sacked, and replaced by JH. I knew of him from reading in newspapers about his work for the players union, but was not really excited by his appointment. How wrong was I?

Tom Dentith remembers the day vividly and was immediately excited: 'In our office at Armstrong Whitworth Aircraft at Baginton it was just a normal day with little happening. Then in mid-afternoon the news came through. I think someone bought an early edition of the [Coventry] *Telegraph*, and it was like a bombshell had been dropped. In a flash everything had changed, work stopped and everyone from the boss to the office girls got caught up in the excitement. It was the start of the most exciting time of my football supporting life.'

December 2nd marked Jimmy Hill's first game in charge of Coventry City. A home game against their nearest geographical rivals in the Third Division, Northampton. Since City's relegation in 1952, the Bantams and the Cobblers had met in every season bar two and there was keen rivalry between the clubs. The Cobblers, under the management of their former player Dave Bowen, had won promotion from Division Four the previous campaign and were handily placed in sixth position, seven points behind leaders Bournemouth and four points ahead of the Bantams.

In the match programme Derrick Robins explained the rationale behind the decision to sack Billy Frith and his coaching staff and appoint Jimmy Hill. The board, he wrote, thought it was 'as vital for the manager to pick the team that works off the field as for him to pick the team that goes onto the field'.

Hill himself wrote his first programme notes, headed with a small photograph of himself superimposed on a cartoon-suited man in a swivel chair. He described how the last few days had been amongst the most hectic in his life and how he was honoured to be appointed to manage a club as ambitious as Coventry. Unlike many of his predecessors and past directors of the club, he would not make any promises other than that he and all his staff would work as hard as anyone to bring success to the club. He went on to say he wanted supporters to 'feel part of the club because we cannot get success without your support'.

Hill made three changes to the side that lost to King's Lynn. Mick Kearns came in for the injured Frank Austin at left-half, Mike Grice replaced the injured Peter Hill at outside-right, and Billy Myerscough replaced Brian Hill at inside-forward. According to his autobiography, Jimmy told Brian Hill that 'when he came back into the side it would be to stay, but positively not as a striker'. JH was prophetic even then, as Brian developed into a fine defensive wing-half and one of the best man-markers in the country. He was still playing for the club in 1970.

A crowd of 13,693, disappointingly low as there were 4,000 noisy Northampton fans there, watched the Cobblers dominate the early play, with their twin centre-forwards Pat Terry and Cliff Holton causing havoc. Then in the 21st minute Northampton full-back Tony Claypole broke his leg in a challenge with Ron Hewitt and it began to look like a more even contest. There were, of course, no substitutes in those days, so now it was ten against eleven. Reshuffled Northampton continued to have the lion's share of the game but in City's only spell of real superiority, just after half-time, they scored the vital goal. With a burst of speed left-winger Stewart Imlach went past his man and his cross was headed in off a post by Dixon past keeper Chic Brodie. From then on it was a brave rearguard action which 'Nemo' described in the *Coventry Telegraph*:

'Highest praise goes to Arthur Lightening and George Curtis, for it was their efforts in the face of the Cobblers' big forward guns that prevented Northampton from scoring. Lightening was outstanding. He has never been less showy and more effective. Few goalkeepers would have kept out, as he did, all three of the thundering efforts Cliff Holton despatched with all his considerable shooting power at the City goal.'

The South African Lightening had been a big crowd favourite ever since he joined City from Nottingham Forest in 1958 and helped City to promotion from Division Four, missing only a handful of games in three years. 'Nemo,' however, was astute. Arthur was popular for his daring leaps and diving saves, but this side of his game overshadowed inconsistencies in his performances.

The traumatic events at Highfield Road had overshadowed George Curtis' good news the previous week. The City captain had travelled as a reserve for the England Under-23 team for their match against Holland in Rotterdam. George was understudy to first-choice half-backs Brian Labone (Everton) and Bobby Moore (West Ham), neither of whom had yet won full caps but were destined to win many. Also in the team that won 5-2 were future internationals Alan Mullery (Fulham) and Johnny Byrne (Crystal Palace).

Hill, then, had started with a lucky win but he was impressed with the fighting spirit, and psychologically winning your first game in charge is a massive boost. In the *Daily Herald* on the Monday, Dave Bowen gave JH some sage advice: 'Don't listen to anyone. Have faith in what you believe in and don't let anyone try to talk or force you out of it.'

Hill acknowledged the advice, and later admitted he had valued Bowen's words and practised them. Robins, on the other hand, told the *Coventry Telegraph* that the gate against Northampton was disastrous and convinced him that Friday-night football was the answer. The previous Friday night game (v Crystal Palace) had attracted a similar crowd but included only around 700 away fans. On Saturday, Northampton brought between 4-5,000, meaning that the home contingent was down to around 9,000. Robins commented: 'It was a local derby, we had a new manager, and the weather – for December – was glorious. It was an extremely bad gate.'

Hill's first full week in charge saw his innovations working already. First, on the Tuesday morning, the players were told that it would be an unchanged side for Saturday's trip to Hull. The timing was unheard of at Coventry City before – normally the team would not be announced until the Friday, but Hill wanted to try and inspire some confidence from his playing staff and thought this would be a good idea.

Second, he changed the training regime, bringing the players in on Mondays in future, and concentrating most of the training into the early part of the week and easing off to shorter stints in the two days before a weekend match.

Third, he lifted the club ban on players talking to the press, which had existed at Highfield Road for ten years. Hill said: 'I do not like players being gagged. They are now free to talk to whom they like.' Hill's action upset Football League chairman Alan Hardaker, whom Hill had crossed swords with during the players' union discussions of the previous year. Hardaker penned a letter asking the club to explain the decision. Robins replied, saying the board supported its manager in his decision and also sanctioned Hill to continue writing a column for the *Daily Express*. Nothing more was heard from League headquarters.

That week also saw the appointment of Alfred Downs as temporary trainer. Hill said that Manchester-born Downs would be in place until May, when the man he wanted would be available. Downs, a former England water-polo international, had previously worked under Matt Busby at Manchester United and had just returned from a three-year spell in Australia, where he worked with a Queensland rugby league team. His immediate task was to help clear the injury list, which included Farmer, Satchwell, Peter Hill and Austin. Austin had recovered from a pulled muscle but suffered a bone fracture in his face after a freak accident on the training pitch and would be out for several weeks. Downs only stayed three weeks, leaving to take up a permanent post outside football; Len Brown, the St John Ambulance man, became trainer on match-days.

A 1-3 defeat at Hull on the Saturday prompted 'Nemo' in the *Coventry Telegraph* to write: 'Mr Hill has been left a legacy of a team that fumbles to find its football, yet is not shorn of its spirit. Of course spirit can often conquer all adversity. But something else is needed and that something else City did not possess at Hull.'

City's away record was abysmal, with only two away wins in 22 games in the previous twelve months. Two weeks later, on the Saturday before Christmas, they recorded a third win, 2-1 at bottom of the table Newport, thanks to a brace from Mike Dixon. In between came another 1-0 home win, over Reading, with Ron Hewitt on target, but watched by a pitiful crowd of 8,091. The fans were going to take a lot more persuasion to return to Highfield Road. Hill in his programme notes refused to make excuses for the Hull performance and had some critical words for City's fans: 'in the Northampton match I could hardly hear a cheer at all for our team. The visiting supporters drowned out all we could offer.'

Hill's admonishment appeared to have an effect. Ten days later in the programme for the visit of Grimsby, Hill wrote: 'One thing I did enjoy [in the Reading game] were the cheers that you gave the lads when they scored the goal and during the last part of the game.'

The Grimsby game, on Boxing Day, saw the most successful PR exercise to date. The club decided to invite youngsters under sixteen to a 'pop and crisps' party after the match. They expected a hundred or so youngsters to turn up for a bottle of pop and a bag of crisps and the lure of players' autographs. Following the 2-0 win for City, the players were told to stay on for half an hour to fulfil the club's commitment. Jimmy Hill describes the scene:

'It didn't take us long to realise we were going to be overwhelmed. We counted over 500 kids in the queue and it took over two hours for the players to do their duty. Cooperative as they [the players] were, there was a limit to their patience, so every time a player's glass emptied it was filled in the hope that no one would notice the time slipping away.'

The exercise was a major success, with news of the party spreading around the city, conveying the message that the football club was suddenly interested in the fans. Hill had stated that he wanted the fans to feel part of the club and the 'pop and crisps' was a small step on the journey to win them back.

The first week in January 1962 was so bitterly cold that City's away games at Grimsby and Halifax were postponed. Hill was busy, though, making his first signing. He paid non-league Gravesend & Northfleet £1,500 for 28-year-old forward Roy Dwight, who had played alongside Hill at Fulham for two seasons before joining Nottingham Forest. At Forest, he had played in their 1959 FA Cup final success but broke his leg on the Wembley turf. The leg took a long time to heal and his recovery was extended by a broken arm, following which he was freed by the club. After joining Gravesend, Roy, who could play on the right wing or at centre-forward, scored 21 goals in 23 games. This proved that he had recovered but Hill ensured a full medical was carried out to confirm that.

Hill announced that the club would promote a tournament between representative sides of sixteen local leagues. Each league would select a representative team of under-eighteens, who would play-off against each other behind closed doors at Highfield Road on Sunday mornings. As a finale, the best eleven players would play City's first team. It was a shrewd move guaranteed to give the best youngsters in the area the thrill of playing at a League ground, with the lure of a game against the City team if they were selected. The club would also be able to identify the best local talent with a view to signing them.

Hill's face was already familiar to the football media, and he began to use it for the club's benefit. *Pathe News* was the leading newsreel company, and in those days produced short news items for cinema audiences. Hill invited *Pathe* to spend three days at Highfield Road filming a documentary entitled *A Day in the life of a Football Manager*, culminating in some action from the home game with Southend. The resulting clip was shown in cinemas around the country in early March, and can still be viewed on the internet, as well as on out-takes.

Four minutes of unique footage shows JH arriving at Highfield Road and entering the offices at the back of the old main stand, moving on to him sitting at his office desk reading his mail. George Curtis enters the office, then the action switches to the old players' lounge where Hill uses a flat board with pitch markings to demonstrate a few ideas. Players such as Brian Nicholas, Billy Myerscough and Mike Dixon make contributions. The next action is a training session on a muddy Highfield Road pitch, followed by what looks like an apprentice banging studs onto a boot, and then Dr Coghill tends to a player's ankle in a treatment room. Finally, extracts from the Southend game are shown, and out-takes show City take the field in their white shirts with navy sleeves. Then comes the bizarre sight of the referee halting the game briefly after three minutes. City are instructed to change shirts because they clashed with Southend's blue shirts with white pin-stripes. City change into their red away shirts, but the referee was wrong – he should have made Southend change as they were the away team. The game ended 3-3, the first home point City had dropped in four games since Hill's arrival, with City recovering from 0-2 down.

The match programme for Southend explained changes in the running of the Bantam Lottery following the resignation of the promoters, former players Paddy Ryan and Lol Harvey. As if he didn't have enough on his plate, JH had been appointed 'honorary promoter'. He now planned to build a strong team of agents.

On the Thursday following the Southend game JH married Heather Harding at Paddington Registry Office. The *CT* reported that Hill had spent his wedding eve watching City's reserves at Portsmouth and would be back at his desk on Friday morning, preparing for the trip to Notts County, but hoped to get a couple of days off after that. He saw a thriller at Fratton Park, with Ken Satchwell notching a hat-trick but ending up on the losing side in a 4-5 defeat. City's star was eighteen-year-old Dietmar Bruck who gave Hill a big nudge that he was ready for the first team.

Defeats at Notts County (0-2) and the following Saturday at leaders Portsmouth (2-3) punctured the mood. Hill had named Alan Dicks as his new assistant manager on the eve of the Pompey game. A former Chelsea man, Dicks was still playing for Southend. He was transferred as a player, with City agreeing to pay Southend £100 per first-team match, up to a maximum of £1,000. Although he often played for Coventry reserves, 28-year-old Alan never pulled on a first-team shirt, and Southend went empty handed.

Hill arranged various friendlies in an effort to improve teamwork, but also to bring in some extra gate money. Over 8,000 watched the first, against Czech side Slovan Bratislava, who included five internationals. Among them was Jan Popluhar, who would captain his country to the World Cup finals the following June. Wearing their change red shirts, City won 2-1 with Roy Dwight scoring on his debut. Two weeks later top West German club TSV Aachen were beaten 5-3, but City fans had the pleasure of seeing legendary Yugoslav forward Branko Zebec. In between, a small crowd of 3,500 watched a friendly against the British Army, whose team was packed with league players, including City's Mick Kearns, who was undertaking his National Service. A further planned friendly against Southampton was called off because of the Saints' league commitments. City travelled to Bristol Rovers for another non-competitive match.

These games had the bonus of allowing City to put some players in the shop window.

Hill had begun to make changes to his team. After the Notts County defeat, Ron Hewitt, Brian Nicholas and Mike Dixon were dropped. Dixon had played his last game for the club, despite scoring six goals in eight games since the change in management. JH clearly did not fancy him and it was no surprise that he joined non-league Cambridge United in early April. He played only a handful of games at the Abbey before signing for Weymouth. Hewitt, a strong-willed Welshman who always had something to say for himself, made only one further appearance before a move to Chester in early March.

The following week, Fratton Park also marked the final games for full-back Don Bennett and Billy Myerscough, the latter moving to Chester with Hewitt. Hill was clearing the decks. The replacements included Bob Allen, a left-sided wing-half who had impressed in the reserves, the diminutive Albert McCann, who had been given few opportunities in the first team since his arrival from Luton, the new man Dwight, and briefly Ken Satchwell, a centre-forward who had never reproduced his scoring form of 1959-60, when he netted fifteen goals in 28 games.

Allen and Satchwell were on target in the 4-1 home win over Shrewsbury, played on, according to 'Nemo', 'the worst pitch of the season.' He described the playing surface as 'more a test of brute stamina than skill as players heaved their limbs through a morass which stopped the ball dead even after the heftiest of kicks from only a few feet away'.

Seven days later, at Peterborough, Satchwell scored twice and McCann nabbed the winner in a 3-2 victory, with 'Nemo' describing the goal as 'a touch of poetry'. 'Nemo' also commented on City's away following in what was City's first ever visit to London Road: 'what a change to hear the Coventry roar away from home.' There was silly talk from some about a late run for promotion, but the Posh win was to mark the zenith of the campaign. City won only four of their remaining sixteen games and home gates dropped badly, with under 6,000 present for midweek fixtures against Port Vale and Bristol City.

Tottenham were the top side in England in those years, and after winning the domestic double in 1960-61 were playing in the European Cup for the first time. Their home games were generally thrilling affairs played under the White Hart Lane floodlights in a charged atmosphere, with the Spurs anthem 'When the Spurs go marching on' booming out incessantly. In his programme notes for the Lincoln home game in early March, Hill commented: 'Talking of Spurs and their song ... Just in case we do get in the European Cup – have we a song ready? No doubt the seeds of a club anthem were formed at that time, and what a positive thought, albeit a pipedream.

Some of Hill's bright ideas faced opposition from the authorities. In late February, JH planned City's first away trip by air. His plan was to play a Friday night league game with Lincoln, then fly up to Scotland the following morning to fulfil a friendly with Morton on Saturday afternoon. Within 24 hours the Football League refused permission because 'they do not wish to encourage clubs to play League matches on Friday nights and friendlies on the following afternoon'. That same week the Football Association turned down City's request to stage a big match in conjunction with the Coventry Cathedral opening festival on 14 May. FA chairman Stanley Rous told the club 'the date was out of season' and warned against a match 'because of the congested representative fixtures at that period involving all our international players'. Hill acquiesced, but wondered who City's international players were!

In his programme notes for the Watford game in mid-March, JH accepted that his team was not going to be promoted but wanted to explain to the fans what was in his mind for the 'City'. He was not going to change the complete team, but focused on the forwards. He explained that the departure of Hewitt and Myerscough, and McCann's injury, had left the forward line depleted:

'Two things can happen; firstly one of the players on the present staff can raise their game and fill the breach, or otherwise we will surely have to acquire an experienced player in this position next season. March is certainly not the time to buy players, unless you have money to waste, so the intervening weeks do give me a chance to experiment positionally. In these days of less money and smaller staffs the player who can play the odd game in another position is worth his weight in gold. This is my chance to collect such information for next season.'

One such player was already in Hill's sights, Irish winger Willie Humphries. The 25-year-old played part-time in the Irish League for Ards. He had moved to Leeds in 1957 but returned home to Northern Ireland after two years because he was homesick. JH made several trips to watch him, and on 27 March it was reported that he had agreed a fee with Ards, made an offer to Humphries, and awaited his reply. Comments from the player in that day's *Telegraph*, however, told a different story: 'It's doubtful if I'll agree to go. I've a good job [with Belfast Corporation] and a home to consider and I've no desire to break up either.'

Two days later the *CT* reported that Humphries had turned down the move. Hill had little money to wheel and deal with, and his plan had been to use Ron Farmer as a makeweight in the deal. Farmer had been on the injured list since early October but was nearing full fitness when Hill broached the idea to him. Farmer describes what happened: 'I had not played for the first team under Jimmy, but he called me in and said how did I fancy a move to Ireland ... Whenever we meet he reminds me that he was going to sell me before he'd even see me play.'

Four weeks later Hill flew to Ireland again to watch Humphries, and this time persuaded him and his wife to return to Coventry to 'have a look at the city'. Willie, who had won his first Irish international cap in the interim, stayed at Hill's Kenilworth home and watched Monday afternoon's home game with Bristol City before flying home that evening.

A week earlier Hill had prepared the way for Humphries by dropping his regular right-winger, Mike Grice, and announcing he was on the transfer list. Grice, a big signing the previous summer, had impressed only in patches and, like Dixon, was thought to be 'not one I fancied'. Hill's persistence paid off when Humphries agreed to sign on Friday, 27 April.

Hill told fans in his Hull programme notes that he had made six trips to Ireland to secure Humphries, so many trips that the players thought Hill had a girlfriend there, and his wife was sure he had.

The previous night Hill had flown from Belfast direct to London to make another important signing, Chelsea's 25-year-old full-back John Sillett. The son of former Southampton full-back Charles and brother of England full-back Peter, John had come through the ranks at Stamford Bridge, playing over 100 first-team games and the *Coventry Telegraph* described him as 'a hard defender with a relentless tackle'. Both Humphries and Sillett made their debuts the following afternoon in the final home game against Hull. Despite, according to 'Nemo', Humphries being 'far and away the best player on the field' and Sillett's 'unhurried defending', City were very poor and Hull easily won 2-0.

Another signing went largely unnoticed in March, the arrival from Lancashire League side Nelson of seventeen-year-old Ernie Machin. A hard-working inside-forward with an eye for a goal, he had been recommended by City's north-west scout Alf Walton. Ernie didn't get a first-team game that season, but Hill blooded other raw youngsters in games with little to play for. Eighteen-year-old Dietmar Bruck had debuted at the end of the previous season and was now given six starts at wing-half. Homegrown centre-forward Colin Holder, seventeen, played two games and scored one goal, and teenagers Alan Turner and George Bassett were given debuts in the final games.

The best result of the last third of the season came at home to champions-elect Portsmouth. Pompey arrived at Highfield Road seven points clear at the top with only six games remaining, and only a disaster would stop them going up to Division Two. City's defence had a settled look but the attack included Ron Farmer, a wing-half, and McCann was back from injury. City outclassed Pompey, who were a big disappointment, and Farmer notched both goals in a 2-0 win.

The season ended on Monday, 30 April with a 2-0 win at Halifax, a win that left City fourteenth, seven points above the relegation zone. The crowd of 2,351 was the second lowest to watch City since the war. Brian Hill, who had not played in the first team since the King's Lynn Cup-tie, was rewarded for his patience with his first game at wing-half and, according to 'Nemo', 'put a vice-like clamp on Conway Smith, the ace goal-snatcher of the Shay.' Although they didn't know it at the time, the game marked the final competitive appearance in a Coventry shirt for Bob Allen, Albert McCann, Stewart Imlach and Colin Holder.

The season's average home gate was 10,256, down from almost 12,000 the previous season, and was the lowest since 1928. Gates around the country were lower and City's Friday-night experiment had proved inconclusive. Hill had made it clear that he wanted to revert to traditional Saturday afternoons.

As the consecration of the city's revolutionary and much-discussed new cathedral in May 1962 approached, plans were hatched for a celebration game at Highfield Road. Benfica, the European Cup-winners, were tipped to come, but their extortionate match fee of £8,000 made it unfeasible, so Burnley, one of the country's top teams, agreed to play. The Lancashire side, who had lost the FA Cup final to Spurs just days earlier, gave a thrilling display to win 4-2 in front of 7,000, with the proceeds going to the Coventry Youth Club fund. City featured West Ham and England centre-forward Johnny Byrne as a guest player, and he scored a stunning 35-yarder to cheer up the home fans. Three days later the team left for West Germany for a rare continental tour. Three games in six days against local Second Division opposition were all won.

When Jimmy Hill announced his retained list of players at the end of the season there were few surprises. Twenty-six players were retained and three senior players given free transfers – Don Bennett, Brian Nicholas and Eric Jones. Two of the 26 were on the coaching staff – assistant manager Alan Dicks and new trainer Peter Hill – but would play occasional games, probably for the reserves. Although Mike Grice and Bob Allen were included in the list of retained players, they were unlikely to be around for long. Grice was on the transfer list and likely to be moving on, whilst Allen looked set to leave.

Allen had grown up in north Wales and in his teens was on the books of Blackburn and Wolves. He was doing his National Service with

George Curtis at RAF Bridgnorth when George persuaded him to have a trial at City. Manager Billy Frith was impressed enough to sign the left-footed midfield player but gave him few opportunities.

Allen explains: 'After Jimmy Hill arrived I was a regular in the side and felt I deserved my place. He offered me a new contract but I told him I did not want the insecurity of professional football. I applied to go on a teacher's training course and later become a schoolteacher in south Wales. I played non-league football in south Wales for quite a few years, combining teaching with playing. My clubs were Abergavenny, Bridgend and Sully, and I played up to the age of 48.'

Three of the 26 had not yet appeared for the first team: a young Welsh winger called Ronnie Rees, eighteen-year-old defender Mick Crump, and the young Lancastrian Ernie Machin. Few City fans realised that Rees and Machin would go on to play a major part in the Sky Blue revolution.

Chapter 5. 1962-63 (Part 1)

A New Forward Line

Following the signing of Willie Humphries and John Sillett in April 1962, Hill had more new players in his sights. He was known to be largely comfortable with his defence but wanted more and better forwards – these, however, would cost money. City were still around £60,000 in debt and Hill had warned Robins that it would take five years to build a successful club built on a strong youth policy. Robins, however, was impatient.

The solution to the club's financial conundrum came in the form of a share issue from Robins' company Banbury Buildings. It enabled Robins to 'cash in' some shares and donate £30,000 to the football club. Early that summer Robins outlined his ideas to Hill and invited him to 'invest' in team strengthening, with the proviso that if the team was not successful then his job would be on the line. Robins was hunting a shortcut to success.

According to Hill's autobiography, he had no qualms about spending the money but had other concerns: 'I wasn't in any way frightened of the responsibility of spending that amount of money, but the thought had occurred to me that if we were to announce the gift to the club immediately, the price of any player we might be looking at would inflate and we would not get value for money.' Hill therefore accepted the money, provided it was only revealed once it had been spent. Robins agreed and Jimmy went off to spend.

Humphries had cost around £4,500, whilst Robins had knocked Chelsea down from £4,000 to £2,600 for Sillett. It still left a big slug to spend, but his next move was for a free transfer. Jimmy Whitehouse had impressed Hill during City's game with Reading the previous season, and when Hill discovered that Whitehouse had fallen out with Reading, he joined a melee of clubs chasing the inside-forward. Whitehouse took his time but was excited by Hill's vision for Coventry City. He chose City over nine other clubs.

A week later, in mid-June, Hill flew to Northern Ireland again. This time his target was the Linfield centre-forward Hugh Barr, a six-footer who had headed the Irish League's scoring lists the previous campaign with 46 goals. Barr's scoring feats had not only earned him his first international cap in November 1961 against England at Wembley, but increased his value. City had to pay £8,500 for his services. Barr was an amateur – he had represented Great Britain in the 1960 Olympic Games

– but soon agreed to put his schoolteaching career on hold for the chance to play professionally in England.

Within days Hill was wheeling and dealing again, with left-winger Stewart Imlach surprisingly sold to Crystal Palace and replaced by Brighton's No 11, 24-year-old Bobby Laverick. Hill described both fees as 'reasonable', but that City had come out on the right side. It later transpired that Laverick cost £2,500, but he was to be a rare transfer error by Hill. In his autobiography, Hill describes how he remembered watching Laverick play for Brighton and he rang Johnny Carey, the Everton manager, for his opinion of the winger: 'John thought I should be comfortable paying £2,500 for him because in the past he had been assessed much more expensively,' writes Hill.

Imlach's departure was a surprise to many – he had played in all but one game the previous season and had been one of the successes following Hill's arrival. 'Nemo' in the *CT* indicated that Crystal Palace had been 'interested' in him for 'some time' but Laverick was a 'similar type of winger and he should prove more than an adequate replacement'.

During the writing of his prize-winning book *My father and Other Working-Class Football Heroes*, Gary Imlach, Stewart's son, tried to discover why his dad had left City, bearing in mind his previous good form. He contacted Hill but found the great man's memory of the summer of 1962 in a poor state. Hill mistakenly told Gary that he had signed Laverick from Everton (an earlier club of Bobby's) and that Stewart Imlach had been sold prior to his arrival. When the facts were explained he could not remember playing Imlach or selling him.

With players' contracts expiring on 30 June, transfer activity increased: it was reported that Brian Nicholas had joined Southern League Premier Division side Rugby Town and Don Bennett had signed for Hereford United, another Southern League outfit. These moves followed Mike Grice's exit to Colchester in early June. Grice's transfer request in April had been granted but he had later been retained and the Oystermen, newly promoted to Division Three, paid City a 'small fee', substantially lower than what City had paid West Ham a year earlier.

City's transfer moves had done little to excite the long-suffering fans. The *CT* reported that season-ticket sales amounted to £3,000 (equating to approximately 800-1,000 tickets), poor compared to Peterborough's £12,000. That was to change on Saturday, 7 July, when it was announced that City had paid Peterborough £12,000 for their prolific centre-forward Terry Bly. According to 'Nemo', Hill had been 'making strenuous but unsuccessful efforts to persuade Peterborough to part with Bly' before he flew off for a holiday in Spain. Then, on 6 July, Derrick Robins got a call

5. 1962-63 (Part 1) A New Forward Line

from Peterborough and raced north from Eastbourne where he was on a cricket tour, only to discover that four other clubs were after Bly's signature. The silver-tongued Robins clinched a deal which lit the blue touchpaper under Coventry City. Bly was almost a household name, from his goalscoring feats in Third Division Norwich's run to the FA Cup semifinal in 1959, and then in 1960-61 his 52 goals in Posh's first season in the Football League. His signing was City's biggest in years. City fans suddenly were intrigued by goings-on at Highfield Road, but some wondered where the money for all these new players was coming from.

Hill was also strengthening his backroom staff, and before pre-season training started he appointed a Hungarian coach, Janos Gerdov. Gerdov advertised his wares in the May edition of the *FA News* thus: 'Physical Education Supervisor at the University of Vienna, chief coach to the Austrian First Division Wiener Athletiksport Club and an FA Qualified Coach is anxious to spend a year in England in order to improve his knowledge of the English language and sport. Would anyone interested in availing themselves of his services please write to him at Hahngasse 11/15, Vienna 9, Austria.'

It is probable that Hill saw this advert and made contact. Gerdov's arrival was reported on 26 June, along with the confirmation that Peter Hill had been appointed 'trainer and coach' and Steve Faulconbridge as physiotherapist.

Information about Gerdov is sketchy. It is known that he was a basketball coach for Yugoslav national students in the early 1950s, followed by a spell as coach of leading Austrian team SK Sturm Graz. He later had a spell as coach for Eintracht Trier, a German regional team. He was expected to stay at City for twelve months and in the summer of 1963 he duly moved back to mainland Europe to continue his career. With memories of the great Hungary side of the 1950s still fairly fresh in people's minds, this was seen by many as a progressive move and, hopefully, an indication of the type of football the team would be playing.

Jimmy Hill now had a completely new forward line, and on 11 August they got their first public airing at Birmingham City's St Andrews in a Friday-night pre-season friendly. Playing for the very first time in a smart all-Sky Blue kit, City were a goal up against First Division Blues through Hugh Barr in 30 seconds, and with Terry Bly adding a second, City ran out 2-1 winners. The performance impressed 'Nemo', who wrote the following day: 'Public practice games are notoriously fickle yardsticks of form and it would be the easiest thing in the world to be over-enthusiastic about City's astonishing display last night. But … City's teamwork and 90-minute zest must have surpassed the wildest hopes of their fans.' City had more than twenty direct shots on goal, compared with eight by the home team, and hit the woodwork three times.

On the following Monday, Robins went public on the 'gift' of £30,000 he had made to the club. He explained that he didn't want to wait five years to build for success, and of his conversations with Hill he said: 'I made this gift because I have a deep desire to see top-class football in Coventry.' He encouraged local industrial firms to help by buying season tickets in bulk for their employees and revealed the existence of a new social club 'the Sky Blue Club – because of City's new continental-style strip'. Annual membership would be one guinea with a 5 shilling (25p) entrance fee to gain access before, during and after each home game. The mystery of where the transfer pot came from was solved.

In his preview of the coming season 'Nemo' in the *Coventry Telegraph* wrote: 'Everywhere a spirit of surging confidence and enthusiasm pervades. Many are saying this will be City's season. The all-important question is, just how good are their chances of winning promotion? I am going to take a chance and say that City will be right there battling it out with the teams at the top.'

'Nemo' saw City's threats coming from Alec Stock's Queens Park Rangers ('the strongest side in the division'), Bristol City, Northampton ('always a potential threat'), and Peterborough ('though they may find the departure of Bly a big blow').

News tumbled out of Highfield Road in that week before the season started, and it was clear that Hill, with the help of his press man John Camkin, was cranking up supporters' interest in the opening game. From the Robins' 'gift' on Monday, to a plan to re-level the pitch in the summer of 1963 on Tuesday, then on Wednesday the news that City had received permission from the Football League to kick off Saturday home games at 3.15 instead of the traditional 3pm, by Thursday it was team news following the final private trial.

The pitch news was welcome, after the disgusting state it had deteriorated into the previous season, and even better news was that the supporters' club, so often a major fundraiser in the past, would pick up the bill of around £12,000. The project would also involve levelling the pitch to remove the six-foot diagonal slope from the Highfield Road corner to the Swan Lane corner, which had existed since the ground opened in 1899.

There were two reasons behind the fifteen-minute delay in kick-off. First, Hill revealed he had received requests from shift-workers whose shift ended at 3pm: they could now attend games if the kick-off time was adjusted. The second reason, and possibly the more important, was that the new 4.55pm finish time would fit in neatly with the new 'Sky Blue' social club, which would have a licence commencing at 5pm. Members would not have to hang around for twenty minutes before a drink. Apparently, Hill had been impressed with a similar social club at Torquay the previous season, where the home fans gathered in large numbers to have a drink after the game, missing the worst of the traffic and mulling over the game with a pint. After the first home midweek fixture, City also put back the kick-off times for evening matches from 7.15 to 7.30.

A revamped match programme included a double centre-page spread for line-ups, a larger, more readable typeface, and for the opening game against Notts County a full-page picture of City's squad in their new sky blue kit. In that first programme Hill mentioned that the Sky Blue Club would be open soon and announced a new resident disc jockey called Chick Pritchard. Hill referred to 'rumours ... of many visiting Highfield Road again after a lengthy absence'. There must have been many returning because the crowd of 22,832 was the largest for an opening home game since Jesse Carver's first game in charge in 1955. It was easily the biggest gate in the Third Division that day.

Rod Dean remembers the build-up to the game well: 'Such was the excitement and anticipation I remember falling off my bike on the morning of the Notts County game, but I patched myself up ready for the big match. My dad and I were a little suspicious of dropping the Bantams' nickname, but the new Sky Blue strip was pretty natty and already the Big Four (Villa, Blues, Albion and Wolves) were beginning to look slightly shop soiled.'

With a large, critical crowd present, accompanied by the feverish build up to that opening match, the burden on City's players was enormous. It showed in a nervous display, rescued by late goals from Barr and Bly to give Hill a 2-0 winning start.

The new all-sky blue kit was well received by the majority, with comments like 'smart', 'continental-like' and 'very innovative' bandied about. One reader of the *Coventry Telegraph*, Mr L W Parsons of Leamington, was not impressed: 'The colours look smart, at least for five minutes. The jerseys, in my opinion, are too tight-fitting and the players are constantly pulling up long, tight sleeves, which must restrict movement. Surely a tight-fitting sweat-soaked kit on a cold day will take its toll on the players. Compared to the Swindon side's cool look, City certainly looked hot and bothered.' City also introduced a new 'change' kit of red shirts and red shorts that got its first outing at Colchester.

Three days after the Notts County win the bubble burst when City's new-look team got thumped 1-4 at Swindon by Bert Head's exciting young team, and the cynics scoffed that it was the 'same old City, can't win away'.

After just four games of the new season (and three clean sheets), popular keeper Arthur Lightening was sold to Middlesbrough for £11,000. He was replaced by Reading's Dave Meeson, who cost £4,000. Over the years rumours circulated that Arthur might have been involved with handling stolen goods, and after a court appearance Hill decided that the club didn't need someone with a reputation for sailing close to the wind. The player's move to the Second Division started terribly, Boro losing 1-6 at Newcastle. Lightening returned for good to South Africa the following summer after telling Boro he was going back for his brother's wedding but never returning to England.

Lightening was very much a loner, spending most evenings at the Longford Billiards Hall. His teammates from his time at Coventry are convinced that, with a bit more application, Arthur could have been a top keeper, even good enough for Division One.

Many fans chastised Hill over the sale of Lightening. He explained his decision in the Southend match programme: 'My own reputation depends on success for the club in the near future and I can assure you that I am not stupid enough to sell any player if I think that such a sale will damage our chances of promotion.' He waxed lyrically about Meeson's ability and, with the transfer fees in mind, continued: 'If there is one thing better than a good keeper, it's a good keeper and a few thousand pounds.' Meeson had played around 180 games for Reading in eight years and as a twenty-year-old in 1955 had been a non-playing substitute for England Under-23s against Italy.

The new team had their teething problems, including an early 3-4 home defeat by Southend (despite a hat-trick from Bly) when Dave Meeson was culpable on his debut. 'Nemo' pointed out that 'he was wholly to blame for Southend's first goal, looked slow in going down to the ground shot that reduced City's lead to 3-2, and was concerned in a misunderstanding with George Curtis which resulted in the equaliser'.

Meeson never really recovered from that bad start, and by November had lost his place to Bob Wesson. Hill's transfer mistakes were few and far between, but in his autobiography he admitted that 'it quickly became evident … that Johnny Carey's opinion of Bobby Laverick was out of date. He played a few games and I saw flashes of ability, but not enough to compensate for an apparent lack of passion'.

Hill acted swiftly by dropping the ex-Brighton man after just four league games, replacing him initially with Roy Dwight then, after four further games, with eighteen-year-old home-grown Ronnie Rees. Rees' enthusiastic approach made up for his lack of experience, but he quickly blossomed into an outstanding two-footed winger. Hill was effusive about Dwight: 'he lost almost a stone in weight even before pre-season training. It is typical of the determination he has shown.'

A day after Lightening left, Albert McCann joined Portsmouth. 'Albie' or 'Cowboy' as the players nicknamed him, had impressed the previous season but had lost his foraging role to Jimmy Whitehouse and was grateful for the opportunity to move to the south coast. He went straight into Pompey's first team and City picked up a cheque for £5,000. McCann went on to have a long and successful time at Fratton Park, making almost 400 appearances in an eleven-year career.

City's form in the first two months of the season was patchy and the pre-season euphoria certainly wore off. City's fans were fickle and clamoured for changes in defence following a 1-6 thrashing at Watford in September. Four days later, after a 0-0 draw with Shrewsbury, the same fans were blaming the forwards. Hill thought the early season programme was tough and some players were tired – City played ten games in September, including three matches in one week to meet their League Cup commitments.

Two players who impressed in those early weeks were the Northern Ireland pair of Humphries and Barr, and they were duly rewarded with international caps against Poland in early October. The Irish team travelled to Katowice for a friendly and won 2-0 with goals from Humphries and Derek Dougan of Aston Villa.

The Sky Blue Club opened on 29 September. An old friend of Hill's, former England cricketer Denis Compton, performed the opening ceremony after the Reading game. Coventry's Lord Mayor, Alderman AJ Waugh, also present. Anyone interested in becoming a member was invited to attend between 5-6pm for cocktails. The first licensees and stewards of the club were Hill's parents, Bill and Alice, and the club was situated under the Main Stand next to the dressing rooms.

Chairman Robins was not disheartened by the mixed start to the season, and at the AGM in October he said: 'I honestly feel that we have turned the last corner of this dreary old lane – a lane which has been with us for at least ten years.' However, he urged patience whilst being prophetic: 'Please remember the revolution has only begun to take place.' The club's accounts showed a deficit, but with £11,000 income from the supporters' club and the Bantams Fighting Fund, the loss was £5,000, the lowest for five years.

After fifteen league games City showed fifteen points and lay fourteenth in Division Three. Apart from the defeat by Southend, they were unbeaten at home, but conversely they had not won away. They had, however, gained useful draws, including at Millwall and Bristol City. After a Friday-night defeat at Barnsley, the club were allowed to invoke Football League Rule 23, which stated that any club with two or more internationals could postpone their league game. Humphries and Barr's selection for Northern Ireland meant that City were the first Third Division club to take advantage of this rule, and the home fixture with Bristol City was rearranged for later in the month.

The rest of the team were able to enjoy their longest break since the start of the season. Ahead lay the home local derby with Northampton, and with the Cobblers leading the division with only two defeats there was immense interest in the game. Stand tickets were sold out in advance and an estimated 6,000 fans made the trip to support the Cobblers. City came close to upsetting the leaders, with Terry Bly missing a sitter near the end, but City gave a good account of themselves against strong opponents and the 1-1 draw marked the start of a 23-match unbeaten run that would extend until the end of March.

A win over Second Division Swansea (3-2) in City's second round League Cup-tie earned a trip to Portsmouth, where a 1-5 thrashing – with Hill's reject Albert McCann inspirational – sent City out of the competition, but it did not seem to bother Jimmy Hill.

Shortly after the visit of Northampton, Humphries and Barr again represented Northern Ireland, this time against England at Windsor Park. This was one of England manager Walter Winterbottom's last games in charge before handing over to Alf Ramsey, and his strong team won 3-1 with Mike O'Grady (two) and Jimmy Greaves scoring. Barr scored the Irish goal but it was to be his last cap. Jimmy Hill flew to Belfast to watch his two players and found himself cheering for the Irish. In his programme notes for the Bristol City game he analysed what he saw:

'It was only in the closing stages … when the talented legs of Jimmy McIlroy and Danny Blanchflower began to tire that England really looked the better side. Immediately after Ireland had scored their equaliser, Willie Humphries raced into the middle, leaped to a height of what he swears was over 7 feet and forced Ron Springett to bring off a miracle save at the foot of the upright.'

The ten-day break for the rest of the team proved to be a big tonic, for on the Wednesday night City came out of the traps like hungry dogs and took a 3-0 lead in thirteen minutes against Bristol City. The first goal was momentous – the first penalty awarded to City since Hill's arrival almost twelve months previously. It came when Bristol defender Tommy Casey, later a coach at Highfield Road, handled. Ronnie Farmer stepped

5. 1962-63 (PART 1) A NEW FORWARD LINE

up to 'glide home a splendid spot-kick to the right as Cook [the goalkeeper] moved to the left'. It was also Ron's first spot-kick for the club – the first of many. City eventually won 4-2 to nudge into the top half of the table, five points behind leaders Northampton.

On 1 November it was announced that club secretary Bernard Hitchiner, who had been on the Highfield Road staff for 30 years, was leaving to go into business on his own. Hitchiner, a Coventry man who loved the club, had arrived as an office boy in 1933 and been secretary since Harry Storer's departure to Birmingham in 1945. Bernard would later return to the club as ticket-office manager and would organise the club's Cup final allocation in 1987.

November 1962 was a good month. The FA Cup started and a potentially tricky first-round home tie with Bournemouth was safely navigated, thanks to a Jimmy Whitehouse goal. The Cherries had a reputation as Cup giant-killers and six years earlier had reached the quarter-finals after toppling Spurs and Wolves. Twenty-two-year-old Bob Wesson replaced Meeson in goal and made several good saves as the Cherries sought an equaliser.

Three weeks later City travelled to Millwall's Den for a much tougher assignment. Wesson was again in top form and City's defence again held tight to earn a replay. Over 22,000, paying record receipts of over £3,800, saw City progress to the third round after a gripping game, winning 2-1. In his programme notes Jimmy Hill expressed his surprise at the away following at the Den: 'Sixteen coach loads of City supporters travelled down to support the team. Hughie [Spencer], our coach driver, tells me that this is the largest number of supporters to travel away for two or three years at least ... the cheers went a long way towards encouraging the players during the match.' The third round gave City an away tie at Fourth Division Lincoln – but that would be in January – or so City thought.

In between rounds one and two of the FA Cup, City clocked up two wins, at home to Wrexham (3-0) and the first away win, at Halifax (4-2). Bly scored three goals in the two games to take his season's haul to thirteen in league and cups, and the two victories lifted the team up to eighth place, four points behind new leaders Peterborough.

Sandwiched between those two league games was a trip to Belfast for a friendly game with Barr's former club Linfield, a fixture that was part of the transfer arrangement for the Irish international. City made club history by flying to a game for the first time, and around 9,000 watched City gain a 2-1 win with an attractive performance that impressed the Irish crowd.

The following night saw drama at Highfield Road, when the ground hosted its first ever England Youth international. With just nine minutes played against Switzerland, the referee abandoned the contest as thick fog engulfed the stadium. When it was clear that the game could not be restarted Denis Follows, the secretary of the Football Association, made a well-received gesture to refund all spectators entrance money. The bad weather was an omen for what was just around the corner – the worst winter since 1947.

In another goodwill gesture, three weeks later the FA sent the England Youth team back to Coventry to face City's first team in a friendly. It was believed to be the first time a club side had faced an England international team in a public game. City needed two late goals to overcome an impressive Under-18 team that included future stars Tommy Smith (Liverpool), John Sissons (West Ham) and David Pleat (Nottingham Forest).

Ronnie Rees' meteoric rise continued with his selection for Wales' Under-23s. 'Nemo' noted that he was one of three new caps, the others being centre-forward Wyn Davies (Bolton) and Alan Durban (Cardiff). Those three 'new caps' would go on to win 118 full caps between them. Rees' wing play suited the football Jimmy Hill wanted his team to play. Dietmar Bruck explains: 'JH wanted the wingers to dictate the game and in training had us constantly feeding Ronnie and Willie. They would constantly take on their full-backs and take the ball to the line before driving it across. The front players Bly and Barr and later Hudson said "drive the ball into the penalty area and we'll get on the end of it – and they did".'

December continued where November left off with five league games played and City extending their unbeaten run to thirteen league and FA Cup games. However, they came close to losing their record at Brighton's Goldstone Ground on 1 December. With George Curtis limping gamely on the wing after a first-half ankle injury, City trailed 1-2 until two minutes from time. Then Terry Bly, given a rollicking by Hill at half-time for a lacklustre display, rose to head home Curtis' cross from his 'good' foot to save the point. A week later Bly again looked sluggish in a 3-2 home win over Carlisle, but scored for the fourth game running. Humphries, however, stole the plaudits on a greasy surface with, according to 'Nemo', 'a dazzling performance of wing-play'.

At Notts County the following Saturday the travelling fans saw a new signing. Many of the City following were unaware who the blond-headed No 8 was – Hill had signed Newcastle's Ken Hale for £10,000 in the early hours of Saturday morning. The 23-year-old replaced Hugh Barr who, following a great start (ten goals in seventeen games) had lost his

5. 1962-63 (Part 1) A New Forward Line

scoring touch in recent weeks. Hill explained that the money to buy Hale had been generated by increased attendances and the gate money from three FA Cup-ties. Bly's inevitable goal earned City another away point at Meadow Lane.

Many people ask when City were first called the Sky Blues, and when it was first adopted as the club nickname, replacing the old one of the Bantams. Up until December 1962 the club programme had a section 'Bantam Notes', but there was no mention of 'The Sky Blues' even in JH's programme notes. 'Nemo' first uses the term 'Sky Blues' in his match report of the Bournemouth Cup-tie in early November but before this he had always referred in match reports to 'the City'.

However, on Monday, 17 December 1962 the club announced that a new club song would be launched at the Colchester home game the following Saturday. Hill said that City's increased away following had made such an impression on him and his players that 'a promoting song' was desirable. According to his autobiography, Hill and club director John Camkin identified the 'emotional, lilting melody' of the *Eton Boating Song* and over a few gin and tonics composed some lyrics, thus:

Lets all sing together,
   Play up Sky Blues,
While we sing together,
   We will never lose.

Proud Posh or Cobblers,
   Oysters or anyone,
They can't defeat us,
   We'll fight till the game is won.

The press conference summoned to launch the song was attended by comedians Frankie Howerd and Sid James, who were appearing in the Christmas pantomime at Coventry Theatre, and they joined the players to sing the new song.

At the time, Hill explained his idea that, in the second line of the second verse, the name of that day's opponents would be used. Oysters was, in fact, an old nickname for Colchester, but suited the song better than 'the U's'. The club hoped the fans would sing gustily, and also planned to release a disc, recorded by the players.

The Colchester game was affected by fog and, at half-time, with City leading 2-0 with goals from Ron Farmer (penalty) and Ken Hale, the referee abandoned the game. 'Nemo' thought only around one-third of the

11,803 crowd had seen Hale's goal because of the fog. The referee waited a quarter of an hour after the break to see if the fog might clear, and that interlude provided the City fans with the opportunity to open their lungs. 'Nemo' described the scene: 'the way in which they sang two rousing choruses of the promotion song "Play up, Sky Blues" indicated that it has quickly caught on and that we will be hearing it regularly in the future.'

The fog was merely a prelude to a bitterly cold spell and the Christmas double-header with league leaders Peterborough would be the last games for almost two months. Over 1,000 fans followed the team to London Road and saw one of the best away performances in years. City won 3-0 on an icy pitch and 'Nemo' reported that 'there was a constant chant of "Play Up, Sky Blues".'

Three days later, with snow beginning to blanket the country, only ten games were completed in the whole Football League. The largest crowd of the day was at Highfield Road, where 25,399 – the biggest crowd for three years, paying record receipts of £3,960 – saw a thrilling 3-3 draw on a carpet of snow. City's groundsman Ellick Smith and an army of City fans helped remove the worst of it, and convinced the referee to allow play to go ahead. Posh were determined not to fall for City's same trick again and they led 3-1 with twelve minutes left. City's determination and a switch by Hill to long-ball tactics saw City grab a late point. City's unbeaten run of ten games had them up to fourth, four points behind Posh and well poised for a promotion challenge.

Chapter 6. 1962-63 (Part 2)

The Revolution Takes Off

The pre-Christmas FA Cup victories over Bournemouth and Millwall had set up an appearance in the third round for only the fourth time in eleven years since City had been relegated from Division Two, from when they had had to start their Cup campaign in the first round.

City were paired with Fourth Division Lincoln in a tie scheduled at Sincil Bank for 5 January 1963. City's allocation of stand tickets had been sold out before Christmas and a 2,000 following was expected. Despite snow covering virtually the whole country, Lincolnshire escaped lightly and as late as the previous Wednesday Lincoln boss Bill Anderson had few doubts that the game would go ahead. Then the weather worsened and the game was called off on Friday at 3pm. In total, 29 of the 32 ties scheduled for that day were postponed. The three that took place were at Preston, Tranmere and Plymouth.

City's postponement would be the first of fifteen (a competition record which has stood for almost 50 years) and although Lincoln initially rearranged the tie for the following Wednesday, it was called off after a pitch inspection in the morning, which revealed 'an iron-hard pitch … with daytime temperatures still below freezing'.

January was a desperate month for football, with much of England under constant snow. By the end of the month only fifteen of the 32 third round ties had been played. On Saturday 12th, City's league game at Southend was postponed with seven inches of frozen snow reported on the pitch, and a week later the home game with Millwall was called off after an inspection on the Thursday morning found bad patches of ice.

On Thursday 24th, City managed a game. Hill contacted Birmingham manager Gil Merrick and persuaded him to bring his team to the Sphinx ground for a full-scale 'practice', played behind closed doors. Despite a fair bit of snow on the pitch it was compacted. According to 'Nemo': 'City appear to have lost none of their zip,' and ran out 4-2 winners in a game refereed by Merrick. At the same time City's reserves drew 1-1 with their Birmingham counterparts at the Walsgrave training ground.

The Crystal Palace away game was postponed on the 26th, but five days later when the following Saturday's game at Shrewsbury was also ruled out, Hill grasped the nettle. A call to Manchester United manager Matt Busby resulted in a hastily arranged friendly in Dublin. Hill, always seeking publicity for the club, had realised that Ireland was far less badly hit by the weather, and using his contacts in the fair isle organised this tasty friendly. Hill had first tried Joe Mercer, manager at Aston Villa, but Joe's players were worried about getting injured. Busby, however, was more adventurous and, like Hill, was desperate for his team to get some competitive play. Busby duly put out his strongest team, including his expensive forward line: Johnny Giles, Albert Quixall, David Herd, Denis Law and Bobby Charlton.

On a day when only four games were played on the English mainland, City and United fought out a contest at Shamrock Rovers' Glenmalure Park that belied the two divisions' difference in status. With United's stars rattled by City's enthusiasm, City recovered from an early Quixall goal to lead 2-1 at half-time, thanks to goals from Farmer and Whitehouse. With Humphries and Rees giving Shay Brennan and Noel Cantwell an uncomfortable afternoon, and Brian Hill marking Law like a limpet, City had chances to increase their lead. Charlton finally saved United's red faces nine minutes from time with an equaliser, but Coventry had made an impression and went home with a nice cheque from a 15,000 crowd.

Hill's foresight in playing in Ireland was soon followed by other clubs, and Liverpool flew over that week to play Drumcondra. The following Saturday, again after another early postponement (a home game with Port Vale), City flew to Cork to take on Wolves. Whilst not the force they had been in the late 1950s, Wolves were in the top six in Division One (higher than Manchester United) and fielded experienced internationals Ron Flowers and Peter Broadbent. On a miserably wet day, the muddy pitch suited Stan Cullis' team's style perfectly, and although City had chances in the first half, Wolves' strength and experience told and they ran out 3-0 winners in front of a drenched crowd of 6,500.

On 16 February, City's game at Reading became the seventh successive league game to be postponed, and at Lincoln there was no sign of progress. Every slight thaw was followed by another freezing night. To this point, ten postponements had been chalked up. Hill admitted that it would be likely that his team (and most others) would be required to play two games a week until the end of the season to complete their league programme. What Hill didn't bargain for was a Cup run that would mean virtually three games a week.

A third and final trip to Ireland took place on Wednesday, 20 February to Belfast, with Wolves giving the Sky Blues a football lesson in a 6-3 win in front of 6,000 neutrals. Three days later City were able to stage a league game at Highfield Road, thanks to a £250 investment in de-icing pellets and heavy sanding of the central areas of the saturated pitch. Two hundred volunteers, mainly schoolboys, who helped clear the pitch of straw and snow, were thanked by Hill over the loudspeaker system and given a voucher for free admittance to the game. Barnsley were the opponents, and the game only got the final go-ahead 2½ hours before the kick-off.

The efforts were worth it, as City won 2-0 and closed the gap with leaders Peterborough to just two points. Seven other Third Division games were played that day – the best day weather-wise since Boxing Day. The following Tuesday City put on the rearranged game with Colchester, despite a hard pitch, but missed the chance to pull level with Posh, drawing 2-2 after leading 2-0.

As February ended and March began, the Big Freeze was over. A vital promotion battle at Northampton attracted over 18,000, which ended goalless on a 'gluepot' pitch, and four days later the Lincoln Cup-tie finally got played, after 60 days and fifteen postponements. The Imps were swept aside, with Jimmy Whitehouse opening the scoring after just fifteen seconds and the final score of 5-1 did not flatter the Sky Blues.

Notwithstanding the raft of postponements, the FA had proceeded to make the fourth and fifth round draws, so that after the win at Lincoln, City knew that their next opponents would be either Portsmouth or Scunthorpe (away). The winners of that tie would relish a plum home tie with Sunderland, the Second Division leaders who had won through to the fifth round three weeks earlier. The last third round tie to be decided was on 11 March, when Middlesbrough beat Blackburn 3-1 in a replay.

Portsmouth duly defeated Scunthorpe, and City's trip to Fratton Park was scheduled for the following midweek. Memories of the 1-5 League Cup defeat there in October were fresh in the mind, but Jimmy Hill insisted: 'we are a very different side now.'

With massive fixture congestion facing all clubs, City were forced to play three ties with Pompey in six days – drawing 1-1 at Fratton Park, then 2-2 at Coventry (after extra-time) in front of another 25,000 crowd, before a 2-1 second replay win at neutral White Hart Lane.

Travelling to north London, City already knew that if they overcame Pompey, then Sunderland, a home tie with Manchester United waited in the quarter-finals, and this provided a massive incentive. At White Hart Lane, City fell behind, but goals from Bly and Whitehouse clinched the win with the 2,000-plus City fans in the quarter-full stadium making 'almost-deafening bursts of the Sky Blue Song'.

The victory extended City's unbeaten run to 21 games and took the club into the fifth round for the first time since 1937. As Cup-ties took priority, no league games were played, and City's backlog of fixtures therefore increased. During March, City played six FA Cup-ties and just three league games.

The long unbeaten run had enabled Hill to discover his strongest eleven, and with few injuries incurred his team had a settled look. Dave Meeson had been dropped in favour of Bob Wesson at the start of November, and the younger keeper had done well. At full-back Frank Austin, who had started the season at No 3, had been sold to Torquay in December, and although Frank Kletzenbauer had played a few games Hill had converted Mick Kearns from a half-back to a full-back with great success. John Sillett was a virtual ever present at No 2. In the half-back line Curtis was a colossus at centre-half, and once Brian Hill got in the side he was a fixture, with the No 6 duties shared between Ron Farmer and the effervescent youngster Dietmar Bruck.

In attack, Humphries, Bly and Whitehouse were virtually ever-present, but Barr's place was under threat from new man Ken Hale. The Irishman, however, would get the nod over Hale for the big Cup-ties ahead. At No 11 Laverick was jettisoned early on and would join non-league Corby before the season's end. Once Ronnie Rees got the shirt he was a regular and without doubt the find of the season. In the nine FA Cup-ties seven players played in every game, with Bly and Rees just missing one each.

Six days after beating Portsmouth, City faced Sunderland in what was the biggest post-war game at Highfield Road, with the prize at stake a tie against Manchester United. The Wearsiders were poised for promotion back to Division One, averaging over 40,000 at home games, and a week earlier had hit seven goals past Norwich in the league.

Over 50,000 fans converged on Highfield Road that night and half an hour before the kick-off the turnstiles were closed with thousands locked out. Three gates were broken down by determined fans and hundreds rushed in without paying. The terraces could not cope and there were fans up the floodlight pylons, on the stand roofs, and hundreds on the running track. The official attendance was 40,487 but it was hopelessly short of the mark – seasoned veterans reckoned there were more like 48,000 in the ground.

Those who witnessed the game will never forget the suspense, as Sunderland led through a 33rd-minute goal from Irish international Johnny Crossan. Three thousand visiting fans roared the Blaydon Races as the tie seemed to be going the Roker men's way. City kept plugging away and with eight minutes left they levelled the scores. A long shot-cum-cross by Dietmar Bruck bamboozled Jim Montgomery in the visitors' goal and flew in off the upright, prompting a mass invasion of the pitch by young fans. Three minutes later George Curtis bulldozed his way into the penalty area and met John Sillett's cross with his massive forehead to score with a thunderous header and provoke a second, more

6. 1962-63 (Part 2) The Revolution Takes Off

ecstatic pitch invasion. A booming tannoy left the youngsters in no doubt that referee McCabe would abandon the game if there was any further encroachment, but Curtis' goal was the last of the night and the excited fans waited until the final whistle before a third intrusion. The Sky Blue song finally drowned out the Blaydon Races and the shock result brought Coventry City suddenly to the attention of the country's sports media. This was no flash in the pan giantkilling, this was the first vital rung on the long ladder to the heights.

City fan Peter Lea recalls the night: 'Like many other kids I sat on the running track within touching distance from our heroes in Sky Blue. I was nine years old. The roar of the crowd and the red and white stripes of Sunderland will be with me forever. I could hear the players as they drew breath and grunted into the tackle. A lean, blond-headed man, who I was told was Jimmy Whitehouse, danced and glided around the pitch effortlessly. He seemed to be everywhere. Red and white striped shirts came at him from all angles but he just turned and rode the tackles.'

The city was buzzing, the only topic Saturday's home quarter-final against Manchester United. After the chaotic scenes of Monday night, the game was made all-ticket with a Highfield Road capacity of 44,000. The club planned to put the tickets on sale on the Wednesday evening, but some supporters started queuing from 5.30 that morning. By mid-afternoon, with the rain teeming down, there were massive queues estimated at 17,000 strong meandering all around the stadium. The police, concerned about the welfare of the supporters, requested that the club start selling tickets early, and at 3.20pm a roar went up when the ticket kiosks opened. In just three hours most of City's 30,000 allocation was sold and an estimated 15,000 were turned away empty-handed.

Hill decided to take the players away for a few days. They went to the Warnes Hotel in Worthing, an old hunting ground of Fulham in Hill's days at the club. Hoping to escape from the media circus in Coventry, the players were nevertheless tracked down by the press.

In Coventry, the rain poured down all week. By Saturday morning huge pools of water covered the pitch. When referee Ernie Crawford arrived early and expressed serious doubts about the playing surface, Hill and Robins raced to the ground from the Hotel Leofric where they were lunching. An army of helpers forked the pitch and the pools slowly disappeared. Crawford gave the go-ahead.

The rain finally abated just before the kick-off, but not before most of the crowd who had been patiently standing on the terraces for an hour or more were soaked through. The drenched fans were livened up by comedian Ken Dodd, who appeared on the pitch. Doddy was appearing at the

Coventry Theatre at the time and Hill, always looking for unusual pre-match entertainment, sent him out in a Sky Blue shirt. The roars from City fans turned to boos as he reached the centre-circle and peeled off his City shirt to reveal a red United shirt underneath.

For the very first time the BBC had television cameras at Highfield Road (perched on top of the Main Stand) to record the action. The highlights were shown later that evening on *Saturday Sport*, with commentary from the soon to be legendary Kenneth Wolstenholme.

Five years after the Munich Air Disaster had wiped the heart out of arguably the best post-war English club side, and seriously damaged England's 1958 World Cup hopes, Matt Busby had rebuilt Manchester United. This 1962-63 season, however, was not proving to be a good one. The team might have boasted ten internationals, including England's golden boy Bobby Charlton and British record signing, the Scot Denis Law, but they were floundering in the bottom half of the table and would ultimately miss relegation by a whisker.

Busby teams always played football, but this one had a hard heart with the dominant Bill Foulkes at centre-half and the assertive and muscular Maurice Setters alongside. In those days Charlton played as a left-winger, but was capable of electrifying pace and loved to cut inside and demonstrate his trademark powerful shooting. But his form, like United's, had been patchy as he struggled to recover from a summer hernia operation. United's poor form had exposed an ill-disciplined streak, with the petulant Law and hard-man Setters both in trouble with referees. Since the thaw United, despite progressing in the Cup, were without a win in five league games, and on the day club captain Noel Cantwell was ruled out. City were unchanged from the Sunderland game, with Hugh Barr holding off a challenge for his place from Ken Hale.

City stunned the Reds by going a goal up within five minutes. Bly and Foulkes both lunged for a Willie Humphries cross at the Spion Kop end, and the ball flew into the net. Bly claimed the goal but admitted that 'it seemed to go into the net off both of us'. Later the weight of numbers in the press credited it as an own-goal to Bill Foulkes. For the next fifteen minutes United were in disarray and Ronnie Rees hit an upright when a second goal would possibly have ended United's hopes. Charlton pulled United level after 27 minutes, and four minutes after half-time put United ahead with a moment of individual brilliance.

As the second half wore on, the heavy pitch tired both teams, with some players up to their ankles in mud. Then, with twenty minutes left Bly, bulldozing his way through the United defence, appeared to be pushed from behind in the act of shooting, and as the ball ran loose

Humphries cracked the ball into the net. To everyone's astonishment referee Crawford disallowed the goal and awarded United a free-kick. After the game Jimmy Hill said the ball had struck Bly in the face but Crawford said he handled it. This was one of numerous refereeing decisions that upset City, while he turned a blind eye to some of United's robust and sometimes reckless challenges. This mystified 'Nemo' in the *CT*: 'He [Crawford] was particularly indifferent to outrageous gamesmanship and persistent fouling by Denis Law who set a bad example as skipper of his side, even though I am a great admirer of his playing capabilities.'

Three minutes later a rare blunder by City's defence let in Quixall for a third goal, and although City fought till the final whistle the great FA Cup adventure was over, as was City's 21-match unbeaten run, stretching back to early October.

Hill later mused that without the friendly with United in Dublin during the freeze, Matt Busby's team would not have realised how strong his team was, and they might have caught United napping. United went on to win the FA Cup, beating Leicester 3-1 in the final with future Coventry manager Noel Cantwell lifting the trophy at Wembley.

There was honour in defeat for the tired Sky Blues – their performances had won over the fickle Coventry footballing public and put the club on the back pages of the nation's newspapers. The 44,000 crowd, a post-war club record, paid receipts of £8,614 which, when added to the Sunderland receipts, meant that City were financially stronger than at any time since World War Two.

Hill was not happy, however. Four days after the United defeat, with the transfer deadline approaching and sixteen league games still to play – and a good chance of promotion – he paid a club record £21,000 for Peterborough's prolific scorer George Hudson. Hill made it clear there was no place for the goal-machine Bly, as Hudson would be his first choice No 9. Not since 1950, when the club had paid £20,000 for Tommy Briggs, had City paid out such a large fee.

Hudson had played alongside Bly at Posh before Bly's move to City the previous summer. He had scored 26 goals to Bly's 27. Posh were managed by former City manager Jack Fairbrother, who said that Hudson had never been put up for sale but 'a staggering fee is offered and we would have been silly not to have taken it'. A week earlier Fairbrother had been quoted as saying: 'I will not sell … within the next two seasons Hudson will get an international cap.'

Hill was known to admire Hudson, but had no hint that Posh would be prepared to sell until he read that Middlesbrough and Newcastle were bidding for him. Fearing he would lose Hudson, he moved fast.

Bly, who was told of Hill's intentions whilst watching a reserve game at Highfield Road, was shocked but sanguine: 'Of course I am very disappointed – we have done so well recently, but these things happen in football and you have to face up to them.' He did not ask for a transfer, though Hill made it clear the club would listen to offers, but not for anything under £15,000. Northampton had offered that some months earlier, it was revealed, for the division's leading scorer.

In his autobiography Hill admits he 'had seen signs here and there that, despite scintillating performances for us when he was hot, Terry was inclined to blow cold on other occasions ... I had detected signs that maybe he wouldn't continue to produce the sensational form for us much longer'. Hill believed there was a right time to buy and a right time to sell – 'before other managers recognise the weakening of a player's potency, enthusiasm or capability'. If he was intending to confuse other managers, he certainly confused a lot of City fans. Hill concluded by insisting there was nothing sinister about the events that preceded the sale of Bly (and the later sale of Hudson in 1966): 'it was pure, cold-blooded, unsentimental business for Coventry's balance sheet, but more importantly in the long-term, to win more matches.'

Hudson would be the man to make Coventry fans forget all about Terry Bly. Dietmar Bruck remembers Hudson's arrival at Highfield Road: 'He arrived in a smart grey suit with a velvet collar with his hair in an "Elvis-like" quiff – a real dandy. He had this Charlie Chaplin-like walk and looked nothing like a footballer. Any doubts the other players had went after his first game – he was pure genius.'

The fans were mystified – why had Hill rejected a centre-forward who had scored virtually a goal a game that season? But in time they realised that the manager had pulled off an inspired deal. Hudson scored a hat-trick in the first half of his debut against Halifax to leapfrog Bly in the divisional scoring charts, but Hill faced a barrage of criticism from supporters for weeks afterwards. The fantastic ball-skill and goals of Hudson won the crowd over, however, and he became a great hero of the fans. Bly would move on to Notts County (with City making a profit), but his career was on the downward slope and he was playing in non-league circles for Grantham in less than eighteen months. Bly made one final appearance in City colours – alongside Hudson at Bristol Rovers – and made a scoring farewell in the 2-2 draw. The following morning Hill informed Bly that he wouldn't be appearing in the first team again unless 'forced into it by a devastating injury'.

Jack Patience, secretary of the supporters' club told, the *Coventry Telegraph* that the general reaction had been one of 'reserving judgement'

6. 1962-63 (PART 2) THE REVOLUTION TAKES OFF

but quoted one City fan as saying 'with Jim in charge there's never a dull moment'.

After the Cup run and the dire weather, City's fixture list was impossible. Despite the Football League extending the season until the end of May, the team played sixteen league games in seven weeks. The fifteen-match unbeaten League run ended in a 1-5 loss at Wrexham but Hudson's arrival saw City lose only once in eight games – a 1-2 home defeat by Bournemouth in front of 30,289, the biggest league crowd at the ground since 1952. With seven games left, promotion was still a possibility but many of the players were looking weary, with eighteen-year-olds Bruck and Rees causing particular concern.

An extra game was also inserted into the schedule when First Division Aston Villa came to Highfield Road to play in a Festival of Soccer to raise money for Coventry Boys Club. A crowd of around 5,500 raised close to the target of £3,000. They watched four hours of football, including an International Clubs XI versus a Coventry Leagues XI, culminating in City's 2-2 draw with Villa. In the former game Jimmy Hill turned out but was carried off with torn ligaments in a 3-3 draw. In the main event, eighteen-year-old Ernie Machin gave an impressive performance and scored a late equaliser. Machin had made two league appearances in the previous fortnight, standing in for the tired Whitehouse, and against Villa looked a star in the making.

Ernie had made great strides since arriving from Lancashire League side Nelson a year earlier. Jimmy Hill had recognised something special about Ernie, after responding to his scout Alf Walton's call to 'sign him up before others do'. In his autobiography Hill describes watching the young Machin: 'he looked extremely slow, but nevertheless when he was in possession of the ball he hardly wasted a pass. He didn't seem to be an outstanding athlete, nor did he have the confidence or the luck to do something special ... I said later that the real reason I took him on was because I liked the look in his eyes ... He had a bright eye and he said, "if you give me a chance, I won't let you down".' Hill wasn't going to pay a huge fee for Ernie and offered the chairman of Nelson £50. To Hill's amazement he agreed and 'for decency's sake he quickly added that if Ernie made the first team he would bump it up to £200.

Three days after Villa, City flew to a league game for the first time when, rather than a long coach journey to Carlisle, they took a plane from Birmingham's Elmdon Airport. The club was rewarded with a 1-0 win, and two days later thumped Bristol Rovers 5-0 to rejuvenate promotion hopes. Northampton were six points clear at the top, but the other promotion place was up for grabs and the win took City to one point behind second-placed Swindon with two games in hand. That however was as close as they got, for none of the next six games was won. The sequence was ended with a win in the last game at QPR. Rangers had been playing that season at the White City as an experiment, but the team's poor form had seen gates drop and they had already announced they would move back to Loftus Road for the following season. Just over 3,000 spectators rattled around the famous old athletics stadium, making for an eerie atmosphere. A poor game came to life when the intensive floodlighting system was switched on with half an hour to go, and City rattled in three goals to Rangers' one as QPR sank to their seventh home defeat. City finished fourth, five points behind second-placed Swindon.

After the final home game on 4 May the pitch-levelling project commenced. As it was not anticipated that the work would be finished in time for the opening day of the 1963-64 season, the club provisionally requested two away games at the start of the new campaign. The cost of the project, £15,000, was met by donations from the supporters' club, but although under-soil heating was a hot topic of the day after the harsh winter, any thoughts of that would have to wait for another day.

Before the end of the season the club unveiled plans for a new stand on the north side of the ground to replace the old 'Atkinsons' stand built from the proceeds of the 1910 FA Cup run. The finished stand, built in reinforced concrete, would comprise six sections, and at 360 feet would stretch virtually the whole length of the pitch. The first phase, to be carried out that summer, would see the erection of two separate wing sections either side of the old stand – allowing the continued use for one last season of the old stand. In the summer of 1964, the old stand would be demolished and four middle sections would be erected, with a complete new stand with 5,100 seats available for the start of the 1964-65 season. Derrick Robins' own company, Banbury Grandstands, would be the contractors, using their innovative quick-build methods which would prove enormously successful over the next five years as the face of Highfield Road changed forever. The cost was budgeted at £80,000 and the early indications were that the funds would largely be met by the supporters' club.

Additionally, during the summer the dressing rooms, referee's room and the players' treatment room would be upgraded, and the Main Stand seats would all be made 'tip-up'. Finally, new refreshment bars were erected at each corner of the ground.

Season-ticket prices and match-day admission prices were increased to help pay for the developments. The dearest season tickets were increased to £7 10 shillings, but to assist fans the club introduced an instalment scheme by which fans could pay a 10 shillings deposit and the remainder in fortnightly instalments before the start of the new season. Within a week the new club secretary, Paul Oliver, announced that they had sold 1,750 season tickets, a 50 per cent increase on the total for 1962-63, and worth around £10,000 to the club – and the season had not even finished. By the start of the new season, the number had risen to over 3,000, generating income of over £21,000, almost five times the income from 1962-63. Things were beginning to buzz football-wise around Coventry.

The pitch levelling was completed by the end of June, with the contractors even employing City player Roy Dwight and the club's former international goalkeeper Reg Matthews to help with the work. At the first home game of 1963-64, supporters saw the impact. The excavations had exposed the terrace wall at the north west and east corners which were now a good ten feet tall. The new pitch looked immaculate and the long-standing drainage problems were expected to be solved.

Two days after that final league game at QPR, the City squad flew to West Germany for three 'tour' games, all of which were won. The tour started near the Danish border with a 3-1 win over Neumunster, the town where Wilf Smith, later to join Coventry, was born. Two days later City beat Bad Neuenahr 6-1 and they rounded off the tour with a 2-0 win over Kaiserslautern. Kaiserslautern had recently been awarded a place in the new Bundesliga, which would commence in the coming 1963-64 season, and the team would visit Coventry later that same year for a return match. Willie Humphries did not travel to Germany, as he was winning his seventh cap for Northern Ireland, against Spain in Bilbao.

Whilst construction work continued at Highfield Road, the club's search for a new training base was ended with the purchase of an eleven-year lease on land at Ryton-on-Dunsmore. Plans were drawn up for a floodlit all-weather pitch, to be completed by October 1963, and other grass pitches for all the club's teams and the amateurs who trained during the week. Until the new base was ready the players would continue to train at Walsgrave and Shilton.

The players reported back for pre-season training on 22 July, and it was announced that Hungarian coach Janos Gerdov was leaving to take up a position with German club Eintracht Trier. Gerdov, who had indicated earlier in the year that he wished to extend his one-year stay, had received an attractive offer from the German Regional League club.

In early August former Aston Villa wing-half Pat Saward was expected to join City as player-coach, but Saward's club, Huddersfield, demanded £3,000 for his signature, even though the former Irish international had not played since the previous December. City refused to pay and

Saward was forced to delay joining the Sky Blues. Hill also signed winger John Mitten on a free transfer. Mitten, son of Hill's former Fulham team-mate Charlie, had been freed by Leicester and failed a trial at another of his father's former clubs, Manchester United. Hill explained that he would prove useful cover for Humphries or Rees in the event of injuries. Mitten's football career had begun when his father was manager at Newcastle, and he made ten appearances in the Magpies' First Division team.

One of the biggest rumours around the city that summer concerned City's young captain and centre-half George Curtis. Allegedly Manchester City had offered City £45,000 for George and were willing to pay the 'iron man' £80 per week. Hill denied these stories and reiterated that Curtis was not for sale anyway.

Four new apprentices arrived on the first day of training, John Docker and Pat Morrissey from last year's Coventry schools team, Mick Coop, from Leamington, and Ken Anderson, a wing-half from Cambridge. Coop and Morrissey would go on to play first-team football, whilst Docker promised much but failed to make the grade.

Despite being out of favour at City, Terry Bly trained with the first-team players until, ten days before the new season started, a deal was struck for his sale to Notts County. County manager Eddie Lowe, a former team-mate of Hill's at Fulham, had expressed interest in Bly but a deal hinged on County selling their star striker Tony Hateley. When Aston Villa agreed to pay £22,000 for Hateley, Lowe had his replacement, Bly, ready. County agreed to pay City £12,300 for the out-of-favour striker – a tidy £2,300 profit for the Sky Blues.

The club's financial gain, however, did not placate Bly's fans in Coventry. A week before the new season started Hill told the *Coventry Telegraph*: 'Continual wrangling about Terry Bly is the best way to destroy this club – it is the one thing that can really stop us doing well. I can foresee what is going to happen – every time someone misses a goal, a few will cry "Terry would have scored". I fully expect that some will stand in front of the directors' box, wait for an opportune moment, and shout "Bring back Terry".'

Hill, of course, was proved right. Bly, despite scoring on his debut, had a disastrous time at Meadow Lane and scored only four goals in 27 games in the 1963-64 season, as County finished bottom of the division. Just over a year later he was playing non-league football for Grantham.

Chapter 7. 1963-64 (Part 1)

Counting Bantams

Coventry City's 1963-64 pre-season was a somewhat low-key affair. The pitch levelling ruled out home friendlies, so that the new pitch would be immaculate for a long season ahead. Instead, Hill took the team to Leamington, Rugby and Wellington for what were described as practice games against non-league outfits but played behind closed doors. At Leamington's Windmill Ground, City were beaten 1-2 by Lockheed, at that time one of the strongest Midlands non-league sides, before City trounced Rugby Town 6-0, and Sankeys (Wellington) 6-1.

The first public practice took place at the Butts Stadium when a City team took on a side described as the 'Pick of the Local Leagues XI'. It was gentle stuff and Hill only fielded his first XI up to half-time before replacing them with his youth team. City scored four goals in each half with two replies for the locals. One of the second-half scorers was Bobby Gould.

Finally, five days before the curtain-raiser, the team were allowed onto the new pitch for a private practice match against Second Division Derby. Around 150 fans standing on the terraces in pouring rain saw City beat the Rams 5-3. Hill declared himself happy with the team's performance and the new pitch. The only question about the team was at inside-forward where Ken Hale and Ernie Machin started the game but Hugh Barr, a second-half substitute, made a strong bid for a place in the team with two goals.

As the season opened, expectations were as high as in 1955-56, when Jesse Carver had arrived to much fanfare. Hill had caught the imagination of the Coventry public and over 26,000 saw the Sky Blues open the season with a 5-1 win over Crystal Palace. Palace had prepared well, and like many teams that season tried to muscle the Sky Blues out. Manager Dick Graham's plan failed as his team conceded two penalties, numerous free-kicks, and were booed by the home crowd for their physical tactics. Ron Farmer, who had taken his share of stick from the City crowd, was the hero of the day, scoring the two penalties and a 35-yard free-kick past a dazed Bill Glazier in the Palace goal. Farmer was ecstatic but he recalls that Jimmy Hill wasn't impressed. Ron explains: 'it was a tradition that if you scored a hat-trick you got to keep the match ball, but when I asked JH for the ball he said that because I scored two penalties it wasn't a proper hat-trick!'

The Sky Blues started the season like a train. Six out of the first seven games were won, the other drawn, with 21 goals scored (Hudson netting seven), and only three conceded. City's away following continued to grow with 3,000 at Notts County, 5,000 at Walsall two days later, and an estimated 7,000 travelling to Luton (in a 14,000 crowd). Local bus firms were caught out by the demand, and amid chaotic scenes hundreds of fans were left stranded at the city's Pool Meadow bus station when they were unable to get to Nottingham and Walsall. The head of Red House Motors, the main local coach firm, explained that they were only licenced to run a certain number of vehicles on any day. Both games had stretched them to the limit, 40 coaches having left for Walsall. Demand for train excursion tickets was great, too, and the coach companies and Mr Ronald Salt, the Coventry station master, appealed to fans to book early to avoid disappointment.

The good start also saw a renewed spurt in season-ticket sales. On 1 September, Hill warned that only a few remained and gave fans five days to snap them up. He gave a figure of almost £20,000 in season-ticket receipts. For the midweek visit of Crewe, over 29,000 flocked to see the unbeaten start extended to seven with a 5-1 win. The team were playing fast, exciting football, with the wingers, Rees and Humphries, providing a constant stream of crosses for the goal-hungry forwards.

The run ended with a 1-2 reverse at Hull's Boothferry Park, but only after a controversial late penalty for the home side. Referee Kevin Howley, one of the top officials in the 1960s, judged that George Curtis had handled in the box. Jimmy Hill was sure that George was almost on the touchline when the incident happened and voiced his opinions to the press after the game. In his autobiography Hill explained that it was this incident and the fruitless public dispute about the decision that made him resolve never again to complain about poor decisions publicly. Seven days later newly promoted Mansfield burst City's unbeaten home record and knocked them off the top by winning 3-0.

In early October the club published their accounts for the previous financial year, which showed a profit of £87, the first profit since 1958. Match receipts, boosted by the FA Cup run, were up from £38,000 to £96,000, but expenses increased at the same time. After losses of £5,000 and £16,000 declared in the two previous years, the figures were extremely heartening, and they would have been over £12,000 better if the Bly proceeds had been able to be included. The figures revealed that Derrick Robins' 'gift' of £30,000 had almost single-handedly funded the club's transfer budget, with the supporters' club funding the £15,000 pitch re-levelling.

The players picked themselves up, following the two league defeats, and Hill kept faith with his selection. A nervous draw at Crewe was followed by four straight wins. The 3-2 triumph at Brentford, which Robins described as the 'best away display in 10 years', took the Sky Blues top of the table again. When Willie Humphries was absent playing for Ireland in the Home internationals, John Mitten made his debut on the left wing with Rees switching to the right.

At Colchester on 19 October City lost to a moderate home side, with Hill's reject Mike Grice scoring a fine goal. City clung to top spot only on goal-average from Oldham, but would remain in first place until mid-March.

Three days later poor Shrewsbury took the backlash from the defeat in Essex, hit for eight in City's biggest victory since the 1930s, in which Rees scored his first hat-trick. Hugh Barr, out in the cold until Ken Hale's ankle injury, scored two in his first home appearance of the season.

That month Pat Saward finally joined the Sky Blues as a player-coach. His club, Huddersfield, had been ordered to scrap any fee and permit a free transfer by a Football League tribunal. Hill explained that, whilst Saward's main job would be coaching the youngsters, 'he could come into the first team if the occasion arose.' A week later Saward played in the reserve team. Irish-born Saward, an FA Cup winner in 1957 with Aston Villa and a holder of eighteen Eire caps, would become a popular character around the club over the next few years. He had a reputation for his dapper fashion sense and was always immaculately attired, an attribute he also instilled into his young players. His young teams achieved unprecedented success, reaching the FA Youth Cup finals in 1968 and 1970.

At the AGM Derrick Robins addressed shareholders in more positive mood than at any time as chairman. With the club top of Division Three and financially sound, he beamed at his audience: 'I would submit that during the past 12 months we have seen success in the club beyond our wildest dreams.' He crystallised what the board and Jimmy Hill were trying to achieve: 'This club has an approach to football unlike any other football club which I know.' After listing the new facilities offered to spectators he went on: 'We believe in doing this, that the public will respond and will become very much closer. We believe that this way the club becomes that much greater and we shall thereby achieve our targets more quickly.' He unveiled another initiative, a vice-presidents' club to attract 'important businessmen in the city into such a group'. It would be housed under the main stand, offering refreshment on match-days.

Jimmy Hill had, so far this season, been lucky with injuries, with only five games missed by his preferred starting eleven in the first sixteen games. But in a 2-2 home draw with Watford, Ernie Machin, who had made a dramatic impression in the side, suffered a serious knee injury. Initially, it seemed that Machin, who had already attracted the England Under-23 selectors, would only be out for three weeks, but it was almost a year before he fully recovered and almost two before he would once again be a regular in the first team.

Ernie described the injury: 'There was no one near me when I turned sharply and I felt something go. I went off and it didn't feel too bad, so on I came again. But the first time I reached for the ball with the same leg, it collapsed under me again.'

The draw for the first round of the FA Cup could have seen the Sky Blues meet non-league neighbours Lockheed Leamington. Lockheed, dubbed 'the Brakes' because of their link with Lockheed Automotive Products, were in the hat following a draw with Corby in the final qualifying round. Instead, the Brakes were given a plum home tie with Bristol City if they could win at Corby in the replay, but they lost. Coventry, however, were given a fairytale tie, away to Trowbridge of the Southern League Premier Division.

After some debate about where to stage the tie – FA rules permitted the hosts to be switched if both clubs agreed – a capacity of 12,000 was placed on Trowbridge's Frome Road ground, with City receiving 3,000 tickets.

Before the trip to Wiltshire, City exited the League Cup, 2-4 at Second Division Rotherham, having won at Luton in the previous round. Today's League Cup is a poor relation of the FA Cup, but in the early 1960s it was even more so, with several First Division sides not taking part until 1966-67, when the carrot was dangled of a Wembley final, rather than the existing two-legged affair. Gates were normally much lower than for league games, and it was clear that Coventry were determined to avoid a replay at Rotherham, which would have required an extra fixture in an already hectic programme.

City prepared for the Trowbridge tie with a short break in Worthing, where they had prepared for the Manchester United tie the previous season. 'Nemo' described the daily programme:

'Tuesday: Leave for Worthing and on arrival have a brisk five-a-side match on the beach. Wednesday: A day of golf or sea-fishing. Thursday: Normal day's training for a Saturday match. Friday: Light sprints and limbering up. Saturday: Arrive at Trowbridge for the match.'

JH travelled down to the south coast on the Tuesday evening, after watching City's youth team play West Brom in the FA Youth Cup. City's youngsters came from 1-6 down to lose to a strong Albion side 4-6. John

Docker, City's exciting prospect, caused havoc with his corners, which produced all four goals, including one goal direct from a flag-kick.

The first team comfortably disposed of Trowbridge, 6-1, and the non-leaguers probably regretted not switching the tie as only 6,500 turned up, with 2,700 from Coventry. November 1963 might possibly have been the best month in the whole history of the club. The team won all four league games, scoring fifteen goals, hit Trowbridge for six in the Cup, and scored eight against German Bundesliga side Kaiserslautern in a home friendly. It was a golden month, too, for George Hudson, with the striker netting thirteen goals including three hat-tricks in ten days. The avaricious striker netted three at Trowbridge, repeated the feat against Kaiserslautern, and again at Loftus Road in a 6-3 victory which went a long way to convincing any doubters in the London press that the Sky Blues were going places. QPR boss Alec Stock described City as 'the finest Division Three team I have ever seen', and not only described them as promotion certainties but tipped them to go straight through Division Two. The 4-2 home win over Bristol Rovers was preceded by a minute's silence for the death of US President John F Kennedy, assassinated in Dallas the previous day.

The team remained unbeaten in the league through December but suffered a shock exit in the FA Cup, losing at home to Bristol Rovers, two weeks after thrashing them in the league. JH was disappointed, but Robins more philosophical: 'After the lessons of last season, one cannot help feeling that it might be for the best. If you go on in the FA Cup everyone gets roused, you put everything you've got into it and so on. Financially, it's not too serious a blow.' It was the age-old dilemma of whether a Cup run helps or hinders league form. In City's case, the 1962-63 FA Cup run had taken its toll, but perhaps that was more about the weather.

The hardest league game in December was the 1-1 draw at Crystal Palace. Palace had recovered from the mauling at Highfield Road and lay third in the table. Their tactics in the earlier game had angered City fans, and in the return game the South London side were determined to stop City's free-flowing style at all costs. Left-back Bert Howe was booked for three crude challenges on Willie Humphries that, according to 'Nemo', 'made even hardened observers wince'. Undoubtedly, Howe's behaviour would have earned a red card in the modern game. Humphries, however, got up and proceeded to 'carve up' Palace's left flank, 'often leaving Howe sprawling on the turf behind him.'

The real hero that day was captain courageous George Curtis. Halfway through the physical first half he received a serious gash on his left knee and had to come off. Trainer Peter Hill told 'Nemo': 'As soon as I saw George's leg I told him he would have to come off. In all my experience I've never seen a gash like it. It was about three to four inches long and really deep.'

Curtis shrugged it off as if it were a scratch: 'Stitch it up and I'll be back on'. Just before half-time he returned to the fray, and with City by this time losing 0-1 and under the Palace cosh, he inspired the team to equalise and almost grab a late winner. During the second half his exertions burst two of the stitches. After the game Jimmy Hill said: 'it was the bravest thing I ever saw.'

Hill and Palace boss Dick Graham had a bitter press row in the days following the game. Hill was critical of Palace's style: 'To me it [the result] proved that constructive football can triumph over the purely destructive. And you can quote me as saying that I don't think Palace will win promotion. This is the third time in a row that Palace have adopted these tactics against us. They base their game on the physical side. Last season a Palace director apologised to us and said he was ashamed of his side's display.'

Dick Graham, sporting a fierce-looking crew-cut, and also a former Palace goalkeeper, defended Howe and criticised Hill for 'trying to run not just his own team but everyone else's and the officials as well'.

Curtis sat out a friendly with Hungarian champions Ferencvaros two days later – City won 3-1 with late goals from Hale and Mitten – but was back in harness the following Saturday against Walsall. Over 12,000 watched the friendly on a cold night, among them England manager Alf Ramsey and his squad, which was staying at Birmingham, preparing for an international. Curtis' stand-in, Mick Kearns, did a marvellous marking job on the Hungarian international centre-forward Florian Albert, rated as one of the best No 9s in the world.

The new 'Sky Blue' stand was taking shape. By October the two wing stands were complete and towered over the old 1910 stand, which was still in use. The club could not sell tickets for every seat in the new wing stands because the back rows had a restricted view, but the usable seats added around 1,200 to the seating capacity and helped the club's finances. Work on the centre sections was hoped to be completed in the summer, after the old stand was demolished, so that the completed new Sky Blue Stand would be ready for the first home game of 1964-65. Building work, however, did not close the terraces in front of the stand.

The club continued to be innovative, looking long and hard at pre-match entertainment. Soon after Hill arrived he had identified the young fans as his target audience and replaced the pre-match band with pop music. Hill and Robins met Jill Hanson, who ran a record shop in the Precinct, and Jill agreed to provide the discs so long as she could also provide the disc jockey to look after them. A young local DJ named Frank Pritchard got the 'gig'. Frank takes up the story: 'I was mad about Coventry City and pop music so it was perfect for me. JH wanted to appeal to the teenagers and also change the image of football being for men in cloth caps. He thought that by me playing pop records over the Tannoy system, more youngsters would come. I started by playing for about 45 minutes before kick-off and again at half-time. I only had a single turntable so had to talk whilst changing the discs and was housed in a tiny cubby-hole with the hospital radio man. The Tannoy sound system was pretty dire and we had lots of complaints, mainly about the distorted music. Early in 1962-63 I was playing the UK's No 1 single, *I Remember You*, by Cov Kid Frank Ifield so often that a local reporter wrote that if I played the song any more the club would have to rename the ground "Ifield Road".' It may not sound innovative these days but in 1963 there was little or no pre-match entertainment save for the occasional marching band.

After about eighteen months in the DJ's chair, Frank was replaced by a 'bigger name', former England wicket-keeper Godfrey Evans, along with club commercial manager Charles Harrold, who had a journalistic background. The name 'Radio Sky Blue' was coined. Other entertainment introduced by Hill included netball games, gymnastic displays from the Butlin Girls, trampolining, the Royal Signals motorcycle display team, and Coventry's own 'pop' group, the Mighty Avengers. It wasn't long before showbiz stars, many appearing at Coventry Theatre, were interviewed by Harrold before kick-off or at half-time. Jimmy Tarbuck, Frankie Vaughan and Frankie Howerd all paid visits to Highfield Road as Hill saw the benefits of being connected with stars of stage and screen. In another innovative move, Hill had a telephone installed next to his seat in the directors' box to communicate with the trainer's bench and Radio Sky Blue.

For Rod Dean, it was the best time of his life: 'Nobody talked about anything else in 1963 – Jimmy had managed to mobilise a whole city – every other week there was a new gimmick, some worked, others never got off the ground. In most households in the area there was constant discussion on new signings, new stands, new training grounds, and of course everybody talked about George Hudson, who became bigger news than Jimmy himself. Season-ticket sales doubled, even trebled, and for the first time large numbers of City fans travelled to away games, and remember this was the era before motorways crisscrossed the country.

Hudson was god to all the young fans, and on some Sunday lunchtimes we went to the Mount Pleasant Pub in Walsgrave Road where George drank (not every Sunday, but regularly). We never spoke to him, of course, but to be in the same bar was enough – the man walked on water.'

After an excellent December, City beat Millwall 3-0 in a Friday night game on 3 January 1964, and following the following day's fixtures the top of the Division Three looked like this:

	P	W	D	L	F	A	Pts
1. Coventry	27	18	6	3	68	29	42
2. Watford	27	14	6	7	51	37	34
3. Crystal Pal	27	13	7	7	48	35	33
4. Oldham	26	14	5	7	51	37	33
5. Bournemouth	26	14	4	8	41	26	32

City stood eight points clear and looked odds-on for promotion. Who would have guessed that they would not win another game for almost three months and virtually throw away their promotion chance?

Chapter 8. 1963-64 (Part 2)

Let's All Sing Together

Coventry City have latterly become renowned for their post-Christmas slumps, and the disastrous slump of 1964 was the first major one.

From 3 January until 28 March eleven league games were played without a single victory, and the only saving grace was they lost only four of the eleven. The writing was on the wall in January when Luton, the division's bottom team, led City at Highfield Road until the final two minutes and went away with a point. Four days later the fourteen-game unbeaten league run was ended at high-flying Boundary Park, in front of 20,008, Oldham's biggest crowd for years. Hill gambled by recalling Ernie Machin, but his knee was not right and he limped through most of the second half.

A week later Hill signed Graham Newton, a young inside-forward from Walsall to act as cover. On top of Machin's injury, George Hudson missed three games before undergoing surgery for a groin strain in late January. Although he returned in early February for two games, he looked far from the slick goal-poacher of November. Another forward, Jimmy Whitehouse, was having a rough time, too. One of the stars of the 1963 FA Cup run, Jimmy had inexplicably lost his form since returning to the side in January and was surprisingly given stick by the crowd. Hill defended Whitehouse and asked the fans to stop barracking City players. In March, however, Jimmy, out of the first team again, signed for Millwall. He followed Roy Dwight, who had moved to the Den in January.

Stiff competition for places saw another star of the previous season's Cup run, Hugh Barr, languishing in the reserves. Before the end of the season he told 'Nemo' he was seriously considering returning to teaching, having left the profession to sign a professional contract at Coventry two years earlier: 'I cannot see much future for me here with regard to getting a first-team place. The competition is so fierce.' Barr revealed he had told Jimmy Hill that he would like to return to part-time football so that he could take up his old job as a PE teacher. 'Nemo' concluded that Barr had never repeated the heights of his first half-season as a City player in 1962-63, when he reached double figures ahead of Terry Bly, but it could never be said that Barr's contribution to City's rise was not very useful.

Another defeat, 2-3 at Mansfield, reduced City's lead to three points, with Dick Graham's Crystal Palace leading the chasing pack, and Watford two points further back. Outwardly Hill was calm but, behind the scenes, he was desperate for a solution to the poor results. Chances were still being created but, he argued, the team weren't getting the run of the ball and confidence had suffered. He was prepared to try anything and shuffled his team, dropping ever-present Bob Wesson for Dave Meeson, giving Whitehouse's shirt to new man Newton, and trying Hugh Barr, then Bobby Gould at No 9 for the injured Hudson. Even the ever-dependable George Curtis was struggling. After his boob had gifted a goal to Brentford, Hill said: 'there were gasps and drawings-in of breath every time he went for the ball. Do you think this helped to relieve the tension?' Hill said his players were scared of letting the fans down, and he never missed an opportunity to boost his players in the local press.

At Wrexham at the end of February Hill tried a new defensive system, described by 'Nemo' as 1-5-4 (four forwards, five defenders and a continental-style sweeper). Although City earned a point, the performance was dire and dour. A week later the poor run looked to be coming to an end when City raced into a 2-0 lead against fourth-placed Bournemouth, but they were then held to a draw despite registering 35 shots at the visitors' goal.

One novel idea rejected by Hill was an offer from a hypnotist to 'relax' the players. Henry Blythe from Torquay had caught the attention at the Coventry Carnival the previous year, and now wrote to Jimmy offering hypnotic relaxation to assist the team ahead of the big promotion clash at Watford. Blythe pledged to charge a fee only if the team won, and then would give half of it to charity, but Hill declined the offer. Roared on by 6,000 travelling fans, City played well at Watford and deserved their point, which kept them top of the league, on goal-average from Crystal Palace, with Watford two points behind in what appeared to be a three-horse race for two promotion places. If City's form did not pick up, however, it would become a two-horse race without them.

The Watford result was a false dawn, however. The following Friday evening Southend shattered City's fragile confidence by winning 5-2 at Highfield Road – the first time a Coventry side had conceded five at home since the war. They trailed 0-3 after half an hour, pulled it back to 2-3, then, despite being roared on by a noisy crowd, conceded two more goals. Poor goalkeeper Dave Meeson was culpable, but so were most of the team in a shoddy defensive display, with the usually consistent George Curtis and Mick Kearns taking much criticism both during the game and in the *Pink* postbag.

Prior to the game rumours abounded of Hill signing players before the transfer deadline the following Monday. Big-name forwards were mentioned, like Ken Wagstaff (Mansfield), Ron Saunders (Portsmouth),

Maurice Cook (Fulham), Jimmy Robson (Burnley) and George Kirby (Southampton). Hill scotched the rumours, saying: 'Why should I make a signing?' The Southend result obviously made him rethink, because on deadline-day he paid Southampton £12,500 for Kirby and Tottenham £11,000 for midfield general John Smith. To help pay for the double signing, City sold Jimmy Whitehouse to Millwall for £4,500 (a profit of £4,500!) and Frank Kletzenbauer to Walsall for £2,500.

Thirty-year-old Kirby was a tall, bruising forward who had spent much of his career in Everton's reserves, but he had made a big impression at Southampton after moving from Plymouth in 1962. Excellent in the air, he had appeared on Coventry's radar after scoring a hat-trick for Saints reserves against City earlier that month, whilst gaining match practice after a stomach upset. At first, he turned down Hill's overtures but finally succumbed to the bearded wonder's charms.

Twenty-five-year-old Smith, who could play either at wing-half or inside-forward, similarly had spent a lot of time in reserve football. A prodigious talent as a teenager with West Ham, John joined Tottenham after winning England Under-23 honours, but played only 21 first-team games in four years, thwarted by the form of Danny Blanchflower and John White in Spurs' 'double' side.

That week also saw the departure of Arthur Cox, the part-time 'A'-team coach. Cox joined his former mentor Alf Wood, who had recently been appointed manager of Walsall. Southam-born Cox had been a promising teenage defender with a fierce tackle, but his playing career had ended after he broke his leg in a youth-team game around 1959.

Kirby and Smith made their debuts at Bournemouth on the Saturday, replacing Humphries and Newton, but the newcomers failed to stop the rot. The Cherries won 2-1 to move to within two points of City, who were now four points behind Palace and clinging onto second place on goal-average from Watford.

	P	W	D	L	F	A	Pts
1. Crystal Pal	38	22	9	7	62	38	53
2. Coventry	38	18	13	7	86	54	49
3. Watford	37	21	7	9	68	47	49
4. Bournemouth	37	20	7	10	67	46	47

With Easter's three important games looming, unless something radical happened, City were destined to blow their promotion hopes.

On Easter Saturday, City faced Oldham. Hill made changes, recalling Bob Wesson, Dietmar Bruck, Graham Newton and Willie Humphries, but he dropped fans' favourite and leading scorer George Hudson, who had scored only one goal in six games since the start of the year. Hill indicated that some players were feeling the mental tension, so he would make changes to field his strongest eleven. He expressed satisfaction at the debuts of Kirby and Smith, but said 'if they can settle down the other nine, they will have done their job.'

The changes paid off, with Kirby netting a hat-trick of headers in the 4-1 victory over Oldham, but the Sky Blues were unconvincing for long periods and Oldham keeper Bollands was hampered by an injury early in the game. The win did, however, give the team some confidence and on Easter Monday at Port Vale they looked set for another win, only to concede a late goal in a 1-1 draw. The following evening almost 30,000 turned up at Highfield Road for the return game with Vale, but the visitors' blanket defence smothered all City's efforts and another 1-1 draw ensued. The lost point meant that the table looked thus:

	P	W	D	L	F	A	Pts
1. Crystal Pal	40	23	10	7	66	41	56
2. Coventry	41	19	15	7	92	57	53
3. Watford	40	22	8	10	72	52	52
4. Bournemouth	40	22	7	11	72	50	51

The action moved to Bristol Rovers' Eastville Stadium four days later. City recorded their first away win for four months thanks to a Ken Hale goal straight from the second-half kick-off. 'Nemo' described it as 'a team performance' and wrote: 'It was 1963 since I was last able to report that there was not a weak link in the side,' and his only criticism was that the Sky Blues should have made it at least 3-0. City's three challengers all dropped points, so their standing in the table had improved slightly.

Now it was the turn of City's rivals to suffer promotion nerves. The following Saturday, whilst City were beating QPR 4-2 at home, Palace were losing at home to Barnsley, and Bournemouth also lost. Watford drew again, putting City back on top, on goal-average from Palace, with three games to play. Two days later Bournemouth lost again, at Brentford, so their promotion hopes were virtually ended. Palace, meanwhile, drew their game in hand to edge one point ahead of the Sky Blues.

George Hudson was desperate to play and his presence in the reserves against Bournemouth's second string attracted 4,181, the largest reserve gate of the season. Hudson, for whom Jimmy Hill had rejected a transfer enquiry from Northampton, showed flashes of his old self and was unlucky not to score in a 2-0 win. 'The Hud's' day would come.

8. 1963-64 (PART 2) LET'S ALL SING TOGETHER

Two of City's final three fixtures were away (at Millwall and then Peterborough), with a home game with Colchester on the last day. Palace, too, faced two away trips (Peterborough and Wrexham) with a final day home visit from Oldham. Watford, on paper, had the easiest finish – home fixtures against Reading and Brentford, with a trip to local rivals Luton on the last day.

Excitement in Coventry was at fever pitch and around 8,000 fans made plans for the trip to Millwall's Den. Never an easy ground to earn points, City had not won there in six visits since Boxing Day 1955. Like many Third Division grounds, the Sky Blues pulled in the biggest crowd of the season at the Den, and over 22,000 made for an electric atmosphere. Millwall were desperate for points to avoid relegation and with City equally desperate there was little football played. Two minutes before half-time City were awarded a penalty, and with Ron Farmer's impeccable record with spot-kicks City fans were already celebrating a 1-0 lead. For Farmer it was unlucky thirteen – the previous week he had speculated that keepers were beginning to 'tumble' to his method of always hitting the ball to his right, and that he might have to change direction. He duly changed his direction, sending Alex Stepney the wrong way, but his shot hit the post and bounced out (Ron went on to take a further eleven penalties for the Sky Blues and never missed another). City's 0-0 draw, coupled with Palace's 1-1 draw at Peterborough, meant no change at the top, but Watford's 1-0 win over Reading edged them one point behind City.

Next Monday afternoon in Coventry one would have thought a world war was starting and the city being evacuated, as thousands converged on the railway station and the Pool Meadow bus station. Factories and firms all over the city, and in surrounding towns like Bedworth, Nuneaton, Rugby and Leamington, reported unprecedented interest in City's game that evening at Peterborough. Many workers left work and went straight on to coaches heading to Peterborough. Hundreds of schoolboys who had been among the Sky Blues' most fervent fans went straight from the classroom to pick up coaches or trains. Thousands more travelled by road across country, with endless streams of cars sporting sky blue colours reported on the main roads of Northamptonshire. An estimated 12,000 City fans travelled in probably the biggest away following since the Second Division derbies with Aston Villa in the 1930s.

The fans sang themselves hoarse and the players gave everything they had, but it was not enough. The team lacked firepower up front and the London Road record league crowd of 26,307 inspired Posh to a 2-0 win that belied their mid-table status. Sky Blue fans trailed back to Coventry now knowing that promotion was out of their hands, and that wins for

Palace and Watford in midweek would leave both clubs above the Sky Blues. Lady Luck was smiling, however. On Tuesday night Watford were held at home by Brentford, and on Wednesday Palace were held by already relegated Wrexham. Despite the boost given to City's rivals by the defeat at Peterborough, both failed to capitalise, with tension blamed for their poor results. The results left the top of the table thus:

	P	W	D	L	F	A	Pts
1. Crystal Pal	45	23	14	8	72	48	60
2. Coventry	45	21	16	8	97	61	58
3. Watford	45	23	12	10	78	57	58

The Sky Blues now knew that a win over Colchester in the final game would guarantee promotion, irrespective of what happened to Watford at Luton. In fact, with City boasting a better goal-average, they only needed to achieve the same result as Watford to clinch a return to Division Two after twelve years. 'Nemo' in the *Coventry Telegraph* calculated that a 1-0 victory by the Sky Blues would require Watford to win 12-0 to pip them ('Nemo' was wrong: Watford would need to win 14-0)!

The stage was set therefore for the biggest league game at Highfield Road since the war. Secretary Paul Oliver began preparations by announcing that the turnstiles would open earlier than normal, at 12.30, to meet the expected 30,000-plus crowd. Coventry police appealed for motorists to leave their cars behind on the big day and use public transport to get to the ground.

On the Friday the team news was surprising – George Hudson was recalled. Many fans had wondered why Jimmy Hill had not drafted him in at Peterborough, against his former club. Hill explained in the *Coventry Telegraph* on the Friday evening: 'I asked George if he would play at Peterborough, and he said he didn't feel he was quite ready. He said to me "Just give me another go in the Reserves at Reading on Wednesday, and I should be all right." When I next asked him to play I got a very different answer. George scored a goal at Reading and told me he was ready to come back into the first team.'

Hill confirmed that he wouldn't play a twin spearhead. Hudson had been playing an inside-forward role in the reserves and the plan would be to play him there against Colchester. Kirby, Hill said, was prepared to switch with Hudson if things were not working out. Ron Farmer, who had missed the Posh game, would also return in place of Dietmar Bruck.

Hill's tactical gamble paid off, with Hudson and Willie Humphries carving huge gaps in the visitors' defence before George, looking like the

Hudson of old, netted after 24 minutes. 'Nemo' described the goal: 'A quick thrust down the left, a cross from Rees while the Colchester defence was at sixes and sevens, and it was a blur as Hudson whipped the ball into the back of the net.'

City missed many opportunities to increase their lead, and after half-time, with Colchester rarely looking like troubling City's defence, the 36,901 crowd's attention switched to news of their rivals. With City kicking off later at 3.15, the Palace and Watford games finished before the final whistle at Coventry, and Godfrey Evans announced the final scores over the Tannoy. Watford had led their local rivals Luton for most of the game but let in two late goals to ensure City's promotion. Palace amazingly lost at home to Oldham, which meant City were champions on goal-average. The last ten minutes seemed to drag and finally the referee blew the whistle. Within seconds the pitch had become a sea of spectators with the players disappearing under a mass of young supporters in a repeat of the scenes twelve months earlier against Sunderland.

Somehow the players got off the pitch, soon to appear in the Main Stand, high above the sea of fans, to take their applause. There was no trophy for the track-suited heroes (it was still at previous year's champions Northampton and would not be presented to City until the League's AGM). Derrick Robins' attempt to have himself heard long enough to present George Curtis with the Midland Footballer of the Year trophy ended in a noisy farce as the fans clamoured for Jimmy Hill. Hill, Robins and the players deserved the plaudits for restoring the club's Second Division status after twelve years. For the third time that season, the club's receipts record was broken, with £5,846 being taken at the turnstiles. The final average gate was 26,017, the club's highest since 1950-51 and the highest by any Third Division club since the golden post-war years. The average was the eleventh highest in the whole Football League, and topped all but three Second Division clubs as well as First Division Aston Villa, Leicester, Wolves, Birmingham and West Brom. For the very first time City had the highest crowds in the Midlands and would do so for the next seven golden years.

After the game Hill revealed two well kept secrets. First, he had ordered the players to take sleeping pills on the Thursday and Friday nights and they had 'worked like a charm', with the players more relaxed than they had been in weeks. Secondly, Hill had invited the comedian Jimmy Tarbuck into the dressing room for about 25 minutes before the match. Hill explained: 'I asked Jimmy to crack a few jokes and keep the lads' minds off the game. It helped them to relax in the worst time – just before the game.'

That night the players and their partners were treated to a celebration dinner at the Hotel Leofric, but there followed a hectic week with friendlies in Dublin (Monday), at home to Tottenham (Tuesday), at Bedworth Town (Wednesday), at home to America FC of Brazil (Thursday) – following a tour of the city in an open-top bus – and at Eastbourne (Friday). The two home friendlies took place against a strange backdrop, with the old stand being demolished and the crowd restricted to three sides of the ground.

The Tottenham game, hastily arranged after the FA initially refused to sanction the Brazilian team's visit, gave the fans a chance to applaud their heroes one by one as they were presented in the centre-circle. The team were then joined on the pitch by the manager, chairman and Hill's backroom team, Pat Saward, Alan Dicks and Peter Hill. Robins thanked the crowd for their wonderful support, and led the players in a rendition of 'three cheers' for their loyal supporters. Spurs, missing only Jimmy Greaves and Maurice Norman from their first team, gave a scintillating display of football and won 6-5 in front of 15,638, with Les Allen scoring an eleven-minute hat-trick. Spurs' Welsh international winger Cliff Jones later said: 'It was a bit of an experience to see a crowd of 15,000 turn out so quickly for a friendly match. I don't think I've heard a crowd shout so much at a friendly match.'

By Thursday night the players were on their knees, literally, and the Brazilians turned on the style to win 5-2, with their international forward Zezinho scoring a hat-trick. But the celebrations were not over and on Friday the team travelled to Eastbourne to fulfil a commitment to the local club and contest the Eastbourne Charity Cup, duly won 3-1. A day's rest allowed the team to watch the FA Cup final between West Ham and Preston at Wembley, but for Jimmy Hill there was no respite. He was the 'expert' on ITV's commentary, giving viewers his insights into a rare exciting final with the Hammers victorious over the Second Division Lancashire team by 3-2.

To reward their achievements, the players, wives and girlfriends were treated to a two-week holiday in the Spanish resort of Gandia, but Hill even managed to organise a friendly – against Spanish Second Division club Onteniente. The trip was generally welcomed, but one player later revealed it wasn't a totally happy camp:

'JH liked us to do everything as a group – it was part of his management approach – and one evening he wanted to take us all to Benidorm, where it was more lively. Someone suggested that a top Spanish singer, perhaps even Julio Iglesias, was performing and Jimmy organised a coach. Two of the wives kicked up a stink: "Why should he [Hill] tell us what to do?" and the evening was soured. A couple of days later Hill called the players together and told us that he and Derrick had decided that the wives wouldn't be going on any more holidays with us. When we went to the West Indies in 1967 they all stayed at home.'

Following another night out in Spain, an inebriated Pat Saward revealed a hidden singing talent on the coach journey back to Gandia. A player takes up the story: 'Nobody knew Pat could sing but he gave a fantastic rendition of *Some Enchanted Evening*. We all shouted for more and he sang it again and again and again. After the fourteenth time we shouted "Sing something else" and he shouts back "I don't know anything else".'

Back at Highfield Road, work continued on the £90,000 Sky Blue Stand. In January, Derrick Robins and vice-chairman Phil Mead had received financial backing for a number of projects. The board gave the go-ahead for the completion of the Sky Blue Stand, including the provision of bars, new toilets, a pools office and supporters' club facilities underneath. The terracing in front of the new stand would also be remodelled, with a new wall constructed, under which 120 spectators could be seated in the dry. This pitch-side area was used by invalid cars (a common sight at football grounds in those times), whose owners were permitted to drive their vehicles around the pitch and watch the game in the comfort of their cars.

On the opposite Main Stand-side of the ground some modernisation would take place. At a cost of £10,000 a covered promenade behind the stand would be built that summer, enabling ticket-holders to file in from either end instead of through the entrances along the front of the stand. Underneath the promenade a new ticket office was planned, as well as a club shop. Inside the 30-year-old building, the boardroom would be expanded, and in all parts of the stadium toilet facilities would be upgraded. A private bar – the Viking Room – would be opened for a new vice-presidents' club, with its own entrance into the main stand.

The most exciting news was the plan for the Kop. This was more of a long-term idea and involved, at a potential cost of £150,000 a double-decker stand providing another 5,000 seats, with the possibility of a dance hall, shops and petrol filling station underneath. Hill was keen to stress that nothing had been definitely planned but said: 'We hope to get it off the floor within two years – and by that I mean not get it built, but get it approved.' He said that, at its most optimistic, they might make a start in the summer of 1966.

It was amazing how much, in less than eighteen months, the club's ambitions and aspirations had changed. The team's success on the pitch over two successive seasons, which had been supported by the Coventry public, in terms of attendance figures, had given the directors the confidence to develop this impressive strategy. The role of the supporters' club during this period should not be under-estimated either. Between 1957 and 1971 it raised over £117,000 for the club, which equates to £1.2 million at today's prices. Hill and Robins were perhaps the only club officials who fully recognised the importance of a harmonious relationship with an influential group of the supporters, who were superbly led by Jack Patience.

Demolition of the 1910 Atkinson's Stand commenced within hours of the Colchester game and took ten days to complete, but the work did not interfere with the *Coventry Telegraph* Cup final and the two friendlies.

The construction of the four centre blocks of the Sky Blue Stand was soon under way, the contractors having promised that the completed stand would be ready for the opening day of the new season. City had acquired the site of the old mining gravel pit at Ryton in the early 1960s, when the club's then property consultant Harvey Williams identified it for visionary manager Jimmy Hill, who wanted the players to train away from Highfield Road.

Hill, and then chairman Derrick Robins, invited the owner, Alderman Featherstone-Dilke, to a match, whereupon agreement was reached to buy the then 25-acre plot – which included the land where the Sky Blue Connexion sports centre now stands – for £10,000, to be paid at £1,000 a year for ten years with no interest.

A month after the end of the season the club announced that every seat in the ground had been sold, bar 250 for emergencies. Season-tickets netted the club over £60,000, three times that of the previous season, in advance sales. 7,200 seats in all were sold, and ground season tickets bumped up the final figure.

City fans awaited the Second Division fixture list with excitement and trepidation. Some pundits tipped the Sky Blues to go straight through the division and win promotion to Division One at the first attempt.

Chapter 9. 1964-65 (Part 1)

The Wheels are Wobbling (I)

Most Second Division clubs were delighted that the Sky Blues had joined them from Division Three. With City's huge following and attractive style of play, it would be a welcome shot in the arm for a division that had lost two big clubs, Leeds and Sunderland, both promoted to Division One. That is not to say that other big clubs weren't lying in wait for the Sky Blues in Division Two – Newcastle and Manchester City had fallen on hard times in the early 1960s but were showing signs of emerging from their slumbers. Another former giant, Bolton, had been relegated after 30 years in Division One and would now face Coventry for the first time in league football. Coventry's old rivalries from Division Three would be renewed in the shape of Northampton, Southampton, Swindon, Ipswich and Norwich.

Southampton manager Ted Bates summed things up during the close season: 'Coventry's impact [on Division Two] will be a great one. With their enthusiastic approach, and the wonderful support of their fans, they will be welcomed with open arms.'

There was little news of playing matters in the close season, with just one low-key arrival – Belfast youngster David Clements joining for 'a small fee' from Wolves, where he had been a reserve-team player. Eighteen-year-old Clements had come to Hill's attention during 'A'-team games against the Sky Blues' third team the previous season. Another inconspicuous import was 28-year-old physiotherapist Norman Pilgrim. He moved from London to join the club and would be a valuable and popular member of the Sky Blues 'team' over the next few years, involved with the serious injuries sustained by George Curtis, Bill Glazier, Ernie Machin and others.

Three days before the curtain-raiser the club announced that Charles Harrold's role had been extended and he been promoted to 'manager of administration'. Amongst his roles would be to develop Radio Sky Blue and build up the club's money-raising activities. Jimmy Hill's title became 'general manager' and many of his administration duties would be assumed by former Fleet Street journalist Harrold.

Highfield Road was buzzing with activity. Two weeks before the season started 'Nemo' reported that the improvements made to the ground since April were 'staggering'. He described the now-completed Sky Blue Stand as 'giving an atmosphere of a big, thriving football club that was lacking before'. He continued: 'equally praiseworthy have been the quick-fire alterations to the facilities in the main stand, including the promenade for easy admission, the new bars, and offices and boardrooms underneath, which have been increased in size and modernised.'

As he looked around the ground 'Nemo' found it difficult to believe all the work would be ready for the first home game two weeks hence: 'But then I had only to realise what had been achieved since a previous "inspection" made in mid-May to convince myself that where Coventry City are concerned, almost anything is possible. Everywhere is the busy sound of workmen, each with his own task of completing the finished article. In the midst of all this apparent chaos the lush green pitch is being watered to make it perfect for the re-entry into Second Division football – a prospect that has excited the footballing populace of Coventry to such an extent that over £60,000 has been taken in season tickets. The Sky Blue colour scheme pervades everywhere. I must say it is most agreeable, and lends splendour to the whole place'.

Secretary Paul Oliver who was overseeing all the projects remarked: 'I think we shall all be relieved when the season gets under way.'

In a pre-season interview with the *Coventry Telegraph*, manager Jimmy Hill stressed the need for the club to not go heavily into debt and reminded fans that the fruits of the last two seasons had been ploughed back into the team and the stadium. He revealed that he was looking for a new goalkeeper but had not found the right one. His closing message to the fans was simple: 'Learn the new words of our Sky Blue Song!' Now that the Sky Blues were in Division Two, the song's two middle lines had to be amended to incorporate names of new opponents. The song was now:

Let's all sing together,
   Play up Sky Blues,
While we sing together
   We will never lose.

Preston or Cobblers,
   Argyle, or anyone,
They can't defeat us,
   We'll fight till the game is won.

On the field, pre-season was frustrating, with a 2-4 defeat at Southern League Cambridge United followed by a 0-0 at another Southern League club, Wellington. The team wound up their preparations with a 1-0 win at Watford, whom they had pipped for promotion in April. Ernie Machin had returned from injury and played a big part in the first two friendlies but limped off at Watford with a recurrence of his knee problems. It was going to be another frustrating season for Ernie. His substitute replacement, John Smith, scored the winner at Watford and on the opening day of the season scored in the 2-0 win over Plymouth.

On that opening day, 'Nemo,' writing in the *Coventry Telegraph Pink*, analysed the Second Division opposition and tipped Bolton and Preston for promotion. Relegated Bolton had been unlucky to go down, and 'Nemo' reminded readers of their three experienced internationals: goalkeeper Eddie Hopkinson, inside-forward Freddie Hill, and centre-forward Wyn Davies. 'Nemo' felt that if Preston had not had an FA Cup run on their minds (they reached the final, losing to West Ham), they would have given Sunderland a closer run for the second promotion place. 'Nemo' tipped Manchester City and Southampton to make a strong challenge. Strangely, the two teams who ultimately were promoted – Newcastle and Northampton – were not on 'Nemo's' radar.

The new Sky Blue Stand was ready for the season's opener against Malcolm Allison's Plymouth. In the match programme Hill listed twenty projects undertaken during the close season, and praised the whole of the club's staff for the fact that every one had been completed on time.

With two points in the bag, City were then directed by the fixture list to the two teams relegated from Division One – Ipswich and Bolton. City won both games 3-1, outclassing the East Anglians, playing their first home game under new boss Jackie Milburn, but finding Wanderers a tougher nut. City weathered a storm before taking the points on the club's first ever visit to Burnden Park. One blot on the copybook, however, was an outbreak of vandalism by City fans returning by train from Bolton. Coventry stationmaster Ronald Salt stressed that it was not on the destructive scale seen from Liverpool and Manchester United fans the previous season (Liverpool fans caused train services to be removed after outbreaks) but that senseless 'swinging on luggage racks and the throwing of small articles were popular pastimes'.

Over 34,000 had watched the first home game with Plymouth, but that was now topped for the midweek return game with Ipswich. Almost 38,000 saw a a scintillating demolition of Milburn's Ipswich, in what was considered one of the finest examples of attacking football seen at the ground in living memory. The Sky Blues thumped the visitors 5-3 to cement top spot in the early league table.

That night, visiting Wolves directors told Hill that they had not experienced an atmosphere like that at a football game since their club's memorable battles with Honved and Spartak Moscow in the 1950s. Things were not going well at Molineux. After almost unbroken success since the war, Wolves had made a dreadful start and, two weeks after the directors' trip to Highfield Road, manager Stan Cullis, the architect of the post-war success and one of the most respected managers in the land, was sacked. Jimmy Hill was strongly linked to the vacancy. Hill, however, reassured the fans via 'Nemo': 'if I couldn't be manager with Coventry City, I wouldn't want to be manager anywhere. I wouldn't go if they offered me £10,000 a year ... I'd rather work where I'm happy than get a lot more money somewhere else, and not be happy.'

City's superb start was complete when beating visiting Middlesbrough 3-0. Five wins out of five had made them the team to beat, and the first defeat came at Derby in match six, when the biggest crowd at the Baseball Ground for ten years saw a thrilling Midlands derby, with the Rams ending City's 100 per cent record. The bubble was truly burst: the opening five wins were followed by five straight defeats before the season settled into an inconsistent pattern.

When Derby came to Highfield Road for the return game, the biggest home attendance so far, 38,278, paying record receipts of £5,959, saw the Rams inflict City's third defeat in a row. Former City goalkeeper Reg Matthews made an emotional return to Highfield Road for the first time since his big money move to Chelsea in 1956. The game saw another Sky Blue innovation, when the electronic scoreboard and clock was unveiled. Paid for by the *Coventry Evening Telegraph*, the electronically operated scoreboard, the first of its kind in the League, was perched on top of the Spion Kop and displayed the score and the scorer's shirt number in 'brilliantly-lit figures'.

City's perfect start had brought the club and its players to the attention of many. Winger Ronnie Rees was awarded his first Welsh cap in early October, against Scotland at Ninian Park, Cardiff. He failed to do himself justice and was dropped for the following game, a World Cup qualifier in Copenhagen, but injuries to others meant the twenty-year-old got a late call-up. He gave a much better performance and was a regular in the Wales side for the rest of the season, appearing at Wembley against England in November. During the Sky Blues' disappointing autumn, he was one of the few bright spots in City's team with a string of consistent displays.

A key aspect of City's success under Jimmy Hill was the team spirit, on and off the pitch. The players socialised together and if there was no midweek game it was not unusual to find Hill and his players attending one of the numerous workingmen's clubs around the city. Dietmar Bruck recalls: 'Just like the kids had their pop and crisps autograph sessions, JH wanted to get closer to the city's working-class followers of the team. Most Tuesdays we would go out to the pubs and social clubs and you couldn't get out of it, but it was fun. We played darts and dominoes and learned a few new card games, which came in handy for away trips in the coach. After Tuesday night, few of us had a drink before the weekend. Jimmy didn't have any fixed rules but he used to say to us: 'I don't mind what you do, it's your body and you know what you're capable of. You perform in training and on a Saturday on the pitch and that's fine, but if you don't perform then you're out. He gave us the responsibility and we took it.'

There was undoubtedly a drinking culture in many football clubs in the 1960s and Tommy Docherty famously sent home seven Chelsea players from Blackpool after they were caught drinking against the Doc's instructions in a nightclub just before a crucial game. Dietmar reveals that Coventry followed in Chelsea's footsteps not long afterwards, visited the same nightclub but avoided controversy: 'we loved going to Blackpool for a break; sometimes JH wanted to get us away from Cov and all the pressure there. This one time we had a hard training session on the beach and afterwards he said, "come on lads, we'll have a night on the town," we went out to a club in the town and got back pretty late, but nobody drank too much and it was a great bonding session. The following Saturday we won 5-1. Often, though, the trips to the seaside were hard work with two training sessions a day and we were too knackered to go out on the lash.'

Jimmy was also a supporter of local amateur football, organising tournaments for local teams with the final stages played at Highfield Road. The best players in the tournament were selected to play against the City first team at Highfield Road and several local players were signed up for the club. Tom Dentith was playing for Standard FC, the team of the Standard Motor Company in the Coventry Works League in the mid-1960s and remembers JH: 'He came to our annual dinner and presentations evening, and the first team [of which I was a member] received their runners-up plaque from Jimmy. I was so proud. After the awards he stayed for the dancing, enjoying himself immensely, signing autographs and mixing with everyone.'

Back on the pitch, City were unchanged for the first seven games, but the slump after the great start convinced Hill that improvements could be made. Despite the club's robust finances (in early October a record profit of £11,000 was announced), he was anxious to wheel and deal and not carry too big a first-team squad, but also make room for promising youngsters. He had made no secret of his desire for a new goalkeeper, and his scouts had watched several young custodians, including Peter Springett (QPR), Bill Glazier (Crystal Palace) and Peter Wakeham (Charlton). Hill had consistently praised Bob Wesson in the press, but after a single error in the home defeat to Northampton, Hill dropped him in favour of Dave Meeson. Meeson's stock had never been high with City fans and his errors at Southampton and Swansea sealed his fate. Hill opened talks with Bournemouth for their highly rated David Best. After a meeting at Dean Court lasting more than three hours, Hill failed to persuade the Cherries' directors to sell. Bournemouth had rejected offers from Arsenal and Stoke the previous season, and believed that keeping Best was essential for the club's Third Division promotion hopes.

A sure sign that a signing was imminent came on 2 October, when the club agreed terms with Swansea for the sale of George Kirby. The Swans paid City 'about £11,000 – £1,500 less than they paid for him' the previous March. Kirby had done his bit to get City up, but with Ernie Machin returning to fitness and a young Bobby Gould scoring for fun in the reserves and champing at the bit, Kirby was expendable. Hill thanked Kirby: 'We're very grateful to him for helping us clinch promotion. But now that George Hudson is showing signs … of coming back to his best form, the position was that Kirby could not get a place.'

Kirby had been City's twelfth man at the Vetch Field for the midweek draw and Swans manager Trevor Morris approached Hill after the game. 'Nemo' predicted that a bid for David Best was to be expected shortly. Hill, however, had another iron in the fire and the following day it leaked out. Hill had cooled on Best and switched his attention to Crystal Palace's Bill Glazier. The national press reported that Palace had turned down an offer of £35,000, a world record fee for a goalkeeper, and City had been thwarted.

The bad run ended with a 3-2 home victory over Swindon, the first win in seven league games, but seven goals were shipped in three home games in a fortnight, whereupon Hill and Robins decided to act. After a two-week hiatus, further calls were made to Palace, with Robins ringing their chairman Arthur Wait (like Robins, a building mogul). The press reported that 21-year-old Glazier, reluctant to move at first, had decided it was too good a chance to miss and signed for Coventry on Friday, 16 October in time to make his debut at Portsmouth's Fratton Park the following day. What may have swung the day is that, recently, the rules on signing-on fees paid to players had changed. Clubs could now pay unlimited 'sweeteners' to sign them. It was also later revealed that the club had awarded Bill a five-year contract, something virtually unheard of in English football at the time.

City fans were stunned by the size of the fee, around £14,000 more than the club record paid out for George Hudson, but Hill was sanguine about the huge deal: 'When you want the best you have to pay for it – and believe me Glazier is the best.' He reminded 'Nemo' light-heartedly that the *Coventry Telegraph* reporter had been saying that if the club wanted to get anywhere they needed two new players: 'Well this is one of them!'

Glazier kept a clean sheet on his debut, helping City to a 2-0 win with 'four brilliant stops'. Bobby Gould, on his first league outing of the season, netted his first league goal, three days after his first senior goal against Mansfield in the League Cup. Another goal followed a week later in a 2-2 home draw with Manchester City, but following another couple of appearances he went back to the reserves.

Despite being first-choice keeper before Glazier's arrival, Meeson was made available for transfer, with Hill publicly proclaiming Wesson as Glazier's understudy: 'In many ways Bob has as much natural ability as Bill [Glazier]. But it's a question of application. He lacks confidence in himself, and this is reflected in his play – particularly his poor kicking.' Meanwhile, things were getting even better for Glazier – less than two weeks after joining City he was called up as a reserve for Alf Ramsey's England Under-23 side, as understudy to Everton's Andy Rankin in a team that boasted some of the country's glittering young stars, such as Alan Ball, Martin Chivers, Norman Hunter and Cyril Knowles.

The victories over Swindon and Portsmouth were the only league wins in a run of sixteen games in three months. Although three League Cup victories took City to the last eight of the competition for the first time, all was not well at Highfield Road. Hill, who had reverted to a more negative 4-3-3 system after the five defeats in September, with Curtis and Kearns playing as joint centre-halves, had been criticised for being too negative.

A 0-3 defeat at Charlton was followed by a scrambled home draw with Leyton Orient, but worse was to come at Bury on a wet Friday night. Colin Bell and Ray Pointer ran City ragged and thumped five past Glazier – the Sky Blues were sliding into the bottom half of the table. Earlier that week a 4-2 League Cup win over Sunderland had raised hopes of a resurgence of league form, with Hudson and Ken Hale rediscovering their scoring boots with two goals apiece, but the hopes did not materialise. After the Gigg Lane nightmare, a 0-0 draw at home to Crystal Palace and a 0-1 defeat at Norwich left City just four points above bottom club Portsmouth, and a League Cup quarter-final with Leicester looming.

Injuries were a factor in the slump – Dietmar Bruck, John Sillett and Brian Hill had been out for periods and Ernie Machin had not recovered his pre-injury form. Several players, including George Hudson, Ron Farmer, Ken Hale and Willie Humphries, had received stick from the Highfield Road crowd and been rested, whilst England youth full-back John Burckitt, a great hope for the future, had struggled in his five appearances in the first team. City had scored just one goal in seven and a half hours of league football, and that was a penalty. The team were anxious and it showed.

Amidst the gloom, Highfield Road was chosen to host an Under-23 international for the first time. Alf Ramsey, presumably with a view to a big crowd and a lively atmosphere, promoted Glazier to the starting line-up. Over 27,000 witnessed an excellent 5-0 win for England with young Alan Ball demonstrating that he was a strong candidate for the full England team in the 1966 World Cup finals. The media were positive about City's hosting of the game, with the *Manchester Evening News* sad that more internationals could not be played at Highfield Road: 'The Coventry crowd entered into the spirit of the match. They chanted England, England – and when did we last hear that at Wembley? ... In addition to the support from the terraces, the club staged the game magnificently. Everything from the illuminated scoreboard which carried scorers as well as the score to the informative background commentary by the club's excellent publicity service gave the game a real show-biz touch.'

The home League Cup quarter-final tie with Leicester proved to be a bigger disaster than Bury, as the Foxes, albeit a major force in Division One at the time, won 8-1 – inflicted the biggest home defeat in the club's history. City played half the match with ten men – captain George Curtis for once, could not play through the pain barrier – and two inexperienced full-backs, Bill Tedds and John Burckitt, were badly exposed. With Ron Farmer and Ernie Machin also missing, it seemed that every time Leicester attacked they scored. The result was pounced upon by the cynics, who claimed it was evidence that the Sky Blues were well short of top-flight quality.

In the club programme four days later Jimmy Hill was almost Churchillian. After praising the City fans for their 'wonderful' support on a black night, he put a positive spin on the bad result: 'While the ten men left were fighting desperately hard to hold Leicester at bay, I thought to myself that perhaps this might well mark the end of our black period. If you drop a ball, it has to hit the floor before it can bounce back. No one can deny that we were on the floor on Tuesday evening, yet somehow during the second half, I became certain in my mind that things would be alright, partly because of the wonderful support that the crowd gave us, and partly because of the way in which our own players fought under crippling circumstances, but mostly because I could feel there were enough people there who still had the true Sky Blue Spirit (I even heard the song again). I think the 1-8 loss might do us a favour and produce in the team the fight and fire that is typical of the British when their backs are against the wall.'

Despite Hill's bulldog stance, things did not improve immediately. Days later Rotherham took City to the cleaners at Highfield Road, winning 5-3, with the Millers' debutant John Galley taking advantage of Curtis' continued absence by giving stand-in centre-half Mick Kearns the runaround and scoring a hat-trick.

Hill made changes. He had already signed full-back Allan Harris, brother of Chelsea hard-man Ron, spending another £35,000, and he quickly shored up the left flank. He dropped John Smith and recalled Dietmar Bruck, and Sillett and Brian Hill returned during December to give the defence a stronger look. The manager also signed veteran centre-forward Ken Keyworth from Leicester. Keyworth had been a prolific scorer for the Filbert Street team before a bad car crash had cost him his place. Hill beat off competition from ten other clubs to sign him on a free transfer, and the player quickly rewarded Hill's faith, scoring in his first two games. More importantly, he seemed to rekindle George Hudson's zest after a relatively barren spell. Days after Keyworth's arrival 'Nemo' had speculated that Hill would probably accept £15,000 to sell Hudson, the enigmatic forward who was out of touch in front of goal. Keyworth only played seven games in a City shirt, and in retrospect his career was on the wane, but he played a small but key role in City's rejuvenation in December 1964.

The FA Cup third round draw gave City a plum tie at Villa Park. By coincidence, on the day the draw was made City's youth team pulled off their best result since the club had first entered the FA Youth Cup in 1955 by winning 1-0 at Villa Park. A goal from the prodigious John Chambers sealed a satisfying win for City's youth coach, Pat Saward, a former Villa player.

The run of bad league results (seven without a win) ended in a 3-2 win at Plymouth, Malcolm Allison's side's first home defeat, but after the customary loss at Deepdale on Boxing Day, the team's upturn took off in the return game with Preston two days later. On a freezing night on a pitch resembling an ice-rink, George Hudson mastered the conditions and gave one of the great individual performances at Highfield Road. In the 3-0 victory over one of the strongest sides in the division, he scored with a nonchalant chip, made another goal, and generally led the visitors' defence a merry dance. The 'Hud' was back to his best.

'Nemo,' in his annual review of the year, made Ronnie Rees his player of the year for 'his outstanding consistency and skill in 1964'. He noted, however, that Rees' form of late had dipped and, but for injuries, Brian Hill, the previous year's winner, would have run Rees close. 'Nemo' made John Burckitt, on the verge of becoming the club's first England youth international since George Curtis in 1956, his 'most improved player'. The 5-3 thrashing of Ipswich was his match of the year, and the 1-0 win at Bristol Rovers his team performance of the year.

The year had ended on a high note and the club had an exciting January 1965 to look forward to. The Cup trip to Villa Park would perhaps show the critics after the Leicester debacle that that was a one-off result, and City could hold their own against the best. Tough but tempting games against the top two sides in the division, Newcastle and the old enemy, Northampton, also loomed in the month ahead.

Chapter 10. 1964-65 (Part 2)

Time to Catch Breath

Twenty thousand Sky Blue fans travelled confidently to Villa Park for the FA Cup third round tie on 9 January. The teams had not met in a competitive game since the 1945-46 FA Cup, when Villa had won a third round contested for the only time over two legs. It was almost 30 years since the clubs had met in the Second Division, in 1936-37 and 1937-38, when the four games had ended honours even (one win each, and two draws) with massive crowds attending the titanic tussles.

City confidence was well-placed – Villa were 21st in the First Division and looked extremely vulnerable to relegation. They had lost 1-5 at Blackburn the previous week, whilst City had won 3-2 at Middlesbrough. After the Leicester League Cup disaster, Hill's men had something to prove, despite City fielding a weakened team in the League Cup-tie.

On a miserably wet day in Birmingham, Jimmy Hill sprang a major surprise by dropping Ken Hale, and playing a defender, Brian Hill, at inside-forward. Hill's gamble failed, and before half-time he had as good as admitted it, by pushing Dietmar Bruck forward and pulling Hill back into defence. JH's thinking had been that the pitch would cut up in the wet and Hill would be perfect in gluepot conditions, but it was also a cautious approach against a side which was one of the lowest scorers in the whole Football League. The pitch, which had been inspected by City's team and staff before the game, was perfect.

City started the game well and Rees hit the crossbar, but they were stunned by Tony Hateley's thirteenth-minute goal. In the second half City improved and at times looked good enough to level the scores, but Hateley's second after 66 minutes sealed the victory before MacLeod's late third goal. The City contingent in the 47,000 crowd – the second largest to watch a City game since the war – who had made such a cacophony before the game and for a while in the second half, were silenced and the Villa fans chanted 'Easy, Easy'.

Dietmar Bruck remembers the game well: 'We really let the fans down that day. There were so many City fans it was like a home game and the Holte End was all sky blue. I can't remember JH making many mistakes, but he got it wrong that day. Brian Hill was never a strong inside-forward – his strength was marking the opposition's star forward. But the players didn't do themselves justice and we were so annoyed because, apart from Hateley, Villa weren't a good side.'

Hill accepted the disappointed fans' criticism for changing a winning side, and for playing a defensive formation with Hill, a defender, in the forward line. Other fans questioned George Curtis' performance against Hateley, and John Sillett's lack of speed against lively Johnny MacLeod. It wasn't the first time that 'Sill' had been vulnerable to a speedy winger, Plymouth's Nicky Jennings had exposed him a few weeks earlier.

In response to the biggest *Pink* postbag in years, Jimmy Hill explained that he put Brian Hill at inside-forward to counteract the strong running Villa left-half Dave Pountney, but had left his decision until just before the kick-off in case Pountney was at centre-half. He held his hands up and admitted it hadn't worked.

A week later Hill axed Sillett and, with Machin injured, recalled Ken Hale and Bobby Gould. His changes paid off and City ended league leaders Newcastle's seven-match winning streak in a classic. When Ronnie Rees scored after 66 minutes City held a flattering 5-1 lead. The Geordies never gave up, however, and with City a bag of nerves they reduced the lead to 5-4 with three minutes left. The game continued to fluctuate and Dietmar Bruck's thunderous shot bounced off the crossbar before Jim Iley's last-minute free-kick went inches wide.

City survived their next big test, seven days later, holding second-placed Northampton to a 1-1 draw at the County Ground. The Cobblers, under Dave Bowen, were unbeaten at home and looked good bets to reach the First Division for the first time in their history. Hill's plans had been thrown into disarray on the eve of the game when Bill Glazier burnt his hand in a kitchen accident at his girlfriend's house in Birmingham. Bob Wesson deputised and gave a excellent display after three months in the reserves. City soaked up the home team's pressure, restricting them to one goal at the break, and eighteen-year-old debutant Dave Clements snatched an equaliser. Hill had preferred the strongly built Clements to Bobby Gould at inside-left on the heavy ground. 'Clem' had impressed for the reserves for some time and his left-foot piledrivers had netted a good number of goals for the 'stiffs'. The Northern Irishman had been released by Wolves the previous summer and had been on the verge of joining Watford until Hill swooped to sign him for a meagre £1,500. The Belfast lad, who earned a call-up for his country's Under-23 side just days after his dazzling debut, would prove to be a key man in the unfolding Sky Blues story.

A week later, on his home debut, Clements scored a late equaliser against Southampton and prompted 'Nemo' to write: 'Clements has an ideal temperament, and a knack of pouncing on anything loose in the penalty-box and turning it to good advantage.'

Clements' goalscoring form followed him into the international arena and he scored on his Under-23 debut in a 2-2 draw with Wales, and followed up with his third City goal in three games at Huddersfield on the following Saturday.

Hill was determined to keep his wage-bill down, and the emergence of Clements and the improvement of Gould meant he could release two more players. Graham Newton joined Bournemouth for £5,000, less than a year after arriving from Walsall, and Hugh Barr, a hero of the 1963 Cup run, left for Cambridge United, then a Southern League club, for around £1,000. His new club allowed him to play part-time so that he would be able to resume his teaching career. For the time being, Barr continued to train with the Sky Blues, along with two other ex-City men, George Kirby (Swansea) and Reg Matthews (Derby). Despite leaving the club in 1956 for Chelsea and later Derby, Matthews had always lived in Coventry and was a 'piece of the furniture' at Ryton.

Poor old Ernie Machin's knee was giving him more problems in early 1965; he had a cartilage removed in February after half a dozen games on the sidelines. He had played just fourteen league games in sixteen months and had failed to regain the form he had shown in 1963 as a teenager. Jimmy Hill defended Ernie, who had had his critics on the terraces: 'I've heard some of them shouting at Ernie during the matches. I hope that when the operation is over he can come back to show them what he can do'. His operation meant a two-week hospital stay and no more football that season, a far cry from the keyhole surgery of the modern day with players returning from cartilage operations in three or four weeks. It was hard to realise that Ernie was still only twenty, but his absence opened the door for thrilling reserves like Bobby Gould and Dave Clements.

Following the Villa Cup defeat there was a mini-run of five games unbeaten, which came to a halt with three successive defeats and a rare event at Huddersfield's Leeds Road. George Hudson became the first player to be sent off in a competitive game since Jimmy Hill arrived, over three years previously.

'Nemo' described the incident as follows: 'A minute before half-time Hudson punched Town's Peter Dinsdale after the players tussled for possession. Hudson won the ball but, as Dinsdale wildly swung his legs in an attempt to retrieve it, catching Hudson across the shins, the City man turned and struck him. When Dinsdale got up there was blood streaming from a cut eye-brow and referee Parkinson [of Blackburn] had no alternative but to order Hudson off. It was a rash loss of temper which Hudson obviously regretted as he sat out the second half in the dressing room.'

'Nemo', from his position in the press-box yards from the incident, believed Hudson had been provoked, something the referee didn't see. Hudson, who had only been booked once in his career previously, did not request a personal hearing and told 'Nemo': 'I just lost my head.' He served a fourteen-day ban for the offence but as City had their game at Leyton Orient postponed because of a waterlogged pitch he missed only one game.

Two more defeats, at Swindon and at home to defence-minded Portsmouth, had City fans again looking over their shoulder, but four out of the bottom five lost on the same day, leaving the Sky Blues five points clear of the bottom two. Nonetheless, Hill rang the changes the following week at Rotherham, dropping Kearns, Smith, Bruck and Humphries and making four positional changes. Hill was vindicated with a 2-0 victory with the ace marker Brian Hill blotting out the dangerous Albert Bennett, and George Curtis 'doing a job' on the hat-trick man Galley. The win sparked a six-game unbeaten run which took them well clear of relegation worries and fringe players Keyworth and Mitten got run-outs.

Dave Clements continued to impress at inside-forward and by the season's end he had notched nine goals and won his first two full international caps for Northern Ireland. His first, in Belfast in mid-March, was against Holland and the Irish won the World Cup qualifier 2-1. Willie Humphries also played in that game, but only hours after signing for Swansea in a transfer which stunned City fans for its speed. Days after being dropped at Rotherham, Willie handed in a transfer request, which was granted with two days to go before the transfer deadline. Hill apparently thought long and hard about agreeing to let Humphries go, but concluded that the diminutive Irishman's form since the early part of the season had been patchy. Besides, he had a good young reserve winger in John Mitten, and Clements was really a winger playing as a striker.

Permission was granted by City's board to sell Humphries, but only if a big fee was obtained. On deadline day Swansea manager Trevor Morris flew to Belfast, where the Irish team were preparing for the international, to conclude negotiations. City pocketed a cheque for £15,000, a profit of over £10,000 – in retrospect a great piece of business as Humphries' career, like Bly's, slumped. Morris saw Humphries as the man to save the Swans from relegation, to link up again with George Kirby and provide the ammunition for much-needed goals. In the event, Humphries and Kirby were unable to save the Swans from relegation.

The season was petering out and home gates slipped away. Under 19,000 saw the Bury game on Grand National Day, 27 March, the lowest home crowd for almost two years. A respectful crowd observed a minute's silence in memory of City's 1930s legend Jock Lauderdale, who passed away the previous day. Away followings dipped too, but there was usually a hardcore of 500-600 City fans travelling to watch away games.

More international honours came the way of Clements and Rees. They squared up in the Home International between Northern Ireland and Wales in Belfast, with both wearing the No 11 shirt. Rees won eight full caps during the season – a club record – and several big clubs were rumoured to be interested in him, with First Division Stoke widely mentioned. In February 'Nemo' speculated that Rees would command a fee of around £50,000 if the club did decide to sell, but he had it on good authority that he was part of the club's long-term plans. Meanwhile, John Burckitt's promising career was rewarded with selection in the England Youth squad to play in the 'Little World Cup', which was actually the European Youth Championship finals, to be played in West Germany during April. John, who had made six first-team appearances that season at full-back, was named in a strong squad, captained by future Coventry player Wilf Smith, that included future full internationals Peter Osgood and John Radford. England reached the final, only to lose 2-3 to East Germany, and John played in all but one game, including the final. Another promising Sky Blue teenager, Pat Morrissey, helped the Republic of Ireland to the quarter-finals.

City's star in the spring of 1965 was, however, Bill Glazier. Good, consistent league performances earned him three Under-23 caps, and in each game he kept a clean sheet. 'Nemo' speculated that his club and country form possibly put him third in line behind Leicester's Gordon Banks and Blackpool's Tony Waiters in Alf Ramsey's 1966 World Cup plans. Glazier's third cap, a 0-0 draw with Czechoslovakia at Leeds, earned him more plaudits, but tragedy was to strike ten days later at Maine Road.

Just before half-time, with City trailing 0-1, Glazier came rushing out to dive bravely on a through ball, but collided heavily with Glyn Pardoe. It was immediately apparent that it was a serious injury. Bill was stretchered from the field with Ronnie Rees donning the keeper's jersey and playing a blinder for the best part of 50 minutes, helping City gain a 1-1 draw. Glazier's left leg was broken in two places (fibula and tibia), which meant he would miss the Under-23 summer tour to Europe and the start of the 1965-66 season. His break necessitated a five-week stay in Manchester Infirmary and he would be in plaster for almost three months. As it turned out, he was out for almost a year and his hopes of inclusion in the World Cup squad were in tatters.

Jimmy Hill was full of praise for Glazier, his record signing: 'Bill has got plenty of physical and mental courage and this is an important factor in a case like this. We certainly hope it will be an early recovery rather than a long one.' He also praised the City following at Maine Road: 'as Bill was carried off, the opening notes of the Sky Blue Song came forth from our bugler somewhere in the stand as some sort of signal to the players to start fighting a rearguard action, and fight they did.'

The first team's inconsistencies turned the spotlight onto the reserve side, which won promotion to Division One of the Football Combination. A free-scoring team scored 96 goals in 36 games, including two sevens, a six and five fives. Crowds for the reserve games averaged an amazing 4,820, with 12,132 attending the final home game – a 1-0 win over QPR that as good as clinched promotion. Hill cheated somewhat by strengthening his team for the vital game with several first-teamers, including Harris, Rees and Clements. Bobby Gould scored the all-important goal to take his reserve tally to 24 in 25 games, to add to his four in nine for the first team. The gate against QPR was a Highfield Road record for a reserve game, topping the 11,700 who had watched Arsenal in August 1936. To put the attendance into perspective, there were only 10,800 at Maine Road four days later to see City's first team play.

Part of the attraction of the reserve games was the entertaining and exciting matches. Assistant manager Alan Dicks had marshalled and guided a blend of experienced players, unable to get a first-team game, with what seemed to be a constant flow of talented youngsters. The former Wolves boss Stan Cullis was a regular at reserve games that season and said to Hill: 'You know Jimmy, these matches are so entertaining, you should charge double the admission price.'

The same week that City attracted a 12,000 gate for the QPR game, Portsmouth announced that they were scrapping their reserve side the following season, on cost grounds. It is hardly surprising that City spent the best part of the next 35 years in the top division whilst Pompey languished in the lower divisions for all but one season during the period.

The youth team were also setting records, by reaching the last sixteen of the FA Youth Cup for the first time. Pat Saward's superbly organised team included internationals Burckitt and Morrissey, plus promising defender Mick Coop and the exciting left-wing pairing of John Docker and John Matthews. They followed up their pre-Christmas victory over Aston Villa with an away win at Derby before losing 2-3 to a strong Stoke side.

The first team sent Swansea down to Division Three in City's final home game. Swansea needed at least a point to ensure safety but City won 3-0 against a poor side which neither Humphries nor Kirby could improve. Four days later George Hudson, who had scored two of the

10. 1964-65 (PART 2) TIME TO CATCH BREATH

goals against Swansea, scored a hat-trick to end the season on a flourish as City won their final game 3-1 at Leyton Orient to finish the season in tenth place.

Then, in a repeat of the previous season's friendly, they entertained Tottenham, who this time won comfortably 3-0 in front of almost 14,000, prior to a three-week break and a trip to Iceland where all three friendly games were won.

The final average home league gate was 26,621, up only 500 from the previous season. Once again City were the eleventh best-supported club in the whole Football League, and only the champions Newcastle topped them in Division Two. Local rivals Northampton finished as runners up and reached the First Division for the first time in their history, also becoming the first club ever to climb all the way from Division Four to Division One.

The final act of the season was for Hill to announce his retained list of players. There were no big surprises, with 25 full-time professionals retained and just two, Bill Tedds and Dave Meeson, released. One newcomer near the end of the season was a fifteen-year-old Scots-born Cambridge schoolboy called Willie Carr. Only 5ft 1in, with ginger hair, he was described as one of the most significant schoolboy captures the club had made since the war. 'Nemo' reported that Carr, amazingly, was the first Scot on the club's books since Stewart Imlach.

'Nemo' summed up the feelings of fans at the end of the club's first season back in the Second Division: 'In their hearts, only a handful of City supporters expected promotion this season. Some hoped, but most felt a comfortable position would be adequate at the first attempt.'

Jimmy Hill thought he knew what had gone wrong: 'unlike Northampton, we have not sneaked points on our off days. In fact we have let points slip on our better days as well.' He continued: 'as far as next season is concerned, there is no side we have met this season that we have cause to fear next term. I think we will show the crowd we deserve their confidence.'

George Curtis added: 'We feel we have learned a great deal this season ... it's surprising how much more knowledge we have gained in this division. I'm sure it will stand us in good stead next season.'

In his final *Pink* column of the season, 'Nemo' reminded his readers of his August prediction: 'they [City] will be content with a position just above half-way in the table.'

Chapter 11. 1965-66 (Part 1)

The Sky Blue Special Pulls Out

In 1965-66 Coventry City got as close to the First Division as they had ever done – they finished third, just one point behind Southampton, who were second and promoted with champions Manchester City.

There were high expectations within the club, amongst the fans, and even in the national press regarding Coventry City's promotion hopes in the summer of 1965. There were no major summer additions to the squad, but Hill felt he had a strong pool of players. He told 'Nemo' at the end of July: 'The fight for places … will be intense. It is up to every player to show me that he is worthy of a place in the pool.'

'Nemo' named 21 players who he thought would be 'pushing for recognition'. That number didn't include seven up and coming youngsters named by 'Nemo' as: Dudley Roberts, Peter Denton, Pat Morrissey, John Chambers, John Docker, Dave Matthews and Dennis Oakes. However, it did include Tom Anthony, described as an experienced triallist from Brentford, who played at full-back. Sadly nothing came of Anthony's trial at Ryton. Two players left before the start of the season: Dave Meeson joined Southern League Wisbech on a free transfer, and Ken Keyworth left after only eight months, Swindon paying £3,500 to take him to the County Ground. The latter move was another good bit of business by Hill, as Keyworth had cost nothing. One move that didn't happen was John Sillett to QPR. The west London club were interested and many thought the lure of a move back to London might appeal to John. After much deliberation he decided to stay in the Midlands.

Football League clubs had finally voted for substitutes to be used in league games from the start of the 1965-66 season. Each club could use one named substitute, but only if a player was injured and not for tactical reasons (that proviso was unenforcible and was lifted two years later). Jimmy Hill, a long-time proponent of the twelfth man, welcomed the innovation: 'But I don't intend to make use of the idea at all if I can help it, unless injury forces my hand. It might be a big temptation at times, but the system must not be abused.'

In the context of Hill's hectic three and a half years at the club, the summer of 1965 was quiet, although progress on making Highfield Road even more comfortable for spectators advanced steadily. Under the Sky Blue Stand a new 350-capacity Continental Bar was nearing completion, as well as a state-of-the-art toilet block, paid for by the supporters club.

PFA chairman Jimmy Hill briefs the press corps during the PFA's dispute with the football authorities in 1961

City's team pose at the start of the fateful 1961-62 season. Billy Frith (centre) is pictured with his team and coaches Alf Wood (left) and Ted Roberts (right)

Ron Farmer nets a late equaliser at Shrewsbury as
the clouds gather over Frith (September 1961)

George Curtis lunges in vain and Arthur Lightening is stranded as
Tony Hateley nets for Notts County (January 1962)

In the last game before the big freeze, Jimmy Whitehouse heads City's second goal in a 3-3 draw with Peterborough (December 1962)

Terry Bly has a close-range shot saved by Barnsley goalkeeper Alan Hill in City's 2-0 win as the thaw arrives (February 1963)

Penalty king Ron Farmer sends Crystal Palace goalkeeper Bill Glazier the wrong way in the 5-1 home win (August 1963)

City pile pressure on the Barnsley defence at Oakwell (December 1963)

Ron Farmer's header spells trouble for Hull as the Tigers defend in a 2-2 draw (February 1964)

George 'Iron Man' Curtis leads out the Sky Blues for the vital Colchester game. George captained the side from Division Four to Division One (April 1964)

City clinch the Third Division championship with a 1-0 win over Colchester in front of 36,901. Willie Humphries goes close (April 1964)

George Kirby leads the charge against Colchester (April 1964)

George Hudson nets the winning goal against Colchester (April 1964)

On the way to an away game on their luxury coach (approx 1964)

City's championship squad attract a record crowd to Bedworth Town's Oval for a testimonial game (May 1964)

The 1964 championship side at Highfield Road. Back: George Hudson, Bob Wesson, John Sillett, Jimmy Hill, Dave Meeson, Mick Kearns. Middle: Willie Humphries, Graham Newton, George Curtis, George Kirby, John Mitten, Ronnie Rees. Front: Ron Farmer, John Smith, Hugh Barr, Brian Hill, Ernie Machin, Dietmar Bruck (May 1964)

The championship team get a heroes' welcome in Broadgate in their open top bus (May 1964)

City's players jet off to Spain with wives and girlfriends as a reward for winning promotion (May 1964)

George Hudson steers in City's third goal in a thrilling 3-3 draw with Manchester City (September 1965)

Bob Wesson and Brian Hill are helpless, and City's FA Cup hopes are in tatters after Everton's Alex Young scores in the 3-0 win (March 1966)

Jimmy Hill gives a pre-season pep talk at Highfield Road (July 1966)

Captain George Curtis wins a heading duel at Bolton's Burnden Park (October 1966)

Bobby Gould heads in at Bury, but his effort is disallowed
(February 1967)

Bobby Gould celebrates a goal made by a mazy Ronnie Rees run against Bolton
(March 1967)

Bobby Gould's goal clinches a vital 1-0 win over Huddersfield as the Sky Blues home in on promotion (April 1967)

The 'Midlands Match of the Century' and Ernie Machin beats Wolves' John Holsgrove to the ball (April 1967)

The Wolves game again. The ball hits the net for Gibson's goal and the young fans cannot contain themselves (April 1967)

A different view of City's second goal against Wolves, scored by Ian Gibson, No 10 (April 1967)

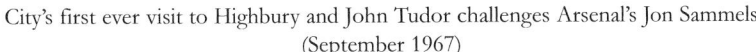

City's debut in the First Division and John Tudor heads towards the Burnley goal
(August 1967)

City's first ever visit to Highbury and John Tudor challenges Arsenal's Jon Sammels
(September 1967)

Bobby Gould soars above Newcastle's Bobby Moncur and John McGrath to head goalwards (September 1967)

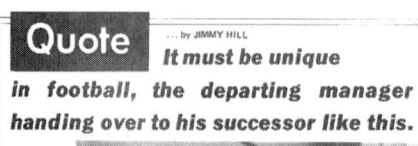

> **Quote** ... by JIMMY HILL
> *It must be unique in football, the departing manager handing over to his successor like this.*

All smiles as Jimmy Hill (left) hands over to new Coventry manager, Noel Cantwell.

Jimmy Hill hands over the managerial reins to Noel Cantwell, to mark the end of an era (October 1967)

The cost of the bar was eased, too, by a sizeable donation by Mitchell & Butlers, the brewery. For younger members of the playing staff the club had installed a jukebox under the main stand. Season-ticket sales were steady, with the vast majority of the 6,500 stand seats sold, leaving only around 700 unreserved seats in the ground. Ground season tickets also sold well, and the takings in total were over £60,000 for the second season running.

Summing up the prospects for the new season, 'Nemo' was prophetic again in the *Coventry Telegraph*. He expected the Sky Blues to 'be right in there fighting it out with the teams at the top' but he was at the same time cautious: 'Yet I still have a nagging doubt whether City are going to be good enough without any further new blood ... I believe the Sky Blues need someone of the calibre of Jim Iley in midfield.' Iley had been the play-maker with champions Newcastle the previous season. 'Nemo' tipped Bolton, Huddersfield and Wolves as the front-runners for promotion, but felt 'less than enthusiastic' about the fortunes of Manchester City, where new manager Joe Mercer 'has a mountainous task ahead of him'.

City fans were unused to seeing their team play home pre-season friendlies, and it was a surprise to hear that the club had arranged to entertain First Division Nottingham Forest a week before the league season started. The reason was money. Earlier in the summer the Football Association had revised a rule where all proceeds of pre-season trials had to be given to charity. Under the new rules, the clubs could retain 65 per cent net gate, with the other 35 per cent going to the FA and county associations. A crowd of 13,500 saw City win 4-3, with George Hudson netting all four City goals. 'Nemo' described the game, thus: 'The factor that tipped the scales in City's favour was the relentless finishing of George Hudson, who came as near to giving a centre-forward's dream performance as I can recall. He not only hit Forest for four – two of them being quite the most brilliant goals he has scored for the club – but long before the end had reduced Bobby McKinlay, usually a model of Scottish reliability, to a state of rare uncertainty.'

Forty-eight hours later the Sky Blues were brought down to earth with a bump, beaten 1-2 at Cambridge City in their final warm-up game, having won 6-0 at Kidderminster Harriers the previous week in their only other friendly.

Hudson had the scent of goals in his nostrils and followed up his four against Forest by scoring two late goals in the opening league game. Wolves visited Highfield Road for the first time in 40 years and were beaten 2-1 in front of almost 37,000 fans. Ernie Machin was fit again after his cartilage operations, but was soon, along with Ken Hale, the butt of the boo-boys in the crowd.

City were unchanged for the first four games and were unbeaten with two home wins and two away draws. After the second home win, over Bury, an unconvincing 1-0 with Hale and Machin both struggling, Hill let rip in the *Coventry Telegraph*: 'I really am astonished that our players are being criticised in the middle of virtual success. It's a pity that the people who profess to show faith in my judgement won't do just that, instead of moaning about our inside-forwards.' He said he was pleased at the way Machin was 'standing up' to matches following his knee operations and expected him to reveal his best form in the next few weeks. He put his faith in the two men by naming an unchanged side for the visit of Manchester City.

The Manchester City game saw Dietmar Bruck become the club's first used substitute. Bruck, wearing a shirt with no number (the No 12 shirt was introduced the following season) came on at half-time in the 3-3 home draw after Ron Farmer fractured his cheekbone in a collision with Johnny Crossan just before the break. In total, City used only nine substitutes in that first season.

Despite his name, Dietmar was a Coventry kid and had come through the ranks at the club. His father had been in the German Army during the Second World War and was killed while returning home to Danzig to see his new-born son. After the war his widowed mother met his future step-father, who was stationed in Germany with the RAF, and the family moved to Coventry, where he grew up as an English boy but keeping his German surname. An outstanding schoolboy footballer, Dietmar played as a pacy inside-forward for Coventry Boys and signed schoolboy forms and subsequently apprentice forms for City. He played for the youth team in the infamous 1-9 defeat by Aston Villa in 1961, but had already made his first-team debut as a seventeen-year-old in the final game of the previous season against Swindon. In his own words, his performance was 'nondescript' and he wasn't ready for the first team.

When Hill arrived, Dietmar's career was in the balance. His three-year apprenticeship had just months to run and it was touch and go whether he would be offered full professional terms. Bruck grasped his chance with both hands and impressed Hill to such an extent that he not only earned a two-year contract, but also got a run out in the first team before 1961-62 ended. Hill converted him, first to a wing-half back, and later, at the start of 1966-67, to left-back, where his pace was not wasted.

Four days after the draw with Manchester City, the Sky Blues travelled to Southampton, who were forced to use their substitute when keeper

John Hollowbread collapsed with a knee injury after 28 minutes. Outfield player Cliff Huxford took over in goal with substitute Ken Wimshurst coming on. City, who had dominated the early play, were unable to take advantage of the situation and slipped to their first defeat of the season, 0-1, at a ground that rarely yielded points for City.

A week later, following a 1-1 draw at Bristol City, where they were perhaps the better side but failed to take their chances, the return game with Southampton produced one of the best results of the Hill era. The Saints, who arrived as Division Two leaders, were swamped 5-1. Three of the goals were memorable, but the first, by George Hudson, would be discussed for years. 'Nemo' described it as follows: 'A Saints thrust broke down on the left when Sydenham screwed his cross too far back. Machin quickly moved the ball out of defence to Rees, who sent right-back Mick Kearns surging down the right wing. Kearns timed his cross to perfection and it went straight to Hudson who flicked it up in the air to beat his man [Tony Knapp], rounded him and nonchalantly headed it over the oncoming goalkeeper Tony Godfrey's head into the net. It was the sort of goal that lives in the memory and even two of the Southampton players applauded it as the crowd exploded with excitement.'

Dietmar Bruck's goal, City's second, was almost as good as he raced 40 yards 'like an advancing tank' before 'unleashing a thunderbolt-shot'. Hill, having persevered with the maligned Ken Hale, had dropped him in favour of youngster Alan Turner, who looked off the pace and picked up an Achilles injury. The No 8 position was proving to be a problem for Hill, and in the next game he gave John Smith a rare appearance that did not impress, but few spectators realised it was Smith's last in a Coventry City shirt. Ten days later he moved back to London, signing for struggling Leyton Orient with City pocketing a cheque for around £5,000 – a loss of £6,000 after just 33 games in the first team. Smith was probably one of Hill's few failures in the transfer market, although it could be argued he helped steady the unstable ship in the 1963-64 run-in.

City's topsy-turvy form was demonstrated when Crystal Palace inflicted a first home defeat (0-1), using a packed defence which again proved unbreachable to Hill's forwards. Southampton, meanwhile, recovered from their Highfield Road mauling to regain top spot with a 9-3 thumping of Wolves. The openness of the promotion race was illustrated by the fact that four points covered the leading thirteen teams in the division, and but for the Palace lapse the Sky Blues would be in second place.

After the previous year's dazzling set of financial results, the news that the club had lost over £16,000 in the year to May 1965 may have come as a shock to many, but at the AGM in October chairman Derrick Robins reminded shareholders of the two big signings made the previous season. Glazier and Harris had cost a combined £70,000, and although fees had been received for Humphries, Newton, etc, the deficit was largely down to transfer dealings. Donations of over £13,000 from the supporters' club helped defray some of the losses, but promotion had meant an increase in players' wages, from £60,000 to £84,000.

The meeting was presided over by the club's new president, the Bishop of Coventry, Doctor Cuthbert Bardsley. He had replaced Walter Brandish the previous June, and Robins thanked Brandish for 30 years valuable service to the club.

At the meeting, both Robins and Hill urged shareholders (and fans) to be patient. This was a period of financial consolidation after the big expenditure on Glazier and Harris, but Robins said it did not mean that they would not buy a player in certain circumstances. He went on to say: 'No body of men is more determined to get to the First Division than the whole of Coventry City.'

Hill reiterated Robins' view, saying: 'If we don't grab at this thing, it will come either this year, next year or after. We mustn't get over-excited or impatient.' The following day City eased into second place by virtue of a 3-1 home win over Charlton. Following the Palace defeat, the side won seven of the next nine league games, despite rarely hitting top form. On top of that, wins at Leyton Orient and Manchester City earned an attractive fourth round home League Cup-tie with WBA.

Before that game, however, the club's latest two innovations had the nation's football media providing massive coverage of the Sky Blues. That summer City had explored the feasibility of beaming an away match back to Coventry for the benefit of fans who had neither the time nor the money to follow the team away. Early applications to the Football League for the experiment were rejected on spurious grounds, but in September the club received approval from the League and the Football Association to relay the match at Cardiff. It had been rearranged from the previous Saturday, a Home International day, as both clubs had players called up, and was rescheduled for Wednesday evening. With the high cost involved and a serious risk of technical difficulties, the financial risk was borne by Viewsport Limited, which purchased the necessary equipment and would retain any profit on the project but, more importantly, would shoulder any losses.

Amid an unprecedented hive of activity, the screens, three in front of the Sky Blue Stand and a fourth in front of the main stand (for VIPs), were erected at the conclusion of a reserve game the previous evening. The workmen, hampered by fog, toiled all night long and a dummy-run

11. 1965-66 (PART 1) THE SKY BLUE SPECIAL PULLS OUT

by the projectionists had to be cancelled. More fog on match-day meant not only that the team had to cancel their chartered plane trip to south Wales and travel by coach, but back at Highfield Road the whole experiment looked doomed to fail.

The fog thankfully lifted in time for the kick-off and the crowd were treated to pre-match entertainment in the shape of interviews with players and pictures of the players warming up at Ninian Park. City wore red and white striped shirts, borrowed from Stoke (and used in the football soap opera *United*, for which JH was the technical advisor), to avoid any confusion to viewers on the black and white transmission. Former Spurs and Northern Ireland star Danny Blanchflower gave his views on screen at half-time, and the evening ended in true Coventry drama with a late goal to clinch a 2-1 away win, sending the Coventry fans delirious at both venues. A crowd of 10,295 watched at Highfield Road and an estimated 500 saw it 'live' at Ninian Park.

The pictures were clear and everyone agreed that the experiment was a great success and definitely the way football would go in the future. There was huge interest amongst other English clubs, thirteen of whom attended the screening, and also from abroad – in France, the football magazine *L'Equipe* devoted half a page, plus pictures, to the pioneering night.

City staged another closed-circuit game later that season when they played Charlton at the Valley. This time the gate at Coventry was higher, 11,321, while 15,000 watched the live action in south-east London. With the lighter evenings, the kick-off time had to be put back to 8.30pm. This time, however, City lost 0-2, a result which all but ended their thin promotion hopes, and the crowd were much more subdued. Viewsport again accepted the risk and it was reported that they had broken even, but Jimmy Hill was not convinced: 'It is a matter of finding the right time to relay and everything would depend on how well the team was doing at the time.'

Three days after Cardiff a club train, the 'Sky Blue Special', ran for the first time. Using ex-British Railways rolling stock, the train was manned by the club's own stewards. This experiment was a response to British Railways suspending 'football special' trains the previous season in the wake of serious and well-publicised damage by Stoke, Manchester United and Everton fans. City decided to take the commercial risk, not to mention the damage risk, and run their own trains with Radio Sky Blue piped through the carriages, Sky Blue catering, and bingo to keep the fans occupied. The first trip was to Preston in October, priced at a competitive 24 shillings (£1.20), and was an unqualified success, with all 600 seats sold in advance. Sky Blues' administration manager Charles Harrold, the man behind so many ideas emanating from Highfield Road, commented: 'We are confident that this move will stamp out hooliganism. After all, anybody who causes damage will be hitting at Coventry City, and not at British Railways.' For the trip to Middlesbrough in December, a local pop group, the Midnights, provided entertainment and dancing in a special converted carriage. In all the trips run over a period of four years by the 'Special' there were no reported incidents of hooliganism. The travellers on the first trip saw City gain a 0-0 draw at Deepdale.

That Preston game saw the debut of homegrown Dudley Roberts, a centre-forward like his famous father Ted, who led City's line with aplomb in the late 1940s. After a promising debut, Dudley was retained in the side and did well in the League Cup win at Maine Road. Then, on his home debut seven days later, on his twentieth birthday, he scored two goals in a 3-1 win over Charlton. Many years later he reminisced: 'I still can't remember the first goal as I was concussed when I scored it. George Curtis and I clashed heads going for a cross and the first half of the game was a blur to me. The second goal, though, is vivid in my memory. I headed in a Ronnie Rees cross.'

After the game his father Ted said: 'I think he did very well – better than I thought he would.' Competition for places in City's forward line was intense, however, and despite scoring six goals in thirteen starts, Dudley could never become a regular choice.

Sad departures in the autumn of 1965 were Jimmy Hill's parents, Bill and Alice Hill. They had been the steward and stewardess of the Sky Blue Club for three years but had decided to retire and move back to London. They were guests of honour at a party in the Sky Blue Club after the Carlisle match, which was attended by many of the players and officials and the couple were presented with gifts.

Bill Glazier's recovery from his broken leg was going well. Then he fractured a cheekbone in early November, just weeks from his first-team return. Fortunately, Bob Wesson was in superb form as his replacement and had few off-days. Bob had been at Coventry since 1958 when, whilst playing for a railway side in his home town of Thornaby-on-Tees, he was recommended to the club by his in-laws who lived in Coventry. Bob was invited down for trials and after three days was offered a professional contract. He was under-study to Arthur Lightening for two years before getting his chance in 1961 when Arthur was injured. Then, after Lightening was sold in 1962, he had to be patient behind Dave Meeson before making the position his own. Bob however knew that once Glazier was fully fit he would be relegated to the reserves.

11. 1965-66 (Part 1) The Sky Blue Special Pulls Out

October 1965 was an excellent month, with five league wins and a draw, plus the League Cup win at Manchester City. The last Saturday of the month saw City beat promotion rivals Portsmouth with the aid of a controversial injury-time penalty from Ron Farmer to go top of the table for the first time, on goal-average ahead of Manchester City. The Maine Road win set up the big League Cup-tie with WBA the following mid-week. After the disasters against Leicester and Villa the previous season, Hill was anxious to see if his team had progressed, and whether they could hold their own against a top-division club. The game was made all-ticket and at one stage the club hoped to set a competition attendance record. In the event there were just over 38,000 at Highfield Road, 2,000 short of the record set by WBA earlier that season against Walsall.

City acquitted themselves well, and once they had attuned to the First Division pace they more than matched their illustrious neighbours from the Black Country, who had led the First Division a month earlier. A 1-1 draw was a fair result but it gave the Baggies the advantage for the replay. Seven days later City looked comfortable for an hour, but were destroyed by four goals in eighteen minutes by one of the best home sides in the country and exited the League Cup by a 1-6 margin.

That defeat came days after the Sky Blues had lost their top spot in Division Two, losing 2-4 at Bolton, courtesy of a Wyn Davies-inspired performance. Davies had been one of the best headers of the ball in the country for some time, and it surprised many that no First Division club had swooped for the Welsh international. Conceding ten goals in two games brought City's sceptics and knockers out of the woodwork again. The normally solid defence had had two off-days in a row and memories of the previous season's back-to-back collapses at the hands of Leicester and Rotherham were recalled. Jimmy Hill, as ever, was positive following the defeats. He told 'Nemo': 'It would have been wonderful to have won and gone on to a match with Villa [Albion's opponents in the last eight]. But our defeat is a source of great relief to me. There are two ways of looking at what happened at the Hawthorns. There's the amateur attitude: isn't it awful to lose 1-6; and the professional attitude: so we're out of the League Cup. We're taking the professional attitude.' On another positive note, City profited to the tune of around £9,000 from the two games with Albion.

City recovered well, winning their next two games to regain top spot, with Ipswich beaten 3-1 and a 1-0 win at Birmingham. Hill recalled Bobby Gould for the injured Hudson, and Gould netted in the former game and won the penalty in the latter. Hill also handed a debut to young right-winger Peter Denton, in what was probably the youngest forward line in the club's history, with Machin and Rees at 21, the veterans. Norfolk-born Denton had improved enormously over the previous year in the reserves and impressed with his speed and enthusiasm, not to mention his crossing, which resulted in more shots at goal (34) than in any game that season. Denton played four games, then switched back to the reserves before another short spell in the first team later in the season. Sadly, Peter didn't make any more appearances for the club until one game early in 1967-68, which turned out to be his final game for the first team. Later that season he joined Luton.

City's stay back in pole position was short-lived. A disappointing home draw with bottom club Leyton Orient and another dropped point at Middlesbrough was followed on the first weekend of December by a dreadful 0-3 home loss to the new leaders Huddersfield. That game was significant because it was the first visit to Highfield Road of any reigning British Prime Minister – Harold Wilson was born and bred in Huddersfield and a keen Town fan.

The defeat heightened the criticism of City's attack – Hill had shuffled his forward line endlessly and yet it was failing to produce the goods. Hudson had lost his early-season spark and when paired with Gould did not look comfortable playing at inside-right. Ken Hale was out of touch and Clements' form of the previous campaign had dissipated. JH, however, was already on the case. Instead of accompanying the team to City's previous match, at Middlesbrough, Jimmy left his assistant Alan Dicks in charge and went scouting. He watched Plymouth v Bury, with 'Nemo' speculating that Hill could be lining up a new inside-forward. Plymouth's Mike Trebilcock and Bury's Colin Bell were the possible targets – both valued at £30,000. The fact that Hill had a meal with Bury's officials on the way back north could have meant something or nothing. A week later Hill lunched with Blackpool manager Ron Suart and the rumour machine said Alan Ball was on his way to Highfield Road (Ball did move at the end of the season, but to Everton for £110,000). 'Nemo' reported that a signing was possible but that big money (and that is what Hill wanted) was not *yet* available for a signing.

The postponement because of a waterlogged pitch at Charlton meant Huddersfield now led the Sky Blues by five points. However, it gave JH some breathing space. News that Bury were not prepared to release Bell ahead of their January FA Cup-tie would have disappointed Hill. Then, on Christmas Eve, Hill ended three weeks' speculation by signing another Bury player, centre-forward Ray Pointer, for a reported fee of £20,000. Twenty-nine-year-old Pointer had made his name in the Burnley side that won the League Championship in 1960. He had also won several England caps around that time. His star had fallen in recent seasons after injury and he had joined Bury the previous summer. With seventeen goals to his credit, he was third highest scorer in the Second Division at the time. Hill explained that the fee was higher than he had expected to pay because the club was paying 'on terms' – in other words, over a period, not in one go. Pointer made a scoring debut in a 1-1 draw at Norwich on Boxing Day, becoming the sixth different player to wear the troubled No 8 shirt since September.

Pointer's arrival certainly perked up the team, and two home wins in five days after Christmas were a great present for the fans. Pointer showed his class with a hat-trick in the second victory, 5-1 over Preston on New Year's Day. With Huddersfield losing at St Andrews and Maine Road over the holiday period, City were level on points with Huddersfield and only second on goal-average. However, the pack on their shoulder looked threatening:

1. Huddersfield P24 32Pts; 2. Coventry P24 32Pts; 3. Manchester City P23 31Pts; 4. Wolves P25 31Pts; 5. Southampton P24 29Pts; 6. Bristol C P24 28Pts.

The battle for promotion to Division One promised to be one of the tightest races for years. Could Jimmy Hill's men last the pace and reach the top division for the first time ever?

Chapter 12. 1965-66 (Part 2)

Hudson's Shock Departure

January 1966 was a good time to be a Coventry City supporter. Other than a defeat at Ipswich, the Sky Blues convincingly won two home league games, scoring five goals on each occasion, and won the crucial Midland derby at Molineux, as well as an FA Cup-tie at Swindon. Bill Glazier made his long-awaited return from his broken leg, playing for the 'A' team. A minor blot on the copybook saw the youth team knocked out of the FA Youth Cup by Stoke for the second season running.

Glazier's return was at West Brom's Spring Road, Smethwick training ground, on a Saturday morning. There were more spectators from Coventry than home fans, among them six schoolgirls who made the trek to see Bill's first game since he suffered the injury in April the previous year. He was inactive for long spells as City outplayed WBA and ran out 6-0 winners. Five of the City outfield players would go on to play for the first team, including centre-forward John Tudor, a triallist from Ilkeston playing only his second game in a Sky Blue shirt. Four days later Glazier was in goal for the reserves, but was on the losing side as a Northampton side ended the 'stiffs' unbeaten home record, winning 4-2. Bill's appearance boosted the crowd to 5,586 on a bitterly cold night, and although he was disappointed to concede four goals, the game gave him confidence. Afterwards he reported no reaction. A number of scouts and managers were present, primarily to run the rule over Ken Hale, who had been transfer-listed following the arrival of Pointer.

John Tudor tells of his first day at Coventry City in his autobiography *King For A Day*. His first encounter with Jimmy Hill was in the club's reception area and illustrates Hill's approach to discipline and standards. Having asked Tudor if he was being taken care of, Hill demanded 'Is this your bag and do you intend to have your hair as long as it is now?' Hill gave Tudor 2s 6d (12½p) and sent him round to Sweeney Todd's, the hairdresser used by all the City players, and ask for a 'Coventry City haircut'. He emerged with shorn locks sometime later.

Peter Denton's early form had fallen away, so Hill decided to rest him, giving John Mitten his longest run in the first team on the left flank, with Ronnie Rees switching to the right. The pair gave the side a better balance and were crucial in the two big home wins. Mitten was an enigma – one day he looked an extremely skilful player making fans think: 'Why isn't he in the team all the time. The next, he can scarcely be in the game.'

An unchanged side travelled to Third Division Swindon for the FA Cup-tie and City overcame their hoodoo at the County Ground – they had lost 1-4 in two previous visits under Hill – despite a snow-covered pitch producing conditions described by most of the players as 'the worst we have ever played on'. Towards the end of the game, as dusk fell, the centre of the pitch became an ice-rink but the experienced referee Leo Callaghan decided to let the game finish. City won 2-1.

Prior to the match Hill introduced another innovation, this one not so popular with the players. For some time he had wanted City's opponents filmed to aid his preparation for future games. He had spoken to local film societies to see if it could be done. Meanwhile, he became aware via John Camkin, who was a commentator for Anglia TV at the time, that the station had film of the Ipswich game from two weeks earlier, and of Swindon's game at Peterborough the previous Saturday. Hill and the players made a 260-mile round trip to Anglia studios in Norwich to view the recordings.

Seven days after beating Swindon, City pulled of a famous victory at Molineux to leapfrog Huddersfield into second place behind Manchester City. Only Joe Mercer's league leaders had previously won there, and Wolves were the division's highest scorers with 66 goals. City soaked up enormous early pressure, and then Ray Pointer scored with only City's third attack, a looping header from a John Sillett cross. City deserved their win in front of over 44,000, the biggest league crowd to watch City since the war. This included some 15,000 of their travelling fans, with 'Nemo' describing the victory as the best all-round performance in Jimmy Hill's reign. The national papers were not so complimentary, with several saying City were negative and nowhere near ready for Division One. 'Nemo' remarked that the enthusiasm of the fans matched that of 1964, and that the noise of the Sky Blue Song sweeping around Molineux was a big factor behind the victory and must have shattered the hopes of disconsolate Wolves fans. February, however, would test City's promotion credentials with a trip to Maine Road, Manchester, and a visit from fifth-placed Bristol City looming.

Before the trip to Manchester, however, the team enjoyed narrow escapes on successive Saturdays. First, a late Pointer goal was needed to rescue a home point against Rotherham, after a wretched display; then, City were two minutes from a shock FA Cup exit at Crewe when Rees equalised to bring the Railwaymen back for a replay. Curiously, the Gresty Road tie was played under the old Highfield Road floodlights, sold to Crewe in 1957. With the minutes ticking away, many of the 2,000 travelling City fans had resigned themselves to defeat, but City lived to fight another day and ran out 4-1 winners in the replay two days later. City were now in the fifth round of the FA Cup for only the second time since the war, and faced a tough but lucrative trip to First Division Everton.

Another Sky Blue innovation in early 1966 was the introduction of a song for the ball-boys. Around a dozen ball-boys were on duty at every home match, entrusted to return the ball to players quickly. At Corley Residential School for Delicate Children a housemaster came up with the idea of a song and had the boys from the school record it. Lyrics were composed to the tune of *There's Something about a Soldier* and the record was played for the first time at the Bristol City home game as the ball-boys marched out onto the pitch.

In six months Joe Mercer had transformed Manchester City from also-rans to promotion favourites. Having recruited Plymouth manager Malcolm Allison as his number two, he had assembled a blend of outstanding home-grown youngsters, such as Alan Oakes, Neil Young and Glyn Pardoe, with some relatively expensive signings – George Heslop, Mike Summerbee and Johnny Crossan. The mix was potent, and City looked good bets to regain their First Division place after three seasons in the Second. The average attendance at Maine Road had almost doubled from the previous season's 14,000 and was higher even than Coventry's. They were unbeaten at home, apart from Coventry's League Cup win in September, and had not lost anywhere since early December. With Coventry having lost only one of their last ten, the game was a true match of the Titans.

Despite a gritty performance from Coventry, it was Mercer's men who won a hard game 1-0, with Coventry missing good chances to have drawn or even won the match. Over 40,000 watched the intriguing clash, including around 8,000 Coventry fans.

A week later Bristol City came to Highfield Road and grabbed a point. The balloon was about to go up. In the second half Jimmy Hill moved George Hudson to the right wing, exasperated by the No 9's first-half input. 'The Hud' scored City's second equaliser, but on the Monday Hill named Hudson in the reserve team to play Southampton the following evening. With the FA Cup fifth-round tie at Goodison looming, speculation rose that Hudson might be dropped. 'Nemo' explained that it was the first 'official admission that Hudson's form has been below par' and he reminded supporters that Hudson had scored only five goals in his last eighteen appearances. Reading between the lines, it is difficult not to conclude that Hill had been concerned for some time. For many fans, however, George could do no wrong and they chose to overlook these statistics because Hudson was their god.

Almost 8,000, swelled by hordes of club scouts, watched City's reserves thump Southampton 7-1. Hudson scored one goal but was put in the shade by young Bobby Gould, who scored two and ran the Saints' defence ragged all night.

The next morning Hill took a phone call from Northampton boss Dave Bowen, who offered a large fee for Hudson. The Cobblers were having a hard time in their first ever season in the First Division and were trying to keep their head above water near the foot of the table. With games running out and the transfer deadline approaching, Bowen saw Hudson as the man who might just save them. The transfer deadline was less than two weeks away and Hill knew this was the time when fees were inflated by desperate buyers.

Not for the first time, Hill made an unpopular decision and faced the wrath of the supporters. He agreed a fee of £28,500 with Northampton – a profit of £7,500 and then spent weeks trying to justify his decision to angry fans. He knew that time would be the judge of his actions – and he was ultimately proved right – but City's stuttering form to the end of the season didn't help his cause.

In his book *Miracle in Sky Blue*, Marshall Stewart sums up Hudson: 'He was a rare combination: a player without personal glamour who attracted the fans' adulation by his disregard of the unnecessary and his ability to reap the maximum effect from the most discreet amount of effort. He had star quality without the spotlights …'

Several coach-loads of City fans travelled to Northampton to see Hudson's debut against Leeds, rather than travel to Goodison to support City in the FA Cup. ATV television rubbed salt in the wounds by showing the highlights from Northampton, with Hudson at his cultured best and scoring a superb goal in the Cobblers' 2-1 victory.

Hill justified the shock sale: 'With every player, there is a time to sell and a time to buy. I give the fans this assurance – I would never do anything against the interests of Coventry City.' It was a virtual re-run of the Terry Bly scenario, and Hill had been proved spot-on in his judgement of Bly. Looked at in retrospect, Hudson, despite scoring a few goals, failed to keep the Cobblers in the top division and was sold to Tranmere for £15,000 less than a year later. Apart from helping dump City out of the FA Cup in 1968, he never made a big splash again, and his golden days were undoubtedly seen at Highfield Road. In the short term, City missed out on promotion but they banked an inflated fee for Hudson, which went towards team strengthening in the summer. In young Bobby Gould, Hill had a ready-made replacement who, whilst not a charismatic player like Hudson, would score the goals that got City promotion in 1967.

The sudden sale of Hudson thrust nineteen-year-old Gould into the limelight. The two were like chalk and cheese. Hudson was the cultured line-leader who rarely chased a ball and would not have looked out of place in a continental side. Gould lacked Hudson's panache and cool, but he would give everything he had for 90 minutes and headed everyone's list for endeavour, enthusiasm and unlimited quantities of never-say-die.

In all the drama of that week, the departure of Ken Hale passed many fans by; he joined Oxford for £8,000, a small loss on the Geordie inside-forward who had joined City in November 1962 for £10,000. Hale had given sterling service to the Sky Blue cause, but his form that season had slipped away so badly that it meant one less option in the forward line for Hill. The knockers questioned this sale too, arguing that Hale was a better bet than Ernie Machin.

With the proceeds from the two sales banked, speculation was rife that Hill would sign a replacement for Hudson before the 16 March deadline. After a board meeting on 3 March, however, the priority was to finish paying off the debt on Pointer's purchase, and to settle some outstanding debts from the ground improvements. At this stage Hill believed that promotion was still achievable and was reluctant to buy players at inflated prices in the deadline mayhem.

At Goodison Park on the Saturday, Ray Pointer took Hudson's No 9 shirt and Gould came in at No 8. The Sky Blues were knocked out of the FA Cup, beaten 0-3 by an Everton side on their way to Wembley triumph over Sheffield Wednesday in May. The scoreline flattered Everton somewhat, with Gould having a goal disallowed when the score was 0-1, but it was a lacklustre display by City. Again, as at Villa the previous year, Hill baffled the fans with his team selection and tactics. Machin and Farmer were played as defensive midfielders to counteract Everton's strong midfield. The 60,350 crowd, however, the biggest to watch City since the Villa Park games in the 1930s, guaranteed City a £4,000 pay-day.

So now City just had promotion to focus on. With twelve games remaining, the top of the Division Two read as follows: 1. Manchester City P30 42Pts; 2. Huddersfield P30 40Pts; 3. Coventry P30 38Pts; 4. Wolves P31 37Pts; 5. Southampton P30 36Pts; 6. Bristol City P30 36Pts.

'Nemo' predicted that 56 points would be enough to get into the top two promotion places (he was almost correct, 54 would ultimately be sufficient) and therefore City needed eighteen points. Against City was the fact that seven of their remaining games were away, and City's away form (only four wins in fourteen) was not one of their strengths. 'Nemo's' assessment was that if City wanted promotion, they would have to strengthen the forward line.

12. 1965-66 (Part 2) Hudson's Shock Departure

A week later a 1-0 win at Crystal Palace cheered up depressed City fans, and a hard-earned draw at Carlisle the following Friday night kept City third, but leaders Manchester City, parading their new £45,000 signing Colin Bell from Bury, won at Derby to go clear again at the top, and with a game in hand. Some City fans eyed the Colin Bell saga enviously, comparing the Manchester club's desire for promotion with Coventry's sale of Hudson. Some made the same accusation that had been heard in the late 1930s: 'City don't really want promotion this season.' Hill replied: 'If we go up, I shall get an increase in salary as well as the players. If anyone thinks I am going to pass up a chance like that, they must think I am a very funny person.'

Down in the 'A' team, City's youngsters were running away with the Midland Intermediate League. In February 'Nemo' reported that the youth team needed a stronger league, having won sixteen out of their nineteen games with a goal record of 64-13. The latest victory, an 8-0 thumping of Shrewsbury, saw triallist John Tudor hit six goals. Tudor's star was rising and he would soon be knocking on the first-team door.

The youth team were attracting interest overseas, too; in March they were invited to take part in the prestigious Easter international tournament in Amsterdam for Europe's best youth sides. Pat Saward's young lions gave a good account of themselves, and one of the blossoming stars of the team, sixteen-year-old Willie Carr, won the player of the tournament award, just weeks after deservedly receiving his reserve-team debut.

The departure of Hudson, coupled with FA Cup defeat at Everton, had temporarily left many fans embittered, and attendances took a definite dip for successive Saturday home games against Cardiff and Bolton. Almost 10,000 fans had stayed away, compared to the Bristol game a month earlier, and despite three points gained, those turning up saw unconvincing performances that looked anything like promotion form. True, Cardiff were beaten 3-1, but only a late goal salvaged a draw against defence-minded Bolton.

Easter was disastrous for the Sky Blues, with two away defeats by mid-table teams seriously denting promotion hopes. On the Saturday, City flew by plane to Portsmouth and a lop-sided attack showed little penetration against the home side which, aided by a rare Wesson error, won 2-0, to add City's scalp to that of Huddersfield gained earlier in the week. On Easter Monday at Derby, Glazier made his long-awaited return but could not stop a late goal sending the Sky Blues to another defeat. With the injured Pointer missing, City's attack again looked out of touch, and Hudson's sale was again the main talking point.

City won the return against the Rams 3-2 the following night with a gritty display, and when Jimmy Hill looked at the league table the following morning he realised that things were not as bad as had seemed on the Monday evening. Manchester City had lost at Bury, and although City were down to fourth, behind Wolves, they had a game in hand over the Molineux men. Ominously, Southampton were three points behind the Sky Blues and, with two games in hand, were poised to take advantage of further slips by the top four.

Another home win, 4-3 over resurgent neighbours Birmingham, with Pointer back in the team, pulled City level on points with Huddersfield and Wolves – the former having lost 1-4 at Derby. Like a Tour de France cyclist, the Saints were tucked in the leaders' slipstream and another win boosted their chances.

It was the away form that proved to be City's downfall. The following Saturday, Leyton Orient, already doomed to relegation, nine points adrift at the bottom of the table, held City 1-1. Despite the relentless cajoling of never-say-die skipper Curtis, City just could not break down a proud but inept Orient side which refused to roll over. Now, though, City would have to rely on their rivals slipping up, and were grateful to hear that Wolves had lost at Portsmouth and that Huddersfield, Manchester City and Southampton had all drawn, too.

Three days later things went from bad to worse, as Charlton defeated the Sky Blues 2-0 in a game relayed back to Highfield Road, where 11,321 watched City's three key attackers all suffer injuries. Gould was substituted, and Rees and Pointer ended the match limping. 'Nemo' summed up his view: 'last night they seemed to me to be absolutely drained of the verve and fire that has kept them in the hunt for so long. They looked a side with whom the strain of the whole race had finally caught them up and I believe it's asking the impossible now for them to do anything but finish in a respectable position.'

The table after defeat at the Valley looked thus: 1. Huddersfield P40 51Pts; 2. Man City P37 51Pts; 3. Coventry P40 49Pts; 4. Southampton P38 48Pts; 5. Wolves P40 48Pts.

Hill was forever optimistic, and when the attendance at the final home game, a 2-1 victory over Middlesbrough, dipped below 20,000, he had harsh words. 'Some supporters have deserted the club at the last lap. I cannot describe how I feel about them giving up supporting the lads who have taken us to the last game, which could well mean promotion. It looks to me as though the city does not deserve a First Division club.'

Middlesbrough's defeat almost certainly doomed them to relegation with Orient, but 'Nemo' identified their captain Ian Gibson as a fine prospect, describing him as 'one of the best inside-forwards we have seen on the ground this term'. On the same afternoon, Manchester City virtually secured promotion with a 3-1 win over Birmingham, but Huddersfield choked, losing at Carlisle. Southampton's 1-0 home win over Charlton meant they were still one point behind the Sky Blues, with two games in hand and a superior goal-average.

City's promotion hopes had been scuppered by taking just one point (and one goal) from four away games against teams in mid-table or worse. On the final Saturday, City finally hit some away form, winning 2-0 at Huddersfield to give themselves a prayer of promotion. They had to rely, however, on their old Division Three South rivals Southampton dropping points in their final three games, all away from the Dell. It was not the first time City and the Saints had been in the promotion mix together – in 1960 two defeats by Grimsby over Easter had blown City's hopes and handed promotion from Division Three to Southampton. This time the Saints had again profited over Easter, gaining three lucky points from Bristol City in two games still raw in the collective memory of Ashton Gate, for they robbed the Robins of top-division football. If Bristol had got the four Easter points their two performances deserved, rather than the one they actually got, they would have been promoted.

As City's 3,000 travelling fans invaded the pitch following City's last-day win at Huddersfield, the Tannoy announced the final score from Home Park: 'Plymouth Argyle 2, Southampton 3.' 'Nemo' described the scene: 'A heart-rending groan went up and the mounting hope that had welled up suddenly ebbed away.' In the City dressing room someone optimistically said: 'we could still do it.'

Forty-eight hours later at Leyton Orient, a Terry Paine goal earned the point that made virtually certain that Southampton and not the Sky Blues would be promoted to Division One for the first time in the club's history. Thousands of Saints' fans converged on Brisbane Road, and the result meant Southampton would have to lose their final game at Maine Road 0-6 for the Sky Blues to go up. As it turned out, they drew 0-0 and the Sky Blues finished third – the highest final position in the club's history, though many City fans failed to appreciate what had been achieved.

As had become the norm, the Sky Blues played a raft of friendlies and testimonials after the end of the league season. George Hudson returned to Highfield Road with relegated Northampton for Mick Kearns' testimonial. Hudson was not fully fit and the much-vaunted clash between him and George Curtis was a timid affair. Over 13,000 watched a benign 2-2 draw almost devoid of tackling. Then the team flew to Dublin for a testimonial with Shamrock Rovers. Hill gave an outing to his former

Fulham team-mate John Key, a right-winger released by Fulham, and after the 2-0 victory Key agreed to sign for the Sky Blues. Other testimonials took place at Bedworth (a 4-3 win) and Ilkeston (a 4-4 draw).

Before the summer break the club undertook a tour of Europe to promote Rover Cars with the blessing of Prime Minister Harold Wilson. Rover provided eight sky-blue Rover 2000 cars which were driven on a 2,500-mile tour of Frankfurt, Vienna, Zurich and Brussels, stopping off at 'promotional conferences' in each city. Games were staged against a local team in each city. The tour matches were generally benign affairs, except for that in Frankfurt against Offenbach Kickers, who lived up to their name. Ronnie Rees, tired from a tour of South America with the Wales team, got himself sent off for a bad tackle.

One player missing from the cavalcade of Rover cars was Allan Harris. The full-back, who had enjoyed an outstanding season, had asked to move back to London and he rejoined his brother Ron at Chelsea for £45,000, a profit of £10,000 in eighteen months for Coventry. At one stage a swap, with England international forward Barry Bridges coming to Coventry, was on the cards but Bridges decided he would rather join Birmingham. Coventry therefore got cash rather than a new player.

Following his return to Stamford Bridge, Harris struggled to get a regular place in the team, although he did appear in the 1967 FA Cup final. Later he was a successful coach under Terry Venables at Crystal Palace, QPR and Barcelona, and much later managed the Malaysian national team.

Coventry's average home league attendance was 25,370, down by around 1,200 from the previous season, but was again the eleventh highest in the whole Football League and second highest in the division, behind Manchester City.

As the country prepared for the World Cup, staged in England for the first time, Hill and Robins knew that they needed to strengthen the team to win promotion to Division One. Despite the excellent gates and a raft of other money-making enterprises, another major source of funding was needed if City were to gain promotion and compete with the big boys. That summer a new Sky Blue Pool was launched, with the aim of generating £100,000 a year. Launched as 'Rocket The Sky Blues into Europe', chairman Robins donated £10,000 to kick off the competition, which boasted a £1,000 weekly first prize by the coming Christmas. The aim was to recruit 250,000 members from the city and surrounding areas.

Chapter 13. 1966-67 (Part 1)

The Wheels are Wobbling (II)

Transfer speculation had been rife throughout the summer of 1966 but Jimmy Hill knew he had no magic pot of money and would have to wheel and deal to strengthen his squad for another attempt at promotion. Looking to the future, the directors knew that to compete at the highest level another, alternative, source of revenue was required. The new 'Rocket the Sky Blues into Europe' would raise £100,000 per year to go towards signing players. Hill explained: 'We wanted Charlie Cooke, the Dundee inside-forward who this week signed for Chelsea for £70,000. And I had another player in mind, who would have cost only a little less, who would almost certainly put us into Division One. But sadly the money was not available. My board of directors decided there and then that I must have the cash in future; I know the players to buy and I haven't made a bad transfer yet.'

Numerous players were linked with the Sky Blues, including Preston's young star Howard Kendall, Tottenham's Alan Mullery, and Grimsby centre-forward Matt Tees. Hill, however, refused to comment on any rumours, not even that Arsenal wanted him as their manager to replace Billy Wright, who had been sacked in June.

The sale of Allan Harris boosted the coffers and a further £5,000 was raised when John Sillett joined Plymouth in July, another profit in the transfer market. Sillett had the task of replacing Tony Book as Argyle's right-back, Book having joined newly promoted Manchester City.

Season-ticket sales had been excellent, and by early July the previous season's total of 5,500 had almost been reached. Then, in the first week of July, with football fans preparing for the World Cup about to start, Hill pounced and paid a club record £57,000 for Middlesbrough's Scottish Under-23 midfield player Ian Gibson. Although Boro had been relegated to Division Three the previous season, 'Gibbo' had been outstanding for them in City's last home game and impressed City fans with his skill and industry. Had Hill managed to persuade Barry Bridges to come in part-exchange for Allan Harris, it is unlikely that the Sky Blues could have afforded Gibson.

Twenty-three-year-old Gibson had been one of the youngest players to appear in the Football League when he made his debut for Accrington at the age of fifteen. In 1962 he joined Middlesbrough from Bradford for £20,000. Boro had rejected £40,000 from Hibernian in 1963 and the player subsequently turned down Birmingham and Southampton, prior to signing for City.

Hill was one of the BBC 'experts' for the World Cup and appeared several times on TV during the competition, making comments and giving interviews. Many in the broadcasting world were impressed with his performances in front of the camera, but few City fans could have imagined that Hill's future career would be in that world. He recalled in his autobiography that on the day of the final he stood next to Joe Mercer at Wembley and both of them were in tears at the final whistle as England beat West Germany 4-2.

The club's youth scheme was churning out talent by the bucket-load, and that summer Benny Glover, Malcolm Keley, John Tudor and Howard Moore became full-time professionals. The 'A' team, which had romped away with the Midland Intermediate League the previous season, entered the West Midlands League, and would meet local non-league sides rather than the youth teams of other Midlands clubs. The 'B' team stepped up to take their place in the Midland Intermediate League. The problem Hill and his staff faced was meeting the ambitions of so many talented youngsters. The reserves would regularly feature a mix of senior professionals and youngsters, and could hold their own against any reserve team in the Football Combination, which included all the top London clubs as well as teams like Nottingham Forest, Leicester and Birmingham. Two regular reserves were unhappy with their lot; goalkeeper Bob Wesson and winger John Mitten both made transfer requests which were granted.

England's World Cup triumph had ignited interest in the game across the country, and in Coventry the anticipation was even greater after narrowly missing promotion the previous term. 'Nemo' penned his usual preview, noting that his City forecasts in the past two seasons had been correct. He now predicted that the Sky Blues would win promotion to Division One. Many pundits tipped Birmingham to be promoted, but 'Nemo' thought not, preferring Blackburn as City's strongest rivals, with Wolves 'particularly if Ernie Hunt is buzzing' to be one of the main bunch.

'Nemo' justified his prediction: 'After last season, which they began with a forward line that frankly wasn't good enough, yet managed to get within a hairsbreadth of promotion, they must tackle 1966-67 with every confidence, particularly now that a player of Gibson's calibre is helping the cause.'

A low-key pre-season – a 1-1 home draw against Bulgarian team Varna; away games at Hereford (5-1) and Dudley (1-1) – was marred by a training incident which left Ernie Machin sidelined for several weeks with a knee problem. Machin's misfortune gave Hill various options. His line-up for the opening league game showed four changes to that which ended the previous campaign. Brian Hill was fit again and started alongside George Curtis at the back, John Key made his debut on the right wing, with Rees on the left, and new man Gibson was in for Machin. Pointer, expected to be reserve following Gibson's arrival, was reprieved for the time being. Key suffered a dead-leg after five minutes and although he carried on he was subsequently out for over a month. With Allan Harris departed, Dietmar Bruck had been converted to a left-back and he took to the new role like a duck to water using his attacking flair.

For the fifth season running, the Sky Blues started on a winning note, beating promoted Hull 1-0 on a scorching hot day. Bruck's bobbling 35-yard shot bamboozled the Hull keeper for the only goal, and Hull's skipper Andy Davidson was sent off after striking Gould. Hull's chairman, local gravel magnate Harold Needler, was trying to emulate Derrick Robins, a personal friend, and bring success to a big-city club who had never played in Division One. Boasting two of the best strikers in the business, Chris Chilton and Ken Wagstaff, they had raced away with the Third Division title, scoring 109 goals. Although the Tigers came close to promotion in the coming seasons it would be another 40 years before they reached the top flight.

City's 2-4 defeat at Plymouth was followed by a Gibson-inspired victory at Portsmouth (2-0), and although Plymouth were beaten 1-0 in the return game it was an unconvincing win. 'Nemo,' however, pointed out that their form might have been unimpressive but they had six points out of eight, a good start. In the fifth game, a 1-1 home draw with big-spending Birmingham, City were by far the better side and looked for the first time like promotion candidates. Bobby Gould scored again, his third of the season, and was not going to give up his place without a fight. It was Ray Pointer who dropped out to make way for the returning Machin.

Goals however were hard to come by. Defeat at Millwall (0-1) and a draw at Norwich were followed by a scrappy 1-0 home win over Bristol City, thanks to a penalty. After eight games City lay fifth, three points behind leaders Bolton, but had scored just nine goals whilst boasting the division's best defence (seven conceded). Some fans were getting frustrated and letters in the *Pink* were critical of City's 'defensive' style, Hill's selection of Machin, and Gibson's 'deep' role. 'Nemo,' however, was convinced City were on the right lines, writing: 'I have seen nothing to shake my conviction that Hill's men will be among the front runners next May.'

Ronnie Rees was going through a bad patch. After the Bristol game, he and Pointer played in the midweek reserve game against Nottingham

Forest. In an experienced forward line, they played alongside John Key, John Mitten and John Tudor. Tudor gave another in a string of good reserve displays, and Hill promoted him to the first team against Bury, in place of Pointer, also recalling Key. City scored three goals for the first time, including a superb diving header from Gould described by 'Nemo' as 'reminiscent of a [Tommy] Lawton special' for his fifth goal of the campaign.

The next two weeks proved to be a watershed in City's season. Away form went from bad to worse, with league defeats at Preston and Carlisle sandwiching a 1-1 draw at Third Division Brighton in the League Cup. A long train journey from Brighton to Carlisle left players bored and tetchy, and the mood in the camp was, for once, strained. Record signing Ian Gibson played poorly in the 1-2 defeat at Brunton Park, and on the following Monday morning asked for a transfer. Hill told the press that 'we just don't see eye to eye on the way he should play in the team'. Gibson told 'Nemo': 'I'm determined to get away – the sooner the better. I'm sorry that things don't seem to have worked out.'

Over the years the truth of what actually happened has seeped out and was partially confirmed in Jimmy Hill's autobiography:

'When the game was over in Carlisle, as fierce as the Coventry players had ever seen me, I chastised Ian, pointing out that his performance left a lot to be desired, or ungentlemanly words to that effect. "It seems to me you are more interested in the result of the three o'clock race at Kempton Park than you are in ours at the same time on Saturday." They were my final words.'

Eye-witnesses describe a physical confrontation in the dressing room and confirm the fall-out was more to do with Gibson's betting habits than his role in the team. Writing the following week in the *Pink*, 'Nemo' suggested Hill had erred by picking on Gibson: 'it would be a blind man who could not see further than Gibson when looking for reasons for City's largely unimpressive showings. When internationals like Rees and Pointer begin the season so out of touch, and other key men like Bill Glazier and Mick Kearns do not turn in consistent performances, it is hardly surprising that the Sky Blues have not done as well as we hoped.'

'Nemo' concluded: 'Let's not delude ourselves that Gibson's departure will solve problems – it will only add to them. Mr Hill made a mistake over Gibson. But he should be finally judged not on this, but on what position the Sky Blues occupy at the end of the season.'

The board rejected Gibson's transfer request, but Hill dropped him from his team. The following night Brighton piled on the agony by winning the League Cup replay by 3-1 at Highfield Road to end a miserable fortnight. 'Nemo' described it as: 'the most abject display since the FA Cup fiasco against King's Lynn in 1961,' and 'only those living in a fool's paradise will refuse to concede that the Sky Blues are passing through a crisis.' 'Nemo' felt that only George Curtis, Bobby Gould and debutant full-back Mick Coop emerged from the replay with any credit.

The Gibson story overshadowed everything else in the local press, so that the departure of City's club secretary passed almost without notice. Paul Oliver, secretary since 1963, decided to leave the club to join the new North American Professional Soccer League. He was replaced by Alan Leather, who had held a similar position at Tottenham.

Despite bright news on the financial side – the club announced record profits of £49,000 – the dream of promotion was fading fast, and over the next month, with Gibson dumped in the reserves, there were few signs of resurgence. Home gates slipped to under 20,000.

Gibson-less Sky Blues got back to winning ways, beating a star-studded Blackburn 2-0 at home, leaving them only four points behind new leaders Hull. The win was the first in a run of four unbeaten games that included a gutsy draw at second-placed Bolton and a win at Derby's Baseball Ground, a bogey ground in the past. John Tudor, deputising for Gibson, scored two goals in the four games, as did the predatory Gould and the steadily improving Machin.

There were no bids for Gibson, although Hill reported that two First Division clubs and a Second Division club had 'made enquiries', but he wasn't prepared to name them. In early November City were strongly linked with Newcastle's Under-23 forward Albert Bennett, but a day later it was revealed that Hill had tried to sign another Newcastle forward, Alan Suddick, in exchange for Gibson, but Suddick didn't wish to leave Newcastle.

Despite 'Gibbo's' absence, Ray Pointer had not appeared in the first team since the Brighton debacle, and City rejected a £15,000 bid from Third Division Oldham to buy him. Bristol City were supposedly interested, too, but for the time being Ray would languish in the reserves.

One player who was happy at City was Dave Clements. The versatile Irishman had switched back to wing-half, following injuries to Ron Farmer and Brian Hill, and his man-marking of sharp opponents like Blackburn's Bryan Douglas and Bolton's Brian Bromley had been crucial in the recent good run. The club rewarded his solid performances with a four-year contract. Until Hill's arrival most players were on one or, at the most, two-year deals. Clements joined Glazier (five years) and Rees (four years) on a longer contract. Hill explained the logic: 'We are encouraging this sort of contract to build up a nucleus of young players who will stay on with the club and enjoy a testimonial. It settles them in their minds and safeguards their future.' Hill had not discarded his patronage of players when he left the Professional Footballers Association. Unlike many in that era, he believed passionately that if you looked after your players they would perform for you. Clements and Rees both showed up well at Derby and were recalled to their respective national teams the following week for the Home Internationals, Rees for his sixteenth cap, Clements for his fourth. Both did their reputations no harm, though they could not prevent defeats. Wales lost 1-5 at Wembley, whilst Northern Ireland went down 1-2 at Hampden Park, where Clements did an effective marking job on one of Britain's finest players, Denis Law.

On 5 November 'Nemo' wrote that Jimmy Hill had told him: 'I have never said that Ian [Gibson] will not play in the team again, as was the case with Terry Bly. If I saw a place where he could improve the side, in he would go.' When 'Nemo' asked why he continued to leave Gibson out, Hill responded: 'we are getting results. Our performances haven't been perfect. But we have picked up five points out of six.' (That day they made it seven out of eight.) 'Nemo's conclusion was that there was a chink of light in the month-old impasse between manager and player, but he worried that the defence, which had shown signs of strain, would crack under the pressure in a side which lacked goalpower.

Seven days later Crystal Palace ended the mini-run, inflicting the Sky Blues' first and, as it turned out, only home defeat, 1-2, leaving City sixth in the table. The irony was that the team gave a better showing than the previous home game against Charlton, which they won. After the defeat 'Nemo' identified the problem as one of 'puny firepower': 'City really have been living on borrowed time. Most of their results this season have been based on defensive effectiveness, particularly at home.'

A week later the defence was under constant siege as City slipped to another defeat, 1-3 at Huddersfield, who had not been enjoying the best of times themselves. The defeat left City in seventh place, five points behind the joint leaders, Wolves and Ipswich. For the first time since the Sky Blue Special train was introduced, the club could not sell all the tickets and the viability of the train was questioned. Few City fans who travelled to Leeds Road on that cold, damp day would have put money on City remaining unbeaten for the rest of the season, but they had just witnessed the last defeat of the campaign.

The conveyor-belt of exciting youngsters never slowed. Although the reserve-team results were not great – the team was, in fact, bottom of the Football Combination in November – the club was oozing talent. The latest to knock on the first-team door were nineteen-year-old Brummie

Benny Glover, who got a place on the bench at Derby after less than a dozen reserve games, sixteen-year-old midfielder Willie Carr, who dazzled against Chelsea reserves, and along with a third super-kid, nineteen-year-old forward Trevor Shepherd, got his first taste of first-team action in a friendly with Morton at the end of November.

With Bill Glazier ruled out with a knee strain, 22-year-old Coventry-born Peter Thomas was called into goal for the visit of Cardiff. Hill had reluctantly sold Bob Wesson to Walsall two months earlier for £10,000, unable to keep the loyal keeper happy in the reserves. Now he had to take a chance with the untried Thomas, who had spent some months on loan to Irish club Waterford, where he had played in a brief European Cup venture. With Dietmar Bruck injured, full-back Mick Coop also got his first league start and the raw Glover was on the bench. Coop and Glover's good news, however, was overshadowed by the return of Ian Gibson, one of five changes from the eleven who had lost at Huddersfield.

The Sky Blues turned on the style to beat lowly Cardiff 3-2, but created enough chances to have thrashed the Welsh team. The crew-cutted Gibson scored two goals and put on a sublime attacking midfield performance. Post-match remarks, however, from both player and manager did little to suggest a reconciliation. Gibson told 'Nemo': 'I am still determined to leave.' Hill noted: 'It's significant that he scored two against Cardiff; before he was dropped he scored one in thirteen.'

One man for whom the Cardiff game did not leave happy memories was John Tudor. The Ilkeston-born centre-forward had netted five goals in nine games. He was beginning to look like a regular and had retained his place after the loss at Huddersfield, with Machin dropped. However, John flung himself into a reckless challenge and dislocated his knee. In the dressing room after the game Jimmy Hill fumed at the prostrate Tudor, calling him an idiot for chasing a lost cause.

December was the crucial month, and the Sky Blues started with two dazzling victories in six days. For the second season running, Wolves, the league leaders, were beaten 3-1 at Molineux. On the following Friday evening, Ipswich, who had gone top themselves, were put to the sword, 5-0. City's swashbuckling display was described by 'Nemo' as: 'probably their best performance in the Second Division and on a par for skill and excitement with the great victory over Sunderland in 1963.' Gibson was the architect and, despite a hat-trick from Bobby Gould, the goal of the night came from cheeky Gibson who chipped the ball over seven defenders to find the the net and guarantee himself cult status with City fans.

After the weekend's games City, suddenly, were not in the chasing pack but in the leading pack:

1. Wolves P20 26Pts; 2. Ipswich P21 26Pts; 3. Coventry P20 25Pts; 4. Carlisle P21 25Pts; 5. Hull P21 23Pts.

Three days after the victory at Molineux, Pat Saward's youth team did likewise, winning 2-0 in an FA Youth Cup-tie. Midfielder Trevor Gould, brother of Bobby, was man of the match, and there were also good performances from two-goal striker Don Peachey, Willie Carr, sixteen-year-old Graham Paddon, and a new find, defender Jeff Blockley.

The first team's third tough game in a row, at Hull, saw City grab an invaluable point, 2-2, against the division's top scorers. Meanwhile, Wolves lost at St Andrews and Ipswich went back on top after a 0-0 draw with Cardiff.

One man in City's camp not happy with his lot was Brian Hill. The 26-year-old defender had been out injured since the end of October, and he had a recurring problem with pulled muscles. In December he successfully came through 'A' team and reserve games before appearing as a substitute on Boxing Day. The following day at Rotherham, however, he pulled a muscle again and would play no further part in City's promotion campaign.

The goals continued to flow over the holiday period. Home wins over bogey team Rotherham (4-2) and Portsmouth (5-1) sandwiched a fighting last-gasp draw at Rotherham, described by Hill as 'the finest away point we have won'. The home victory over Rotherham, on Boxing Day, witnessed an unsavoury incident when a Coventry yob climbed over the terrace wall at the covered end and attacked the Millers' stand-in goalkeeper John Galley and their trainer. Police quickly dealt with the idiot, but the club's reputation for well-behaved supporters was tarnished.

1966 ended with a 5-1 home win over Portsmouth. Pompey, five down with 35 minutes left, were let off the hook somewhat. City were without two of their injured stars, Gibson and Rees, but showed their strength in depth with Tudor and Mitten stepping in and scoring. Right-winger John Key was also finding his feet, after an injury-hit start to his Coventry career, and netted his fourth goal in six games. With their two promotion rivals, Wolves and Ipswich, drawing 0-0, the league table on New Year's Eve saw the Sky Blues second, their highest position of the season so far:

1. Wolves P24 31Pts; 2. Coventry P24 31Pts; 3. Ipswich P25 29Pts; 4. Crystal Palace P24 29Pts; 5. Millwall P24 29Pts.

Chapter 14. 1966-67 (Part 2)

We are the Champions

The FA Cup third round draw gave City a dream home tie against First Division Newcastle. Since returning to the top flight in 1965, the Magpies had not made a big impression, and when the draw was announced on 7 January they propped up the table, boasting just one away win and a pitiful six goals on their travels. In an effort to stem the tide they had spent £140,000 on five players, among them Welsh international centre-forward Wyn Davies for a club record £80,000. The 6ft 2in, ginger-haired striker had, however, taken time to settle on Tyneside. The tie was scheduled for 28 January, and before then there were some tough league games facing the Sky Blues.

City's talented youth team were progressing well in the FA Youth Cup, defeating Swansea 2-1 in a third round replay, with Don Peachey scoring both goals. In the last sixteen a physically stronger Port Vale side knocked City out on a paddyfield of a pitch at Vale Park. With most of City's kids, including Trevor Gould, Carr, Paddon and Blockley, eligible the following season, Pat Saward's young bucks would achieve remarkable things in the coming year.

On 7 January the Sky Blues went top of Division Two with a 1-1 draw at St Andrews. For the third away game in a row they fell behind, but recovered to gain a priceless point. A large City contingent boosted the crowd to almost 37,000 on a miserably wet day. Leaders Wolves' defeat at Ashton Gate meant City were now a point clear at the top. Millwall, by virtue of winning at Northampton, crept into third place, level on points with Wolves. 'Nemo' revealed that a 'prominent firm of bookmakers' – no advertising in the *Coventry Telegraph* in those days – had made City 2:1 favourites to lift the Second Division title, with Wolves priced at 5:2.

In January 1967 'Nemo' abandoned his *nom de plume* and started writing in the *Coventry Telegraph* under his own name, Derek Henderson. The tag 'Nemo' had been employed as a pseudonym for the paper's soccer writer since the early 1900s, with each subsequent reporter adopting it over the decades. At the same time, the newspaper's rugby union writer 'Nimrod' was exposed as David Irvine, and the boxing correspondent, previously known as 'Leftguard', was revealed as Alex Goodman.

Devon-born Henderson had been working as the *Coventry Telegraph*'s main football writer, and covering Coventry City, since early 1958. By 1967 he had seen City in action on most grounds in the Football League, and before his departure from the newspaper in 1973 he would take his tally to 90 of the 92 grounds. He missed Doncaster and Scunthorpe.

City's eight-game unbeaten run was beginning to have an impact on the Sky Blues' fair-weather supporters, and a week after the team went top almost 28,000, the largest Saturday gate since September, were enticed by the visit of Norwich. The Canaries had won only four games all season but gave City a hard fight, and it needed a very late Machin goal to seal a 2-1 win. Wolves dropped a home point to Carlisle but the biggest shock was the home defeat of Millwall by Plymouth – the Lions' first home reverse in 59 games stretching back two and a half seasons to 1964. Plymouth fielded their new signing John Mitten who, having been available for transfer for some months, had left City for £3,500 the previous week. The left-winger's opportunities had been limited, but his sale came less than two weeks after his dazzling display against Plymouth at Highfield Road.

Another imminent departure was Ray Pointer. Out of the team since October, Ray was coveted by both Bristol City and Portsmouth, and Hill, conscious of Pointer's tumbling transfer value and keen to maximise what he could get, homed in on an exchange deal with Pompey's midfield utility player Brian Lewis. Brian Hill's recurring muscle problem (he limped off in a reserve game in January) and lack of cover on the flanks, made this a sensible insurance policy, which could pay dividends if the club won promotion. After two weeks of protracted negotiations the deal was completed and 23-year-old Lewis signed. Derek Henderson suggested that Pointer was valued at £15,000 with City paying Pompey another £20,000 to balance the transaction. The following day JH was full of praise for the new Sky Blue pool, whose profits for that season of around £12,500, had largely paid for Lewis.

Of lesser note was reserve goalkeeper Peter Thomas' transfer to Waterford. Thomas had been the first ever City player to be 'loaned out', when Hill let him go to Waterford earlier in the season. The Irish club were now keen to sign him permanently, and although it left City with only the untried Martin Clamp as cover for Glazier, Hill agreed to the move for a small fee. On the same day, tucked down at the foot of the back page of the *Coventry Telegraph,* was the news that Northampton had sold George Hudson to Tranmere, less than a year after signing him from City, and for half the fee they had paid. The Hudson fans who had criticised Hill for selling their hero began to recognise that the manager had done good business for the club.

For the Norwich game the club introduced a revamped match-day programme. The cover was the same (head portraits of the Second

Division captains around the edge), but inside the team layouts were displayed in columns rather than the old fashioned 2-3-5 formation. There were more pages, new features, a letters page and more photographs. In his programme notes Hill admitted he had always envied the glossy programmes of Chelsea and Arsenal, but he had always believed that the programme had to make a profit for the club. At the recent game at Hull, their chairman had told JH that Hull's new glossy programme made a financial loss but Hill was persuaded to try an experiment. JH expected the new-look programme to make a small loss but hoped that more fans would buy it and thus make it profitable.

Another away draw, at Bristol City, consolidated City's top spot after Wolves, having a dire January, drew 0-0 at Blackburn. George Curtis celebrated his 400th league game by scoring a rare goal, a towering far-post header. Three thousand City travelling fans celebrated as City again came from behind to take a point in a 2-2 draw.

The much-awaited FA Cup-tie with Newcastle was a thriller. Since the draw had been made, the Geordies had picked up points and lifted themselves off the foot of the table. A massive following from the North East began arriving in Coventry on the Friday evening, and the city's pubs enjoyed their busiest weekend for years. Newcastle's Cup reputation had been established in the 1950s, with three Wembley victories between 1951 and 1955, and the mere mention of the competition evoked memories of those golden days.

It was estimated that as many as 8,000 Geordies converged on Highfield Road. They packed the old Covered End terraces where City's vocal choir normally stood, and were sent wild after a sensational start that saw their team score twice in the first three minutes. City were always chasing the game after that, but fought hard, despite losing the influential Gibson after half-time. They even levelled at 2-2, but with wily midfield general Jim Iley pulling the strings, and Wyn Davies giving George Curtis a hard time, and scoring a hat-trick, it was Newcastle's day and they ran out 4-3 winners. One consolation for City was the attendance of 35,748, who paid club record receipts of £9,724.

City fans were generally sanguine about the Cup exit. Their team had put up a proud fight against the famed Cup fighters in a classic match, and although it racked up yet another defeat by First Division opponents, it prompted the corny cliché: 'Now we can concentrate on the League.' But in a season where bread and butter league points were far more important than fleeting moments of Cup glory, the cliché actually rang true. Derek Henderson reminded fans that in the 1964 championship season the team had made an early exit from the Cup to Bristol Rovers.

Few players let themselves down in higher company, but one man, Bobby Gould, had a stinker, missing two easy chances in the second half which might have turned the game City's way. Henderson reported that Gould had been 'roundly booed' by fans half an hour after the game as he walked through one of the bars under the main stand. Jimmy Hill was appalled when he heard and responded in the following week's *Pink*: 'People forget that Gould is in his first full season leading an attack which is expected to win the division. A manager gets accused of having favourites – they're the people I think stand the best chance of winning the match for us … many fans will be surprised to know that Bobby is ten times as severe on himself as the nastiest anti-Gould fan. Wyn Davies was brilliant last week but Bobby has scored more goals than Davies this season.' Nevertheless, Hill dropped Gould to the substitute bench the following Saturday at Bury.

The unbeaten league run continued with four wins in a row. The Bury hoodoo was ended with a late Rees goal, and a week later Gould was back in the starting eleven against Preston, where City trailed North End for almost an hour. Even the most optimistic fans were ready to admit the long unbeaten run was coming to a halt. But City never gave up and finally got their reward against their defensive visitors, the winner coming from Gould four minutes from the end. The Sky Blues now led the league table by two points:

1. Coventry P29 39Pts; 2. Wolves P29 37Pts; 3. Carlisle P30 35Pts; 4. Huddersfield P28 34Pts; 5. Crystal Palace P28 34Pts.

On the Monday following, Derek Henderson wrote: 'First Division status is now within City's grasp. They themselves hold the key to promotion, for the three sides immediately below them – Wolves, Carlisle and Huddersfield – have to come to Highfield Road.' With seven of the remaining thirteen games at home, and several of their rivals also having to play each other in the run in, Henderson predicted a 'grandstand climax' to the season.

Jimmy Hill was keen to reorganise a hectic three-game Easter programme and persuaded Northampton to rearrange the game scheduled for Easter Monday, especially as City had two successive free Saturdays in early March. The trip to the County Ground was changed to Saturday, 11 March, the day of the FA Cup fifth round and a free day for both clubs. Hill was critical of an 'archaic' system that had teams typically playing three games in four days over the Easter holiday.

The trip to Charlton a week later ended in bad blood. The game was littered with 41 fouls and three bookings (a lot in those days). City's approach was undoubtedly uncompromising but Derek Henderson felt this was down to 'their fierce determination not to release the grip they have secured on the Second Division and I certainly would not blame them for that'. Henderson was critical of Bedford referee Peter Bye, whose booking of George Curtis he described as 'unjustified'. Charlton manager Bob Stokoe and the home crowd would have disagreed with Henderson.

The flashpoint came twenty minutes from time, with City leading through a Gould goal. New man Brian Lewis had been booked for a high tackle on home centre-forward Matt Tees and had incensed the crowd. Then Curtis headed away strongly and the momentum of his leap took Tees off the pitch, onto the running track and into the trainers' shelter and the perimeter wall. According to Curtis, the referee ran up to him and said 'Move away, it was a fair challenge'. Stokoe was incensed by the challenge and while the shaken Tees received treatment he angrily shoved Curtis away and remonstrated with the referee, who returned to the pitch and booked Curtis saying, 'I've got to book you for following through – it's only a minor offence.'

Curtis and Lewis were roundly booed every time they touched the ball but City scored again and ran out 2-1 winners. The London papers made a meal of City's 25-foul performance, labelling them 'rough' as well as 'not ready for the First Division'. With City's closest rivals in FA Cup action that day, the only other game in the division saw Blackburn beat Huddersfield 3-0 and leapfrog their opponents into third place, six points behind the Sky Blues.

George Curtis was in the form of his life and determined to lead City to the First Division. He had been a fixture in the side for as long as anyone could remember, and it was hard to realise that he was still only 27 years old. He was the son of a Welsh miner who had left the coalfields of south Wales to move to Kent around the time Curtis jnr was born in 1939. George was a prodigious talent, playing for Snowdown Colliery, a Kent junior side managed by former City star Harry Barratt. Barratt recommended him to Coventry in 1955 and within months George was given his league debut as a sixteen-year-old. It was not until the start of the 1958-59 season that Billy Frith switched him to centre half and kept him there. Over the next nine seasons the 'iron man', as he became known, missed only three league games, a post-war record bettered only by Tranmere's Harold Bell.

In 1967 Curtis was approaching 500 City appearances, but his contribution to the club's rise cannot be measured in statistics alone. That year Hughie Spencer, the club's long-serving team-coach driver, who had probably seen most of Curtis' games over the years, described George's part in the club's progress: 'I often think that, but for George, the club would never have been where it is today.'

Curtis led with his courage and strength, and his example earned the respect of colleagues and opponents alike. Opposing fans booed and baited him, but he was one of those players you wished you had on your team.

When Jimmy Hill arrived at Highfield Road in 1961 Curtis was already the captain of the side and Hill quickly recognised that he had a jewel on his hands. Not only was he a fearsome and courageous centre-half, but he was also a wonderful ambassador for the football club. According to some of his team-mates, Curtis went out of his way to cultivate the captain's role under Hill, acting as the manager's chief lieutenant in the dressing room and as the players' go-between with the manager.

A week after the Charlton victory, against Carlisle, City left their winning goal very late for the third home game running. They trailed almost until half-time. More controversy came when Carlisle's goalkeeper, Alan Ross, was sent off ten minutes into the second half. Ross jumped to claim the ball from a Curtis header, when Bobby Gould challenged him with a shoulder charge. Ross gifted Gould a stunning right-hook which put the Coventry man on the ground. Ross knew he was in trouble and was walking towards the tunnel almost before the referee said a word. Deputy keeper Peter McConnell kept City at bay until the last two minutes, when Ernie Machin scrambled a goal in off a post. It was another vital goal that retained the status quo at the top of the table, despite Wolves, Blackburn and Huddersfield all winning away.

After the game Carlisle boss Alan Ashman became the latest critic of the Sky Blues, accusing them of 'using spoiling tactics rather than skill' and saying 'it is not enough to have skill and courage – it seems you have got to kick as well'. Ashman admitted that the referee had no alternative to send off Ross, but he believed the keeper had acted under 'extreme provocation' from Gould. Jimmy Hill was unrepentant and pointed to the club's excellent disciplinary record – only four bookings all season – and reminded the press that Carlisle had three men facing suspension and had two players sent off in successive games. He described his team as 'pansies compared with Leeds and Liverpool', quickly adding 'not that they are unfair, but I mean in terms of physical strength'.

Hill took his players to Worthing for a four-day break, where the players enjoyed some golf and squash and a five-a-side game on the beach. Winger John Key was nursing ankle ligament damage and was ruled out for a month, and Hill surprised everyone by agreeing to pay Bury £13,000 for another winger, Barry Lowes.

City returned from the coast to play a Friday night friendly against First Division West Ham for the Winston Churchill Remembrance Trophy. At full-time the sides were level at 3-3 and the teams, by prior agreement, staged a penalty shoot-out, the first ever at Highfield Road. Each side took ten penalties and West Ham won 9-7 against City's young reserve keeper Martin Clamp, on as a substitute for Glazier. An excellent crowd of over 18,500 came to see two of West Ham's World Cup heroes, Geoff Hurst and Bobby Moore, the latter receiving the trophy from Mrs J Leese, wife of the editor of the *Coventry Evening Telegraph*. The following day, with City idle, their rivals all won home fixtures, which meant the lead over Wolves was cut to two points, everyone having now played the same number of matches. With eleven games remaining, promotion to Division One was within reach.

Days after playing for West Ham, their goalkeeper, Alan Dickie, joined the Sky Blues as cover for Bill Glazier during the crucial run-in. As the promotion race reached the final stretch, Hill was taking no chances and paid £4,000 for the Hammers' reserve, who had turned down a chance to be Swansea's first-team keeper. City's reserve full-back John Burckitt went on loan to Bradford City the same week – a deal that suited all parties, with John gaining valuable first-team experience and City cutting their wage bill slightly. Over at Molineux, Wolves manager Ronnie Allen was also taking no risks with promotion. That week he paid Leicester £45,000 for Northern Irish centre-forward Derek Dougan. Dougan would pay swift dividends.

The 8,500 Coventry fans who made the short trip to Northampton on 11 March were anticipating another victory on the promotion trail. The Cobblers, relegated from Division One, were propping up the table and looked good bets for yet another drop. But their old foes were not going to roll over. A vicious wind spoiled any football and favoured the more direct Northampton side, who gave City some nervous moments as the ball did some freakish things in their team's penalty area. For just the second time that season, City failed to score, and the game ended 0-0. That extended City's unbeaten run to fifteen games – equalling a club record set in 1937 and emulated in 1962-63. One veteran journalist who had witnessed dozens of such derbies down the years prophesised: 'I fancy it'll be a long time before we see these clubs meet again in a league match.' Derek Henderson reported that new man Barry Lowes had a 'lively' game – 'when he was given the ball' – and was impressed with the ex-Bury man's direct style.

A week later, after another draw against Bolton (1-1), Henderson was less impressed by Lowes, noting that 'his speed ... was never in evidence'.

Lowes, who had replaced Brian Lewis in both games, was promptly dropped and played only one further competitive game for the club. An experienced member of the City team told me that Jimmy Hill and Lowes had a major row after a tour game that summer in the West Indies. Hill accused Lowes of not trying and told the Lancastrian winger he would never play for City again. Before the new season started Hill sold him to Swindon. In his first game for the Robins, Lowes received a crunching tackle from a spiky Brighton full-back by the name of George Dalton and his professional career ended that day. Dalton later became trainer at Highfield Road in the 1980s.

For Bolton's visit, BBC1's *Match of the Day* cameras came to Highfield Road for the first time. The Saturday night programme had been running since August 1964 and in those days showed highlights of only one game. The programme, which had switched from BBC2 following England's World Cup victory, had featured the Sky Blues' 2-0 win at Huddersfield the previous season, so for millions of armchair fans this was a first view of Hill's Sky Blues. The 1-1 draw was not one of City's better performances and they missed a hatful of chances before allowing Bolton to grab an undeserved late equaliser, but City's goal would have won 'goal of the month' if such a thing had existed in those days. Ronnie Rees's jinking run from halfway was reminiscent of great wingers of the past, and the visitors' defence was at sixes and sevens by the time he crossed for Gould to nudge the ball home. The Sky Blues set a new club record for unbeaten games, with Kenneth Wolstenholme, the top commentator of the day, providing commentary from a temporary gantry high in the Sky Blue Stand. It was a point dropped, however, and the four clubs immediately below them all won away to close up on City.

Easter was a crucial period at the top of Division Two. Coventry and Wolves took advantage of slips from all their rivals to consolidate their position at the top. On Easter Saturday, City won 1-0 at Ewood Park, home of third-placed Blackburn, and followed up on Tuesday evening with a 2-0 home win over Northampton. For the second year running Huddersfield were imploding – they lost all three Easter games, including a home reverse to the threatened Cobblers. Crystal Palace, previously still in with an outside chance, lost two home games in three days, and Carlisle slipped up at lowly Charlton. Wolves, like the Sky Blues, were now in the groove, and a Dougan hat-trick on Easter Saturday helped slam Hull 4-0, and they followed up with a double over Huddersfield.

At Blackburn, Lewis replaced Lowes in an otherwise unchanged side in a tough battle that saw Blackburn's winger Mike Ferguson ordered off for punching Dietmar Bruck. Despite a brave performance from ten-man

Rovers, Gould snatched the only goal to clinch a significant victory and send the 4,000 travelling Sky Blue Army into ecstasy. Three days later the poor old Cobblers gave City another tough game. A huge crowd roared the team to a 2-0 win, with goals from Ernie Machin and, inevitably, Gould, with his seventh in seven games. The attendance of 38,566 was the biggest at Highfield Road since 1949 and the fourth highest league figure in the club's history. But Wolves' win over Huddersfield had pushed City down to second place on goal-average. Following the hectic Easter programme the top of the table was:

1. Wolves P35 49Pts; 2. Coventry P35 49Pts; 3. Blackburn P35 43Pts; 4. Ipswich P35 41Pts; 5. Carlisle P35 41Pts; 6. Millwall P35 41Pts; 7. Huddersfield P35 40Pts.

Long-serving fan Rod Dean sums up City's form: 'the hard work was done in February and March, culminating in the hard-won victory at Blackburn, who had thwarted us in 1938-39. Although there were still eight or nine games remaining, the City and Wolves were hot favourites for promotion and as each game was completed that became a certainty.'

Derek Henderson, too, was now convinced City and Wolves were uncatchable and the only unanswered question was which of them would win the title. The two teams were scheduled to meet at Highfield Road a month hence, and although both had four games beforehand, that fixture was shaping up to be massive, possibly deciding the destination of the championship. Henderson pointed out that the task of Blackburn in third place in overhauling City or Wolves was of such a magnitude that if City averaged only a point a game from their final seven matches, Rovers would need to win every game to catch them.

Two more off-field innovations were introduced that month. First, City started selling club merchandise via mail order – they were believed to be the first English club to use this medium for selling to fans. Then they launched Sky Blue Rose – a telephone answering service, keeping the fans up to date with club information. It was planned to be installed by the following season and would consist of 'a taped message lasting between 15 and 20 seconds giving the outstanding news of the day'. The messages would be recorded by Rose McNulty, the club's receptionist, thus the title Sky Blue Rose. It was Jimmy Hill's idea, after he had taken many calls over Easter from fans seeking information. He explained that the service would offer fans information on 'team news, the Sky Blue special train, news of visiting teams and suchlike'. This was yet another far-thinking idea from Hill which predated the modern information age.

At the next home game, a scrambled 2-2 draw with mid-table Derby, obscene chanting was heard for the first time at Highfield Road. Referee

Roy Harper was the target of chants questioning his parentage after some decisions that did not go City's way. A Radio Sky Blue announcement asked the miscreants to desist, adding that the club would 'be happy to refund their entrance money if they would leave the ground'. Organised chanting had become a familiar part of the football scene, but at that time it rarely lapsed into the obscene. On the pitch, the fortunate draw, thanks to another late Machin goal, extended City's unbeaten run to nineteen games, and with Wolves and Blackburn also drawing it was no change at the top, with one less game to play.

A week later, close to 9,000 City fans descended on south London for City's vital game at Crystal Palace. The Sky Blue Special was extended to twelve coaches and all 730 seats were sold within eight hours of going on sale. Red House Motors, the leading coach operator in the city, was ready with 40-plus coaches heading for the capital. Like several other fixtures that day, the kick-off was switched to the evening to avoid the Grand National at Aintree, which might have lowered the attendance – it marked the first ever Saturday evening fixture for City.

The Sky Blues' enormous following boosted the Palace crowd to over 23,000 and created a cup-tie like atmosphere. Playing in unfamiliar orange shirts with sky-blue shorts, City fell behind but rallied with a gutsy and skilful performance to grab another point and keep the run going. Wolves beat Rotherham 2-0 that evening and were now one point ahead of City, with Blackburn, winners over Hull, five points adrift.

The nerve-ends were starting to show amongst City players and it was a stuttering and laboured 1-0 victory over Huddersfield that the BBC filmed for *Match of the Day* the following week. At Palace, Jimmy Hill had rested Ron Farmer and recalled Barry Lowes, but now he preferred fit-again John Key to Lowes, with Brian Lewis continuing in the defensive midfield role where he had been so effective at Palace, marking the dangerous Johnny Byrne out of the game. Gould again scored the vital goal – a typical opportunist effort from close range and his 25th of the season – that finally broke the Huddersfield defensive barrier. Wolves won 2-1 at Preston, but Blackburn's 0-4 defeat at Plymouth meant City were seven points clear of the chasing pack with only four games remaining. Promotion looked virtually certain, and a win at Cardiff seven days later would confirm it.

Preparations were well advanced for arguably the biggest game in the club's history, the visit of Wolves on 29th April. The club resisted calls to make the game all-ticket for fear that that if the weather was bad, many spectators – knowing their entry was assured – would leave it late and cause crowd congestion. Instead, City planned to have crowd packers in operation, to ensure that all areas of the terraces were put to optimum use. Supporters of both clubs were urged to arrive early to watch the pre-match entertainment, which would include a motorcycling display by the Royal Corps of Signals. Club secretary Alan Leather appealed to supporters to 'make a special effort just this once to arrive early. If everyone co operates, the record [attendance] could go by the board'. The record gate was 44,930 set in 1938 for the Second Division visit of Aston Villa, although many believed the 'unofficial' gate for the Sunderland game in 1963 had topped this.

A 1-1 draw at Cardiff's Ninian Park meant that City still needed an elusive point to clinch promotion because of Blackburn's 3-0 home win over Northampton. For Blackburn to overhaul the Sky Blues they would need to win their final three games and City would have to lose their last three – not to mention Rovers' vastly inferior goal-average. Chairman Derrick Robins produced champagne from nowhere and there were 'celebrations' in the Cardiff dressing room, but the unbeaten run wobbled that afternoon. At 1-1, with eighteen minutes left, Cardiff's eighteen-year-old centre-forward John Toshack, missed a penalty, shooting a yard wide in front of the vast City contingent, who did their best to put him off.

In addition to conjuring champagne out of thin air, Robins was also booking tickets for the players' trip to the West Indies, promised by the chairman months earlier as reward for promotion. The players had been dubious about jumping the gun and swigging champagne at Cardiff, but the optimistic Robins told Derek Henderson: 'We are not up – but we do not accept that we can be caught.' His optimism was proved right the following Tuesday evening when Blackburn drew 0-0 with Bolton. Within minutes of the result becoming known a party was in full swing at the chairman's house in Leamington, and all over Coventry fans were out celebrating in the pubs. At the Town Hall Tavern in the city centre champagne was being drunk from half-pint glasses and renditions of the Sky Blue Song echoed through the streets.

Derrick Robins paid tribute to Jimmy Hill and the players: 'It is a wonderful, and a very just reward for the hard work put in by the directors, by Jimmy, and above all else, by the players. There is no doubt there has never been a more dedicated, more disciplined team in the history of the club.' Hill arrived for work the next morning and walked into a Highfield Road besieged by calls, telegrams and messages of congratulation from all quarters. He had much to say, as usual, but made sure everyone knew that the job was not complete: 'We're out to beat the Wolves on Saturday – we would like the title to round it off.' With typical Hill hyperbole he described the game as the 'Midlands Match of the Century'. With both clubs assured of promotion, this game would probably decide which club the title would go to. Two matches would remain to play afterwards.

City's unbeaten run now stretched back 22 games, whilst Wolves had gone fourteen of their own without defeat. As far as the title was concerned, Wolves were in the driving seat, however, with a two-point advantage and slightly better goal-average. Ronnie Allen's team was a mixture of youth and nous, with several players having First Division experience, among them centre-forward Derek Dougan ('the Doog'), speedy wingers Terry Wharton and David Wagstaffe, as well as England internationals Mike Bailey and Bobby Thomson. Injuries to defenders Gerry Taylor and Leamington-born David Woodfield meant that Allen had to switch his captain and driving force Bailey to right-back and bring in the precocious youngster Peter Knowles in midfield.

City, too, had to make a rare change with John Tudor recalled for the injured Bobby Gould. Gould, who had scored in six successive games before Cardiff, had broken the scaphoid bone in his wrist at Cardiff and was put in plaster for six weeks. The plaster meant that could not play any part in the final three games. The club succeeded in keeping the seriousness of the injury from the press, even suggesting he could play with an injured thumb strapped up. In his own words Bobby, who watched from the stand, was 'gutted' not to be playing but at the same time delighted with the outcome.

On a bright spring day thousands of spectators were turned away as the Highfield Road turnstiles were closed fifteen minutes before the kick-off on advice from the police. Hundreds gained admittance illegally by climbing over walls or crawling under gates, and the club felt that around 53,000 actually saw the game. The terraces at both ends were overflowing and many complained of being unable to see the action. Many youngsters were plucked from the seething mass and allowed to sit on the grass and the running track. By the time the teams emerged the youngsters were four or five deep around most of the perimeter, many just a yard from the touchlines. Dozens of fans perched perilously on the base of the floodlight pylons 'like decorations on a Christmas tree', and at one stage more than 50 spectators were perched on the roof of the covered end. Despite loudspeaker warnings that the roof of the tea-bars were unsafe, dozens clambered onto them, and when the roof did indeed collapse on one of the bars at the covered end, four people fell through. Fortunately no one was seriously injured.

It was the greatest day in Highfield Road's long history. And City did not let their fans down, putting on one of their finest displays. A Peter

14. 1966-67 (Part 2) We are the Champions

Knowles goal after 41 minutes gave Wolves a half-time lead, but City came out to blitz the Wolves defence and produce arguably their most irresistible 45 minutes of the season.

After an opening flurry from the much-vaunted Derek Dougan, George Curtis mastered the Irishman and paved the way to victory. After half time, kicking towards the Kop end, Ernie Machin equalised Wolves' goal, and four minutes later Ian Gibson put the Sky Blues ahead. Wildly excited youngsters spilled onto the pitch after both goals. At the second incursion, referee Norman Callender strode to the edge of the pitch and seconds later came a tannoy announcement: 'any further pitch invasions and the referee will abandon the game.'

Despite falling behind, Wolves were not finished and Knowles hit a post as they pushed forward in search of an equaliser, but with five minutes remaining City broke away for Rees to score a third goal. The fans on the perimeter seemed to pause momentarily, but thankfully none encroached. At the final whistle the youngsters raced onto the pitch to acclaim their heroes. The crowd massed around the tunnel, under the directors' box, and the players soon emerged to receive the fans' plaudits. In an emotional scene, a suited Bobby Gould was lifted onto players' shoulders to a large roar. Gould had answered his critics in the best possible way – by scoring goals, the goals that had earned the Sky Blues promotion. Jimmy Hill led the fans in a chorus of the Sky Blue Song, conducting the singing as though he was at the Last Night of the Proms. Derek Henderson in his match report wrote: 'Those who were there will never forget it. Nor perhaps will they ever be able to convince those who were not of the unforgettable drama and electricity of the greatest day in Highfield Road's history.'

The attendance was a ground record 51,455, later adjusted for league records to 51,452. Receipts topped £12,000, a record, with over £10,000 taken on the day and over 20,000 programmes were sold. Some fans were unhappy that their view was obscured on the packed terraces – and a few even claimed to have exited the ground before the kick-off. There were heartbreaking stories too – two boys who got in at 1pm eventually jumped over the perimeter wall because they were scared by the congestion on the terraces, and then being told by police – they claimed – that they had to return to the terrace or leave the ground. They left without seeing the game. On a happier note, the police reported that only four fans were ejected from the ground, amazing when one considers the size of the crowd and the lack of segregation employed.

Jimmy Hill's father, Bill, was so excited after the game he was taken ill with high blood pressure and had to spend four days in bed recovering.

The following Saturday, in the season's penultimate games, the Sky Blues drew 1-1 at Ipswich, to extend the unbeaten run to 24 games, while Wolves beat Norwich 4-1 at home. Those results put Wolves a point ahead of the Sky Blues with a better goal-average going into the final games. Demand from City fans to go to Portman Road was so great that the club put on two Sky Blue Special trains after the first train sold out in two hours. Both trains had the traditional Radio Sky Blue piped through the carriages and bingo sessions, as well as a bar and catering facilities.

Highfield Road staged a big event before the final league game, for Liverpool provided the opposition for the second Curtis/Kearns testimonial. Bill Shankly's Liverpool were at virtually full strength, but were beaten 2-1 by a City side keen to show their critics that they were worth their place in the top division. Before the kick-off Robins and Hill thrilled the crowd by making a bizarre lap of honour; Robins driving the kitted Curtis and Kearns in his Rolls Royce convertible, and Hill in full hunting gear atop a horse. The crowd, still euphoric after the Wolves game, could not get enough of it and visiting Liverpool fans could not believe their eyes.

Ronnie Rees scored the goal of the night, capping a 50-yard run with a rocket shot from just outside the penalty box that left Lawrence in the Liverpool goal grasping at thin air. A crowd of over 25,000 raised £6,000 for George and Mick's testimonial fund. Bill Shankly, in typical acerbic style, declined to make an assessment of the Sky Blues: 'I never discuss performances in friendlies.' Never one for over-statement, he added: 'I was impressed with the whole atmosphere here'. One player not impressed that night was Scottish international forward Ian St John, later to be City's assistant manager briefly under Noel Cantwell. He later recalled: 'Within minutes of the kick-off George Curtis performed a crunching tackle on me. I woke up being carried off on a stretcher. When I "tackled" George about it later he said: "It's a man's game, Saint." And that for a man we were down trying to make a few bob for.'

Four days later it was back to business and the final day of a momentous season. Wolves travelled to Crystal Palace, needing a point for the title, whilst City entertained Millwall, who after a bright spring had lost their way. On Saturday morning Jimmy Hill was quoted as saying: 'The odds must be on Wolves to get a point,' whilst Derek Henderson stuck by his earlier prediction that Wolves would land the top prize. Both were left to eat their words at the end of another afternoon of roller-coaster emotions. The Sky Blues won 3-1 and Wolves crashed 1-4.

Not for the first or last time the later kick-off at Highfield Road added to the drama of the day. Even before the teams trotted out at Highfield

Road for the 3.15 start, Sky Blue Radio had told the crowd that Wolves were already trailing 0-1. George Curtis led the team out to a deafening chant of 'Champions, champions ...' By half-time the team had done their stuff, leading inferior Millwall 2-0 with goals from John Key and John Tudor. And as the second half wore on and Wolves' embarrassment intensified, the mood of the City crowd turned from nervous nail-biting to euphoric celebration. With fifteen minutes left, a steward raced out of the players' tunnel to the edge of the pitch and raised four fingers to the sky. A minute later, the loudspeaker announced that Wolves had crashed 1-4. The Sky Blues, 3-1 ahead and toying with Millwall, were Second Division champions.

Rod Dean remembers: 'there was nothing at stake really, but we thought it would be nice to win the title – although this looked unlikely. The unsung John Key had his greatest ever match; he overwhelmed Millwall's Harry Cripps and scored a well-taken goal.'

At the final whistle the crowd invaded the pitch again, congregating behind a police cordon by the tunnel, shouting for their heroes, who duly emerged in their tracksuit-tops in the directors' box. In a moment to savour Hill, for the second time in two weeks, led the crowd, and the players, in the most emotional rendition of the Sky Blue song. One of the most vociferous singers was Bobby Gould, again dressed in a lounge suit and crisp white shirt. City's top scorer had been forced to sit out the last three games because of his wrist injury. Gould was one of three key players – Brian Hill and Ron Farmer the others – who missed the run-in. Hill was still recuperating from injury, while Farmer was substitute, having lost his place to Brian Lewis.

Derek Henderson summed things up: 'We thought we had seen it all a fortnight before at the Wolves' game. But here were the Sky Blues with that extraordinary flair for the dramatic – landing the Second Division championship at the last hurdle amid scenes of emotional hysteria. Who else but Coventry City could eke out of an already great season, an added final triumph?'

As the crowd slowly dispersed, with the realisation that the Sky Blues would be playing First Division football for the first time in their history, the demolition men had other things on their mind – to pull down the old covered end in preparation for a new west stand. Throughout the weekend the demolition team worked, with the aid of floodlights, and by Monday morning the whole site was flattened.

The decision to proceed with the new stand, estimated to cost £80,000, had been taken by the board in the previous February. Now the race was on to have it ready for the opening First Division home game in

August. The new stand would have a cantilever design, with 3,200 seats, and be built by Banbury Grandstands, a subsidiary of Derrick Robins' Banbury Buildings. The extra seats would raise the total seating capacity of the ground to 10,500, one of the largest in the Football League. The old terracing underneath would remain largely unaffected. With extra season-ticket revenue being generated, the financial plan was for the stand to recoup its cost within three years.

Over 32,000 saw the Millwall game, taking the season's total to over 593,000 – an average of 28,269 and breaking the club record average set in 1950-51. City's gates were the highest in the Second Division and the fourteenth highest in the country.

The reserves, who had fared reasonably in the Football Combination, averaged 5,428 for their home games, believed to be the highest in the country.

City's first team fulfilled an obligation to play a testimonial game at Nuneaton Borough's Manor Park on the Monday evening. Despite miserable weather, over 7,000 turned out to see the Second Division champions take on the Southern League runners-up. John Tudor was deadly, scoring four goals in seven minutes, including a hat-trick timed at four minutes (easily the fastest in the club's history). City won 7-3.

The following evening the club were the guests of honour at a civic reception at the Hotel Leofric in the city centre. The championship trophy was hastily despatched from Maine Road, Manchester, along with the newly struck medals, and the presentations made by Football League president Len Shipman. Hill was named the Westclox 'manager of tomorrow' and received a cheque for £500 to add to the £10,000 bonus paid by the club for reaching the First Division, an incentive written into his very first Coventry contract, according to his autobiography.

Derrick Robins kept his earlier pledge, and at the end of May the first-team players and the management and coaching staff flew off to the West Indies for a three-week break. It wasn't all pleasure though – the team had to play six friendlies, which took in Trinidad, Barbados and Bermuda.

Back at Highfield Road, it was another hectic close season. In addition to the West Stand rearing skywards at breakneck speed, there was work going on in the Main Stand to enlarge the pressbox and the directors' box. The pitch, which had been pretty bare down the centre for the last two months, was re-seeded.

The club announced price increases for the new season, with terrace prices increasing by 6d (2½p). Standing on the Spion Kop would now cost 5 shillings (25p) and all other terraces 6 shillings (30p). The club were expecting to sell the vast majority of the 10,500 seats as season-tickets, although a number had to be retained for visiting supporters. Prices for season tickets were increased and ranged from £5 for a Kop ticket to £15 for a central seat in the Main Stand. The new West Stand seats were all priced at £10.

City's new price structure was similar to Chelsea's and slightly cheaper than at Tottenham, who still priced in guineas. Jimmy Hill told Derek Henderson that the club had tried to fix a price range for the man who wanted to bring along his family: 'We are very conscious that with a family, it entails a lot of money. But when one considers the difference, it really isn't a lot of extra money for a season of First Division football.' Within less than a fortnight the club announced they had sold their entire reserved seating accommodation of 9,800, and taken over £100,000 as a result. The new West Stand had sold out completely and wasn't even built!

Even before City flew off to the West Indies, rumours were circulating that Jimmy Hill would quit soccer to work in television, specifically to replace David Coleman, who was leaving BBC's *Grandstand* programme. When asked about the rumours by Derek Henderson, Hill replied: 'As far as I am concerned, there is no substance to this, simply because I have not been approached.' In the modern game, responses like that can rarely be believed, but back in 1967 Hill's words would have put the fans' minds at rest and quashed any rumours. However, as the summer progressed there was, as the saying goes, 'no smoke without fire.'

With wives and girlfriends left behind at home, the trip to the West Indies was a heady mixture of pleasure and work. The team played five games in eighteen days, winning them all and winning lots of friends along the way with their friendly, down to earth approach to the locals. The only black spot on the tour came when Ronnie Rees was sent off in the fourth match, in Barbados, for what the referee later described as 'violent conduct'.

The players flew back into Heathrow at the end of June to spend a couple of weeks with their families, and in Bobby Gould's case, get married, before pre-season training started in preparation for the greatest season in the club's history in the First Division. Little did they realise that a major shock awaited them before the season started.

Chapter 15. 1967-68

The Top Division: JH Decides to Go

Throughout the summer of 1967, the so-called Summer of Love, with hippies wearing flowers in their hair and psychedelic music everywhere, Coventry City fans were relishing the thought of their team playing for the first time at the highest level of English football. Highfield Road was once again a hive of activity as the new West Stand grew out of the ruins of the old Covered end.

Ground developments continued apace during June and July, and on 8 July Derek Henderson reported that work on the West Stand was a week ahead of schedule. He described the new stand thus: 'it rises, with its stark white concrete, over the terraces.' He described a list of other developments, including a new ground-level bar on the corner of the main stand closest to the west end of the stadium, an extension to the vice-presidents' club, a new 50-seat pressbox to handle the demands of the much bigger coverage the club could expect, and an entrance block to the West Stand from Nicholls Street. With the ticket office working at full stretch to meet the massive demand, the whole ground was buzzing that summer.

Season-ticket sales were phenomenal and excitement in the city was at fever pitch. Many fans expected incoming transfers in preparation for the new season and Rod Dean remembers: 'as the close season progressed we were all somewhat surprised that the expected big signings did not materialise. The club had plenty of money, a wealthy chairman and a squad full of players who had been with the club since the Third and Fourth Division.'

Behind the scenes Jimmy Hill was negotiating a new contract. He had been given a five-year contract in 1964 after winning promotion to Division Two, and now both parties wished to extend that.

According to his autobiography Hill never considered another job and was happy at Coventry: 'I feel I belonged at Coventry City much more than I did at Fulham.' He 'saw no reason why I should not continue managing them for many years to come'. He knew, however, that behind the promotion hysteria there was realism to be faced. Several of the team weren't good enough for Division One. The club's financial resources meant it could not buy success (in those days no club could), so the current squad of players would need to be given time to adjust. Over the past five and half years, Hill had seen glimpses of the fickleness of

Coventry's fans, for example when Bly and Hudson were sold, and again in the autumn of 1966. Then, promotion looked a pipedream. Adulation for Hill had turned to criticism of his methods and occasional bilious outbursts. He knew it would be a rough ride in Division One, but he had no long-term fears about turning Coventry into a team capable of challenging for honours. Hill wanted time and was prepared to give it, but he foresaw a situation where the club's progress stalled, with him made the scapegoat and losing his job.

The board offered Hill £7,500 a year with a five-year contract. The money was not that important to him – he had earned less than £35,000 in his whole time at Coventry – but he demanded the insurance of a ten-year contract. Derrick Robins and the board balked at that – they had heard of the problems at Chelsea and Hull after agreeing ten-year deals with managers Ted Drake and Cliff Britton respectively. Both clubs had acquiesced at times of heady success, but within eighteen months had sacked the managers and been obliged to honour the contract. Hill listened to this argument and was disappointed; he felt his relationship with his club was far deeper than was the case with Drake or Britton.

Surprisingly, the board did not seek to compromise. In his book, Hill says he expected Robins to say 'let's split the difference and make it seven and a half years', but he didn't and Hill wouldn't budge either. The discussions dragged on, with the club's directors urging Hill to change his mind.

The bombshell exploded on the morning of Thursday, 17 August, two days before the season started. No mention was made of any contract discussions. The club's official statement read: 'In the summer Mr Jimmy Hill ... told the club he wished to retire from football management. The directors have made every possible effort in recent weeks to persuade him to change his mind and regret that they have not succeeded. The board appreciated the reason for Mr Hill's decision and, recognising his tremendous work for the club in the past six years, believes it would be wrong further to prolong its persuasion. Mr Hill will retain full responsibility as the club's general manager until the board are able to obtain a new manager of suitable calibre, but he will not stay with the club after the end of the present season. Mr Hill states categorically that he would not dream of joining any club other than Coventry, where he has obtained the complete support of players, staff, directors and fans.'

Derrick Robins was holidaying in Venice when the news broke. He was quoted: 'It is bad, but not disastrous.' He flew back to England to be at Burnley for the opening game and paid glowing tribute to Hill, acknowledged the enormity of what he had achieved, and, at the same time, looked forward: 'This is not the end – we have put our foot on the first rung of the ladder, and are determined to climb to the top. Success in Division One and in Europe, too, are high on the Sky Blue agenda.'

The shock in the city was cataclysmic. Work at the city's factories ground to a halt as the news was debated from every angle. The fans had no inkling and were planning their route and booking their train and coach trips to Burnley for the club's first ever game in Division One. The players were stunned when they were informed at 11.00 on the Thursday morning. Jack Patience, the secretary of the City supporters' club said: 'I have won my bet – I said this would happen. He has done a great job, of course, and whoever takes over from him will have one hell of a reputation to live up to. He's ambitious and I certainly don't blame him, but it will shatter a lot of City fans.'

Many fans criticised the timing of the announcement, and it wasn't until Hill's autobiography was published 30 years later that it was revealed that, throughout the close season, he was hoping to stay. He wrote: 'The last thing I wanted for the club was to bring an end to the progress we had made.'

Outside his home in Canon Hill Road there were children waving rattles and chanting 'We want Jimmy', before a police car arrived to disperse them.

The resignation was national news and the media circus descended on Highfield Road with press conferences and television cameras. The general view was that he had been offered a lucrative job in television or journalism, because he already wrote a weekly column in the *News of the World* and had impressed when called upon to do television work. A gentleman who lived just outside the ground in King Richard Street was sought out by the *Daily Express* to pronounce that it was the biggest shock of his life.

Rod Dean remembers where he was when the news broke: 'In those days any fan could turn up at Ryton on training days and hang around, fraternise with the players and staff. So it was on that sunny morning in August 1967 when I drove up to Ryton and hung around behind one of the goals. Out of the blue Bobby Gould trotted over and openly said to us that 'the boss is leaving' – that was it, the end of the game before it had even started!'

The early names bandied about as a replacement included three top First Division bosses: Don Revie (Leeds), Tommy Docherty (Chelsea) and Ron Greenwood (West Ham), plus Celtic's Jock Stein.

The phenomenal success of the Sky Blue Pool continued that summer. The club announced that membership was up to 125,000, halfway to the target after less than a year's operation. In one week in June over

1,000 new members signed up. A large percentage of them were from outside the city – the agents were scouring Warwickshire with the attraction of top weekly prizes of over £1,700. Some City fans, however, were unhappy with the decision to house all the ground season-ticket holders in an enclosure in front of the Main Stand. Around 2,000 supporters had applied for the £6 season tickets, but many of them wanted a choice of where they stood. The club's reasoning was that concentrating them in a dedicated enclosure would ensure they never got locked out of a big game. The club changed its mind following a meeting at the ground in early July, and instigated £5 season tickets for the Spion Kop with £6 gaining entrance to the rest of the terracing.

The fans were desperate to see the fixture list, but in those days the League did not publish it until mid-July, and it revealed a tough start, with away games at Burnley (champions as recently as 1960) and Nottingham Forest (current runners-up). Sheffield United would be the first visitors to the revamped Highfield Road on 26 August.

The players were back in training on 24 July. Despite vague rumours that City were interested in Swindon's exciting young winger Don Rogers, there were no new signings. The professional playing staff numbered 29, which included four youngsters given their first professional contracts: Jeff Blockley, Willie Carr, Don Peachey and Trevor Gould. John Burckitt had returned from a loan period with Bradford City. One departure was Barry Lowes, who left the club for Swindon for a fee similar to that paid for him the previous February.

Derrick Robins' 25-year-old son Peter joined the board of directors that summer, raising the number of directors to six. Peter was also on the board of his father's company, Banbury Buildings, and Derrick felt it was important for Peter to learn the ropes for a few years in anticipation that he would one day succeed his father as chairman.

For the opening game at Turf Moor the club announced a new Sky Blue Travellers' Club. Limited to 500 members, paying 5 shillings for the season, it guaranteed a seat on the Sky Blue Special for every away game. The club foresaw big demand for away trips in the First Division and had responded to ideas from fans worried about a scramble to obtain tickets. The 500 members virtually guaranteed to fill at least one train, and the club expected sufficient demand to run two trains to most away games. The new club would offer the added benefits of reserved seats and pre-ordered meals and drinks.

Three pre-season friendlies, or trials, as they were known, took place. The Southern League provided the opposition for two of the games with a 2-2 draw at Hereford and a 4-0 win at Cambridge City sandwiching a fixture at Second Division Bristol City. A rejuvenated Bristol side gave City a hard game and won 2-0. Ian Gibson had taken a knock and was unable to play, so Hill gave seventeen-year-old Willie Carr a place in the forward line and the flame-haired Scot gave a good account of himself. Four days later at Cambridge, Carr again deputised but Derek Henderson did not feel he was ready for the First Division the following Saturday if Gibbo was unfit: 'It would be rather like throwing a learner swimmer into the deep end.'

The centre-forward place was also up for grabs. Bobby Gould, recovered from his wrist problem, had not set the world alight in the pre-season games. At Cambridge he was substituted at half-time, John Tudor coming on. Tudor looked far sharper than Gould and scored an excellent headed goal to cement his place in the side at Turf Moor.

Many of the 7,000 fans who travelled to Burnley to see the Sky Blues surrender their 25-match unbeaten run in a 1-2 defeat were still dazed by Hill's bombshell two days earlier. City's run stood just five short of the then Football League record of 30 undefeated games, set by Burnley themselves in 1921. Hill resisted the temptation of throwing in Carr for his debut, so Farmer played in Gibson's place. City's first goal in the top division was a late own-goal by Dave Merrington, scant reward for a good City performance against one of the division's best home sides.

Three days later even more fans travelled to Nottingham. Reserve keeper Alan Dickie played instead of the injured Glazier. After four minutes captain George Curtis was stretchered off with a broken leg following a challenge with Frank Wignall. City's reshuffled side, with Tudor moving back to centre-half and Bobby Gould on as substitute, took the game to Forest. Gould twice put City ahead, only for Forest to equalise, and it needed an Ian Storey-Moore penalty to rescue a point for Forest after Ernie Machin had scored a third City goal. Derek Henderson went into hyperbolic overdrive in his match report: 'I have seen many performances from Coventry City to make the blood tingle in the 9½ years I have covered their games. But never have I seen them rise to the challenge of the hour and defy all the odds as they did at Nottingham last night.' Hill described it as: 'the finest team performance in 5½ years.'

It was soon clear that Curtis' leg break was serious. He was expected to be out for the whole season. Derek Henderson thought the injury a bigger blow than Hill's resignation: 'Luck has finally caught up with the phenomenal man, who only three times since September 1958 had not turned out for Coventry City in League matches.' Hill needed a replacement and quickly, but soon found good 'stoppers' were at a premium. After 48 hours of frantic activity he paid Southampton £25,000 for Tony

Knapp, who had recently lost his place to Jimmy Gabriel. Knapp went straight into the side for City's first home game against the big boys. The visit of Sheffield United also inaugurated the new West Stand. Little did the 33,000 crowd realise that over the next nine months the Sky Blues and the Blades would be bitter rivals at the foot of the table, with the Blades' ultimate relegation ensuring that City stayed up. Twice the Blades led and twice the Sky Blues bounced back. John Key scored the club's first home goal in the top league, a powerful header at the Spion Kop end. Dietmar Bruck saved a point for City after a Glazier howler had let United go in front.

Three days later Forest arrived at Highfield Road and demonstrated the size of the mountain City faced. Forest won 3-1 against a side already handicapped by injuries to key men. Gibson, despite playing two reserve games, had an ankle injury that required a visit to a specialist, and Key, Brian Hill and Farmer were also injured. Knapp pulled a muscle on his debut and Mick Coop had to play at centre-half in the Forest home game. It didn't help that the normally consistent Glazier, recovered from his ankle knock, had a couple of stinkers.

The first win did not arrive until the sixth game, when old rivals Southampton were beaten 2-1 in a contest that marked the full debut of Willie Carr. Four days later a vibrant, Colin Bell-inspired Manchester City thrashed City 3-0 at Highfield Road, showing why they would be contenders for the League title come May 1968.

Following another home defeat to Arsenal in the League Cup, critics suggested Jimmy Hill should quit Highfield Road immediately, arguing that his presence was not helping the team. There was little or no news about the appointment of his successor, but Hill broke the silence: 'The very reason there has not been an appointment is obvious – the board are determined to get the very best.' Replying to suggestions that he should leave immediately, he added: I would be doing the club a disservice if I did that. It would put pressure on the board to make an appointment of any sort rather than the right one.' He also praised the team, saying that he was not embarrassed by their performances but he was hurt that so many people quickly show so little faith in an organisation that has performed miracles at the club.

Ian Gibson finally made his First Division debut at Newcastle. He inspired City to a two-goal lead, only to pull a muscle trying to avoid a scything tackle. Without 'Gibbo', City lost their inspiration and sank 2-3 to leave them next to bottom. Bobby Gould scored again, his fourth of the season, and Hill divulged that he had received two offers for the Coventry-born striker already. Gould's goal at Highbury in the 1-1 league draw had boosted his reputation in north London and before the season was over he would join the Gunners.

Having known almost nothing except five years of winning, City fans were grumbling. Although crowds were up – the first four games averaged over 35,000 – there was a mounting undercurrent of discontent among supporters.

The luck turned briefly at the end of September with a 4-2 home win over WBA, a side City would have the Indian sign over in these early years in Division One. Hill made more changes, giving a full debut to young Irish midfielder Pat Morrissey and welcoming back the evergreen Brian Hill. His pleasure at victory was tempered, however, by another injury to a key player. This time it was Bobby Gould, who suffered a ruptured knee ligament that would sideline him for up to three months. Despite not wishing to sign players likely to be quickly discarded by his successor, Hill was now desperate to reinforce his injury-ravaged side. In the space of nine games in Division One he had lost arguably his three most important players – Curtis, Gibson and now Gould.

The search for Hill's replacement threw up any number of top names. Every top boss in the land was linked with the job, including England manager Alf Ramsey, Celtic boss Jock Stein, fresh from his European triumph with Celtic, Don Revie of Leeds, Chelsea's Tommy Docherty and even ex-Tottenham star Danny Blanchflower, who had never expressed any interest in management. Revie later admitted that he had turned City down.

On 23 September Derek Henderson revealed that 'a man from Manchester' could be the favourite. Henderson wrote that the City board had two young coaches under their spotlight, Manchester City's 40-year-old assistant manager Malcolm Allison, and Manchester United's 35-year-old player Noel Cantwell. Cantwell had turned down a generous offer to become assistant at Aston Villa, and was known to be keen on hanging up his boots to enter management. Henderson assured his readers that if Allison was offered the job he would take it, and he felt an announcement 'will not be long coming'. Whether Henderson had the complete inside track is not known, but he added prophetically: 'when it does, I feel sure it will be a youngish man whose playing days are not that far behind him.' Allison had retired from playing after losing a lung ten years earlier, so Henderson seemed to be pointing to Cantwell.

Meanwhile, Hill's assistant, Alan Dicks, had been offered and accepted the vacant job as Bristol City's manager. Any ambitions of being put in charge of Coventry had been thwarted by the board's insistence on a 'name' manager, and the Bristol opening was perfectly timed for Dicks.

The clubs agreed, however, that, with an appointment imminent at Highfield Road, Dicks would stay at Coventry until things were sealed. Another departure from the Sky Blue family was Ron Farmer, who joined Notts County on 7 October. Farmer had lost his first-team place and was compensated for missing out on a large testimonial at Highfield Road by City waiving a transfer fee. County recompensed Farmer accordingly.

Suddenly, on 8 October, the day after City's 0-4 thrashing at Sheffield Wednesday, a Sunday newspaper revealed that Derby's young boss Brian Clough had turned down an offer to take over at City. According to several people close to Coventry, Clough had 'dillied and dallied' too long, having been made what was described as an 'unbelievable offer'. Clough preferred instead to sign a new three-year contract with Derby. At this time Clough, and his omnipresent assistant Peter Taylor, had been in charge at Derby less than five months, but his reputation within the game was such that he was in huge demand.

Twenty-four hours later Malcolm Allison, Manchester City's young coach, announced to the *Manchester Evening News* that he had been offered and had verbally accepted the Coventry post. Allison's boss, Joe Mercer, confirmed that City had been given permission to talk to Allison, and the long soap opera appeared to be over. But there was a twist in the tail. The same evening Derrick Robins, addressing the press on the subject for the first time in two months, denied that Allison had got the job: 'I saw him and we had a discussion. It was the same sort of discussion I have had with others. He said he would contact us again on Thursday. I stressed [to him] that it must be treated with secrecy. The next thing is that it is blazoned across the newspapers. This is not the way we work.'

Earlier, director John Camkin had told the media that Allison was on a shortlist and the board would be making a final decision on Thursday (12 October). Allison meanwhile claimed that he had the terms of a three-year contract written by Robins on his own notepaper. Whichever way you look at the issue, Coventry City who prided themselves on their public relations, had mishandled things with Allison. It had been a mindless breach of confidence that cost him the job there and then.

Henderson now believed that Ipswich's Bill McGarry was in line for the job. Rumours circulated that there was a rift on the Coventry board, with Robins unconvinced about the Ipswich boss, whose claims were being pushed forward by Camkin.

Finally, on Thursday 12 October, 34-year-old former Manchester United captain Noel Cantwell was appointed. By coincidence, Cantwell had played alongside Allison at West Ham in the 1950s and the two were still friends – Cantwell's appointment must have stretched the limits of that cordiality. Another friendship – between Derrick Robins and Manchester United manager Matt Busby – also came into play. The two had become pally whilst holidaying in Venice, where the persuasive Busby had pushed Cantwell into the race. Busby had two motives, fixing up one of his lieutenants with a good position, while shifting a high-earner off the Old Trafford wage bill. Cantwell, however, must have known he wasn't the first choice for the job, and that if either Clough or Allison had acted with some decorum the Irishman wouldn't have got it. Any negative thoughts, however, would have been assuaged by the salary of £6,000 *per annum* – more than JH had been paid, but less than the £7,500 offered to Hill with the new contract.

When told of Cantwell's appointment, Allison is alleged to have said: 'Had I gone to Coventry I would have taken Noel as my number two.'

Cantwell had had a fine playing career, spending eight years at West Ham, where he captained the side to the Second Division title in 1958, before moving to Old Trafford for £27,000 (a record for a full-back) in 1960. He was a key part in Busby's rebuilding operation following the Munich air disaster and was club captain, leading them to their 1963 FA Cup final win over Leicester. He had won 35 caps for the Republic of Ireland and had recently been appointed manager of the international team – a post he retained for a while after his appointment at Highfield Road. He shared one coincidence with Jimmy Hill – he was the chairman of the Professional Footballers Association – but he would now relinquish that post, terminating his playing career on taking on the Coventry City job.

On Saturday, 14 October 1967 Jimmy Hill formally handed over the managerial reins, prior to the home match against Tottenham. Hill selected the team after explaining his choices to Cantwell. Before the game the pair appeared on the running track, arms held high, and Hill called for 'unquenchable' support for his successor. They sat together in the directors' box and watched a stirring display from the Sky Blues as they came from 0-2 down to pull level, only for a piece of Jimmy Greaves magic to wreck the party with a stunning chipped goal out of nothing to clinch a 3-2 win.

Since the announcement of his departure, Hill had not let the grass grow under his feet. Some weeks earlier it had been announced that once his tenure at Coventry City was over, he would become head of sport at London Weekend Television – a venture which would not be up and running until 1968.

The Jimmy Hill era was over, the Noel Cantwell era had begun, and life at Coventry City would never quite be the same again.

Chapter 16

Post-Hill

Coventry City's new manager, Noel Cantwell, had ten days following the Tottenham game before he picked his first team for the visit to – his old club! Home international matches on the intervening weekend meant the fixture at Old Trafford was put back to the following Wednesday evening. Cantwell made just one change from Hill's last line-up – the experienced Mick Kearns replacing the raw Pat Morrissey at right-half. The Sky Blues held out for half an hour as a crowd of over 54,000 watched, fascinated. With the famous Stretford End blaring out their repertoire of anthems, including a twenty-minute chant of 'We are the Champions', Busby's red-shirted stars turned on the heat. At the final whistle Coventry trudged off, defeated 0-4. Only a late penalty save by Glazier from Denis Law prevented 0-5. The gap in class was enormous, and if Cantwell had had any illusions as to the magnitude of the task ahead, he certainly didn't now.

Derrick Robins sounded the clarion call: 'The fight starts now. We need a point a game till the end of the season to stay up. We are determined that the last six successful years shall not be in vain.'

Within weeks the club had signed winger Ernie Hannigan (from Preston for £55,000), centre-forward Gerry Baker (Ipswich, £20,000), and Cantwell's old United team-mate Maurice Setters (Stoke, £25,000). Setters added steel to a creaky defence and poor Tony Knapp was quickly jettisoned, but results did not improve. Just one of Cantwell's first fourteen games was won – 5-1 over Burnley – and at the end of January the team were anchored at the foot of the table with just sixteen points from 25 games.

On 3 February victory at the Hawthorns signalled a turnaround, and wins over Chelsea and Sheffield Wednesday soon followed. Punctuating these victories was an ignominious FA Cup exit at Third Division Tranmere, which in other circumstances would have been calamitous. Now it came almost as a relief, for survival among the elite excluded all other considerations. One of Tranmere's goals was scored by former City hero George Hudson, whose professional career was winding down. Hill's decision to sell 'The Hud' was now not in doubt.

If City's supporters thought things could not get any worse, they were wrong. On 16 March 1968, Highfield Road's main stand was gutted by fire, leaving among the cinders a melted and twisted Second Division championship trophy and most of the club's archives. The stand was fatally damaged and would need complete rebuilding, but it was hastily patched up to enable the match of the season against Manchester United to go ahead ten days later. A crowd of 47,111 witnessed a famous City victory, secured by goals from Ernie Machin and new skipper Setters.

As the season neared its climax, the Sky Blues found themselves locked in a fight for survival with Fulham and Sheffield United, any two of whom would be doomed. Fulham were the first to perish. With two games left, City led the Blades by one point. Both City's games were away, at West Ham and Southampton. They drew the first 0-0, but Sheffield won at Burnley, leaving the two clubs tied on points going into the final game.

On a nerve-jangling occasion at the Dell, 7,000 City fans roared their team to another backs-to-the-wall goalless draw. When the final whistle blew, ecstatic supporters invaded the pitch, knowing that Chelsea had won at Sheffield to send the Blades into Division Two.

It had been all-change at Highfield Road. Only six of the Second Division championship side which won at home to Millwall twelve months previously took the field against Southampton – Glazier, Bruck, Clements, Lewis, Machin and Tudor.

Of the Big Four who had taken City all the way from Division Four to Division One, Farmer had left for Notts County the previous October. Kearns had been dropped by Cantwell, decided to retire and went off to help run his family's Nuneaton bingo hall. George Curtis had recovered from his broken leg and made two appearances as a striker over Easter before suffering a knock. At 29 his career was far from over and he played a crucial role over the next two seasons before losing his place to Roy Barry and joining Aston Villa for £25,000. It seemed that Brian Hill had been around for ever, but he was still only 27 and had endured another injury-hit season. Hill's appearances became less frequent, but whenever a talented opponent needed marking, Brian would be wheeled out and would generally do his job effectively. Typically, in early 1970 he marked Everton's Alan Ball so well that City won a fine point at the champions-elect. Brian was the only one of the Big Four to play for City in Europe – he played against Bayern Munich, marking the famous Gerd Muller – and played his last game for the Sky Blues on Boxing Day 1970. In early 1971 he left to join Torquay.

John Key played only six games in the top flight and Jimmy Hill's last signing, Tony Knapp, appeared eleven times before being relegated to the reserves. Brian Lewis had started twenty games in Division One, but his appearance at the Dell would be his final one in a Coventry shirt. He left for Luton that summer.

The talented homegrown players Willie Carr and Mick Coop gained valuable First Division experience. Carr became a regular under Cantwell by the end of the season, winning universal plaudits for his buzzing midfield style and drawing comparisons with another red-head, Alan Ball. Willie would play for the Sky Blues until joining Wolves in 1974. In 1968-69 Coop emulated Carr and would be a virtual ever-present for the club until 1981, making more appearances than anyone but George Curtis.

Because of knee injuries Ian Gibson started only fourteen games in Division One that season, but showed that he was not out of place in the higher division. Over the following two seasons his luck with injuries improved only slightly, but whenever he was in the team you were guaranteed some fireworks. His brushes with authority – apparent in October 1966 with Hill – came to the fore every so often with Cantwell, too, and it seemed that 'Gibbo' would 'turn it on' only if he was in the mood. Cantwell's patience ran out in 1970 when, despite 'Gibbo' having played a part in qualifying for Europe, he surprisingly sold him to Cardiff for a cut-price £35,000.

Of the other five who survived that first Division One season, Bill Glazier, Dave Clements and Ernie Machin would all play key roles in the Sky Blues story well into the 1970s. John Tudor, who had been a regular in the first season, often playing out of position as a centre-back, was sold to Second Division Sheffield United for £65,000 in October 1968. He went on to enjoy a very successful career, first at Bramall Lane and later at Newcastle. Finally, Dietmar Bruck lost his left-back place to Chris Cattlin and, with Coop's emergence on the other flank, his opportunities were reduced. In 1970, after two seasons of sporadic appearances, he left to join Charlton.

Cantwell made more signings in early 1968, with forwards Neil Martin (from Sunderland for £90,000) and Ernie Hunt (Everton, £65,000) and full-back Chris Cattlin (Huddersfield, £70,000). It took City's outlay to over £300,000 in under six months, and Second Division heroes Bobby Gould and Ronnie Rees had to be sacrificed to fund it.

In its way, City's performances in 1967-68 were as heroic as any in the ensuing decades.

As for Jimmy Hill, he became a household name on television, bringing his passion for sporting innovation to a national audience.

Players purchased by Jimmy Hill

Date	Player	Signed from	Fee*
Jan 1962	Roy Dwight	Gravesend	£1,500
Mar 1962	Ernie Machin	Nelson	£250
Apr 1962	Willie Humphries	Ards	£4,500
Apr 1962	John Sillett	Chelsea	£2,600
June 1962	Jimmy Whitehouse	Reading	Free
June 1962	Hugh Barr	Linfield	£8,500
June 1962	Bobby Laverick	Brighton	£2,500
July 1962	Terry Bly	Peterborough	£12,000
Aug 1962	Dave Meeson	Reading	£4,000
Dec 1962	Ken Hale	Newcastle	£10,000
Apr 1963	George Hudson	Peterborough	£21,000
Jul 1963	John Mitten	Leicester	Free
Jan 1964	Graham Newton	Walsall	£2,000
Mar 1964	George Kirby	Southampton	£12,500
Mar 1964	John Smith	Tottenham	£11,000
July 1964	Dave Clements	Wolves	£1,500
Oct 1964	Bill Glazier	Crystal Palace	£35,000
Dec 1964	Ken Keyworth	Leicester	Free
Dec 1964	Allan Harris	Chelsea	£35,000
Dec 1965	Ray Pointer	Bury	£20,000
May 1966	John Key	Fulham	Free
July 1966	Ian Gibson	Middlesbrough	£57,000
Feb 1967	Brian Lewis	Portsmouth	£35,000
Feb 1967	Barry Lowes	Bury	£13,000
Mar 1967	Alan Dickie	West Ham	£4,000
Aug 1967	Tony Knapp	Southampton	£25,000
		Total	£317,850

Players sold by Jimmy Hill

Date	Player	Sold to	Fee*
Mar 1962	Mike Dixon	Cambridge U	Free
Mar 1962	Billy Myerscough	Chester	Free
Mar 1962	Ron Hewitt	Chester	£2,000
July 1962	Brian Nicholas	Rugby Town	Free
July 1962	Don Bennett	Hereford	Free
July 1962	Mike Grice	Colchester	£2,000
July 1962	Stewart Imlach	Crystal Palace	£2,000
Sept 1962	Arthur Lightening	Middlesbrough	£11,000
Sept 1962	Albert McCann	Portsmouth	£5,000
Aug 1963	Terry Bly	Notts County	£12,300
Jan 1964	Roy Dwight	Millwall	£2,000
Mar 1964	Jimmy Whitehouse	Millwall	£4,500
Mar 1964	Frank Kletzenbauer	Walsall	£2,500
Oct 1964	George Kirby	Swansea	£11,000
Jan 1965	Graham Newton	Bournemouth	£5,000
Jan 1965	Hugh Barr	Cambridge U	£1,000
Mar 1965	Willie Humphries	Swansea	£15,000
July 1965	Dave Meeson	Wisbech	Free
July 1965	Ken Keyworth	Swindon	£3,500
Sept 1965	John Smith	Leyton O	£5,000
Mar 1966	George Hudson	Northampton	£28,500
Mar 1966	Ken Hale	Oxford U	£8,000
May 1966	Allan Harris	Chelsea	£45,000
July 1966	John Sillett	Plymouth	£5,000
Sept 1966	Bob Wesson	Walsall	£10,000
Jan 1967	John Mitten	Plymouth	£5,000
Jan 1967	Ray Pointer	Portsmouth	£15,000
Mar 1967	Peter Thomas	Waterford	£1,000
Aug 1967	Barry Lowes	Swindon	£13,000
Oct 1967	Ron Farmer	Notts County	Free
		Total	£214,300

* fees are those quoted in the press at the time.

Guide to Seasonal Summaries

Col 1: Match number (for league fixtures); Round (for cup-ties).
e.g. 4R means 'Fourth round replay.'

Col 2: Date of the fixture and whether Home (H), Away (A), or Neutral (N).

Col 3: Opposition.

Col 4: Attendances. Home gates appear in roman; Away gates in *italics*.
Figures in **bold** indicate the largest and smallest gates, at home and away.
Average home and away attendances appear after the final league match.

Col 5: Respective league positions of City and opponents after the game.
City's position appears on the top line in roman.
Their opponents' position appears on the second line in *italics*.
For cup-ties, the division and position of opponents is provided.
e.g. 2:12 means the opposition are twelfth in Division 2.

Col 6: The top line shows the result: W(in), D(raw), or L(ose).
The second line shows City's cumulative points total.

Col 7: The match score, City's given first.
Scores in **bold** show City's biggest league win and heaviest defeat.

Col 8: The half-time score, City's given first.

Col 9: The top line shows City's scorers and times of goals in roman.
The second line shows opponents' scorers and times of goals in *italics*.
A 'p' after the time of a goal denotes a penalty; 'og' an own-goal.
The third line gives the name of the match referee.

Team line-ups: City's line-ups appear on top line, irrespective of whether they are home or away. Opposition teams are on the second line in *italics*.
Players of either side who are sent off are marked !
City's players making their league debuts are displayed in **bold**.

Substitutes: Names of substitutes appear only if they actually took the field.
A player substituted is marked *

N.B. For clarity, all information appearing in *italics* relates to opposing teams.

LEAGUE DIVISION 3 — Manager: Billy Frith > Jimmy Hill — SEASON 1961-62

No	Date		Att	Pos	Pt	F-A	H-T	1	2	3	4	5	6	7	8	9	10	11	Scorers, Times, and Referees
1	19/8	A READING	11,668		L 0	0-4	0-2	Lightening Meeson	Kletzenbauer Goodall	Austin Vallard	Nicholas Walker	Curtis Spiers	Farmer Evans	**Grice** Palethorpe	Hill P Whitehouse	Myerscough Allen	Hewitt Wheeler	Imlach Webb	Webb 25, 71, Paleth'p' 41, Curtis 49 (og) Meeson Ref: R E Smith City suffer the heaviest defeat in all four divisions. Frith orders them in for Sunday morning training. Austin errors lead to the first two goals and Curtis heads in after being caught in two minds. Only Lightening, Myerscough and Grice emerge with any credit from a woeful display.
2	21/8	H SWINDON	13,761		W 2	2-1	1-1	Lightening Burton	Kletzenbauer Jones	Austin Trollope	Nicholas Morgan	Curtis Owen	Farmer Bell	Grice Summerbee	Hill P Hunt E	Myerscough Hunt R	Hewitt McPherson	Imlach Darcy	Burton 23 (og), Grice 78 Hunt R 42 Ref: P Rhodes Burton punches Grice's corner into his own net. Ralph Hunt scores from Darcy's sweet cross. Grice's swerving shot should have been stopped by Burton. City are vastly improved but their fans admire the youthful vigour of Mike Summerbee and Ernie Hunt, who look set for greatness.
3	25/8	H NEWPORT	12,693		W 4	3-0	2-0	Lightening Weare	Kletzenbauer Bird	Austin Herrity A	Nicholas Evans	Curtis Peake	Farmer Bowman	Grice Finlay	Myerscough Robertson	**Dixon** Buchanan	Hewitt Rowland	Imlach Harris	Imlach 6, Grice 36, 46 Ref: K Collinge Mike Dixon makes an impressive start by creating the first two goals and having a goal ruled out, but City squander a chance to improve their goal-average against a poor County who are run ragged by City's wing men. Disappointing crowd for the first Friday night game of the season.
4	29/8	A SWINDON	10,563	8	D 5	3-3	1-0	Lightening Burton	Kletzenbauer Jones	Austin Trollope	Nicholas Morgan	Curtis Owen	Farmer Bell	Grice Summerbee	Hill P Woodruff	Myerscough Smith	Hill B Hunt R	Imlach Corbett	Myerscough 23, Grice 60, Dixon 69 Summerbee 48, Corbett 54, Hunt R 56 Burton Ref: K Aston Bert Head's struggling Swindon look set for a first win after three quick goals, but Grice and Dixon save the point. Grice follows up to score after Dawson saves his pile-driver and Brian Nicholas sets up Dixon. City are robbed of a win when a late Dixon effort is ruled out for offside.
5	2/9	A SOUTHEND	9,372	14	L 5	0-2	0-0	Lightening Goy	Kletzenbauer Shiels	Austin Anderson	Nicholas Costello	Curtis Watson	Farmer Grieveson	Grice Bentley	Myerscough Corthine	Dixon Fryatt	Hill B McKinven	Imlach Kellard	Corthine 75, Fryatt 86 Ref: T Dawes A hot day at the seaside ends in a disappointing loss, with few chances created. Curtis creates City's best with a rampaging 45-yard run into the home penalty area but he has no back-up and shoots weakly wide. Bobby Kellard sets up the Shrimpers' first goal but the second looks offside.
6	4/9	H HALIFAX	13,158	9	W 7	3-1	2-0	Lightening Downsborough Stanley	Kletzenbauer Roscoe	Austin Tilley	Nicholas South	Curtis Fagan	Farmer Priestley	Grice Barnett	Hewitt Burgess	Dixon Large	Hill B Redfearn	Imlach	Dixon 13, Grice 30, Imlach 50 Priestley 47 Ref: K Seddon The early league leaders lose their unbeaten record to an impressive City, who ease off after the third goal. Dixon's header from Imlach's cross is followed by a scorching 30-yard left-foot shot from the excellent Grice. Imlach makes it three after good work by Brian Hill and Dixon.
7	9/9	H NOTTS CO	13,366	11	D 8	2-2	0-1	Lightening Smith	Kletzenbauer Edwards	Austin Noon	Nicholas Sheridan	Curtis Gibson	Farmer Carver	Grice Withers	Hewitt Horobin	Dixon Hateley	Hill B Forrest	Imlach Bircumshaw	Dixon 63, Hewitt 66 Bircumshaw 2, Horobin 77 Ref: J Bullough A superb display from keeper Smith, a Grice penalty miss and a disallowed Farmer 'goal' at the death make it an unlucky day for City. Dixon's tap-in and Ron Hewitt's header put City ahead after Lightening drops a cross for County's first. Curtis is mastered in the air by Tony Hateley.
8	16/9	A SHREWSBURY	7,602	12	D 9	1-1	0-0	Lightening Gibson	**Tedds** Walters	Bennett Skeech	Austin Pountney	Curtis Wallace	Farmer Harley	Grice Kenning	**McCann** Dolby	Dixon Starkey	Allen Rowley	Imlach McLaughlin	Farmer 86 Rowley 67 Ref: J Pickles Frith drops five after the Workington debacle and gives summer signing McCann and 17-year old Tedds debuts. The evergreen Arthur Rowley escapes Austin's clutch just once and heads in. Farmer taps in after Tedds' cross is fumbled, and in the last minute hits a post from a free-kick.
9	19/9	A BRENTFORD	6,119	12	L 9	1-2	0-1	Lightening Cakebread	Tedds Wilson	Bennett Gitsham	Austin Belcher	Curtis Dargie	Allen Coote	Grice Rainford	McCann Brooks	Dixon Higginson	Farmer Edgley	Imlach McLeod	Imlach 89p Higginson 21, Belcher 80 Ref: L Callaghan The Bees tear into a dismal City and deserve their first win of season. The game ends on a sour note as Imlach is booked for raising his fists to Rainford, but then is fouled for the penalty. City's defence looks solid with Curtis superb but the attack is poor with Dixon missing two sitters.
10	23/9	H PETERBOROUGH	19,922	16	L 9	1-3	0-2	Lightening Ronson	Tedds Whittaker	Bennett Walker	Austin Rayner	Curtis Hopkins	Allen Ripley	Grice Hails	McCann Emery	Dixon Bly	Farmer Smith	Imlach Senior	Farmer 46 Ripley 25, Smith 28, Senior 75 Ref: K Tuck The biggest crowd since April 1960 sees the well-drilled Posh outclass City and break their home record. Jimmy Hagan's team look strong promotion bets and, although Farmer's header gives City hope, Senior caps a great game by scoring after Lightening's save from Terry Bly.
11	25/9	H BRENTFORD	10,276	13	W 11	2-0	1-0	Lightening Cakebread	Tedds Wilson	Bennett Gitsham	Allen Belcher	Curtis Dargie	Farmer Coote	Grice Rainford	McCann Brooks	Dixon Higginson	Hill P Satchwell	Imlach McLeod	Hill P 43, Imlach 81 Ref: J Cattlin After an abject first half, City up the pace to see off lowly Brentford, for whom former England man Johnny Brooks stars. Hill nets in a melee from a Grice cross and the aggressive man of the match Imlach seals the win two minutes after Lightening's save from a goal-bound free-kick.

170

#		Opponent			Score	Pos	L	Pts	Scorers / Ref	Attendance	Lightening team										
12	A	PORT VALE	30/9		0-2	16	L	11	Longbottom 20, Poole 33 Ref: C Duxbury	9,821	Hancock	Whalley	Sproson	Ford	Nicholson	Miles	Jackson	Poole	Llewellyn	Steele	Longbottom	Imlach

Another woeful away performance ends in defeat. At 0-0 Peter Hill and Imlach spurn good chances and later Lightening atones for fluffing the second goal with two great close-range saves. Mick Kearns' return gives the defence a tighter look, but unimpressive Vale are off-colour too.

| 13 | H | TORQUAY | 6/10 | | 2-2 | 18 | D | 12 | Dixon 66, 75
Pym 43, Jenkins 49
Ref: W Haynes | 9,445 | Marsh | Bettany | Eckersall | Spencer | Lancaster | Rawson | Astall | Baxter | Northcutt T | Jenkins | Pym | Imlach |

The Friday-night crowd drops below 10,000 as Frith rings the changes to little effect. Lightening prevents a rout as the Gulls outclass City before Dixon comes good. He nets after nudging Marsh into dropping a routine clearance and then hooks in at the far post after Marsh boobs.

| 14 | H | BRADFORD PA | 9/10 | | 3-0 | 12 | W | 14 | Imlach 13, Hewitt 43, Dixon 75
Ref: M Fussey | 7,195 | Gebbie | Walker | March | Scoular | McCalman | Dick | Atkinson | Spratt | Hannigan | Gibson | Bird | Imlach |

The lowest gate since 1958 and City beat a poor Bradford side. Their player-manager Scoular, the former Newcastle captain, is over the hill and only Gibson causes City any grief. Imlach's well-worked goal is the best of the night but nobody can see why Farmer's header is ruled out.

| 15 | A | LINCOLN | 14/10 | | 2-1 | 10 | W | 16 | Green 18 (og), Myerscough 52
Lightening 70 (og)
Ref: J Pickles | 5,009 | Graves | Jackson | Smith | Wardle | Howard | Green | Bannister | Linnecar | Punter | Harbertson | Tracey | Imlach |

City break their away duck with a free-flowing display. Frith thinks Hewitt's head scored the first goal but Green admits it was his. Then Ron Hewitt's header is punched by Smith but Myerscough taps in and no penalty is given. Lightening drops in a cross and City hang on in the end.

| 16 | A | BRADFORD PA | 16/10 | | 0-0 | 10 | D | 17 | Ref: A Edge | 8,681 | Gebbie | Walker | March | Scoular | McCalman | Dick | Atkinson | Spratt | Buchanan | Gibson | Hannigan | Grice |

The first league game under Bradford's floodlights sees a tremendous City rearguard action, with Lightening superb with the wet ball. It's not a game for faint hearts and Curtis is booked, along with Gebbie for punching Satchwell. The impressive Nicholas tames the talented Ian Gibson.

| 17 | H | BARNSLEY | 20/10 | | 1-1 | 11 | D | 18 | Hewitt 55
Smillie 86
Ref: R Leafe | 8,208 | Hill A | Hopper | Brookes | Wood | Sharp | Houghton | McCann | Bartlett | Tindill | Oliver | Jagger | Imlach |

Lightening, the hero from Bradford, misjudges a curling cross and City drop a daft point. Satchwell is off with a badly cut leg for 23 minutes but the later thumps the bar with a 30-yarder and sets up Hewitt's goal. England manager Walter Winterbottom watches Curtis and Kearns.

| 18 | A | QP RANGERS | 28/10 | | 0-3 | 14 | L | 18 | Hewitt 82
Barber 36, 41, Bedford 37, Evans 55
Ref: A Holland | 10,008 | Drinkwater | Bentley | Williams | Keen | Rutter | Angell | McClelland | Bedford | Evans | Collins | Barber | Imlach |

At 0-0 Imlach is bowled over in the area but no penalty is given. After this it is one-way traffic with only the bold George Curtis stopping a complete rout. City have plenty of fight but not the quality to stop an impressive in-form Rangers team of giants, who thankfully ease up at 0-4.

| 19 | A | BOURNEMOUTH | 11/11 | | 1-1 | 14 | D | 19 | Coxon 4
Ref: C Woan | 9,113 | Wesson | Godwin | Arnott | Jones | McGarry | Nelson | Standley | Bain | Bumstead | Dowsett | Archer | Coxon |

Bob Wesson, in for Lightening who has food poisoning, defies the league leaders as 10-man City grab a point at a lucky ground. Satchwell is off after 65 minutes with a leg injury after City had dominated. Satch misses a sitter and twice hits the woodwork. City wear a new strip.

| 20 | H | CRYSTAL PALACE | 17/11 | | 0-2 | 16 | L | 19 | Allen 64p, Uphill 74
Ref: R Harper | 13,757 | Rouse | Long | McNichol | Summersby | Evans | Petchey | Allen | Byrne | Uphill | Smillie | Heckman | Imlach |

Unlucky City hit the woodwork three times. The ref loses control and wild tackles go scot-free. Johnny Byrne shows why he is in the England squad, but former cap Ronnie Allen scores from the spot before the 'offside' Uphill, an ex-City man, seals the win and probably Frith's fate.

| 21 | H | NORTHAMPTON | 2/12 | | 1-0 | 14 | W | 21 | Dixon 54
Ref: G Carr | 13,693 | Brodie | Foley | Claypole | Everitt | Branston | Leck | Spelman | Holton | Terry | Reid | Lines | Imlach |

The Jimmy Hill era starts with a win against the best away side in the division, who finish with 10-men after Tony Claypole breaks an ankle on 21 minutes. Lightening, with three great saves from hot-shot Holton, and Curtis are the pick of a gritty team, who frustrate 4,000 Cobblers fans.

| 22 | A | HULL | 9/12 | | 1-3 | 15 | L | 21 | Dixon 69
Clarke 27, Henderson 37, McSeveney 71 Collinge
Ref: K Collinge | 3,817 | Fisher | Davidson | Bulless | Collinson | Feasey | McMillan | Clarke | Price | Henderson | McSeveney | Crickmore | Imlach |

The lowest post-war crowd at Hull see Hill's team show all their old failings. The home wingers give City's backs a roasting and Lightening keeps the score down. Dixon taps in after Fisher fails to hold Kearns' long shot but does little else. No lack of effort but no punch up front.

| 23 | H | READING | 16/12 | | 1-0 | 14 | W | 23 | Hewitt 77
Ref: R Windle | 8,112 | Meeson | Goodall | High | Kearns | Walker | Evans | Wheeler | Whitehouse | Lacey | Webb | Allen | Imlach |

Lightening is in top form but Hewitt is the hero, scoring the winner after emergency dental treatment at the break. Jimmy Hill asks the fans to be patient but they are restless after a poor first half against lifeless Reading. Mick Kearns is converted to a full-back and marks Wheeler well.

LEAGUE DIVISION 3 — Manager: Billy Frith > Jimmy Hill — SEASON 1961-62

No	Date		Att	Pos	Pt	F-A	H-T	Scorers, Times, and Referees	1	2	3	4	5	6	7	8	9	10	11
24	A 23/12	NEWPORT	3,360	12	W 25	2-1	1-0	Dixon 40, 67 Robertson 59 Ref: J Cattlin	Lightening Weare	Bennett Thomas	Kletzenbauer Rowland	Nicholas Williams	Curtis Evans	Kearns Bowman	Grice Walsh	Myerscough Robertson	Dixon Harris	Hewitt Herrity W	Imlach Smith
								Newport's lowest crowd of the season see City make it three wins in four for Hill on a grassless pitch. Bowman hits the post with an early penalty after Curtis' foul on Walsh. City are on top until Robertson's goal, then it is all County until Grice breaks away and Dixon heads home.											
25	H 26/12	GRIMSBY	11,218	10	W 27	2-0	0-0	Myerscough 79, Dixon 85 Ref: P Bye	Lightening Barnett	Bennett Donovan	Kletzenbauer Keeble	Nicholas Welbourne	Curtis Jobling	Kearns Knights	Grice Scott	Myerscough Cullen	Dixon Purvis	Hewitt Rafferty	Imlach Hill
								City leapfrog the Mariners, who are later promoted, on a bone-hard frozen pitch. Billy Myerscough coolly scores from Hewitt's through ball before Dixon forces an error for number two. Lightening is a virtual spectator. 500 cold, young fans get pop, crisps and autographs afterwards.											
26	H 13/1	SOUTHEND	9,376	12	D 28	3-3	1-3	Dixon 30, Hewitt 50, Imlach 70 Jones 14, 15, Kellard 41 Ref: A Holland	Wesson Goy	Bennett Shiels	Kletzenbauer Anderson	Nicholas Bentley	Curtis Watson	Kearns Grievesan	Grice Wall	Myerscough Jones	Dixon Costello	Hewitt McKinven	Imlach Kellard
								Lightening has bronchitis and new boy Dwight has the flu. Stand-in Wesson has a nightmare, as does Goy. After three minutes the referee incorrectly makes City change into their away kit. City are stunned by Ken Jones but rally with a Hewitt 50-yarder and an Imlach blaster.											
27	A 20/1	NOTTS CO	8,827	12	L 28	0-2	0-2	Hateley 4, 22 Ref: L Hamer	Lightening Butler	Bennett Edwards	Kletzenbauer Bircumshaw	Nicholas Sheridan	Curtis Gibson	Kearns Carver	Grice Moore	Myerscough Forrest	Dixon Hateley	Hewitt Horobin	Imlach Withers
								Goal-shy on their travels, City rarely trouble Butler and apart from Grice the attack is woeful. On a murky wet day, Tony Hateley is on fire and scores two opportunist goals. The ref errs by giving City a free-kick for a handball well inside the box. Hill appoints Dicks as his number two.											
28	A 27/1	PORTSMOUTH	13,506	12 1	L 28	2-3	1-2	Imlach 38, McCann 86 Gordon 20, Dodson 40, 82 Ref: S Yates	Lightening Beattie	Bennett Rutter	Kletzenbauer Wilson	Kearns Brown	Curtis Snowdon	Allen Dickinson	Grice Barton	Myerscough Gordon	Dwight Saunders	McCann Blackburn	Imlach Dodson
								City stun the runaway leaders with a great second-half display, which deserves at least a point. Inspired by Imlach's deadly crosses, City lack a ruthless scorer to capitalise as the chances go begging. Pompey's third is a breakaway but the impressive McCann sets up a grandstand finale.											
29	H 3/2	SHREWSBURY	8,832	11 18	W 30	4-1	2-0	Allen 20, Satchwell 43, Kearns 73, McLaughlin 88 [Morrall 89 (og)] Ref: L Tirebuck	Lightening Miller	Austin Walters	Kletzenbauer Skeech	Kearns Harley	Curtis Morrall	Allen Hemsley	Grice Kenning	Dwight Pountney	Satchwell Starkey	McCann Rowley	Imlach McLaughlin
								On a dreadful muddy surface City find their shooting boots and are rewarded for their attacking prowess. Lots of help from a dodgy keeper, at fault for three goals. Kearns' 30-yard drive is the best goal and Dwight has a big hand in the own-goal. Veteran Rowley is given stick by fans.											
30	A 10/2	PETERBOROUGH	11,751	11 6	W 32	3-2	1-2	Satchwell 2, 66, McCann 83 Curtis 25 (og), Senior 42 Ref: E Crawford	Lightening Wells	Austin Whittaker	Kletzenbauer Walker	Kearns Rayner	Curtis Hopkins	Allen Graham	Grice Hails	Dwight Smith	Satchwell Bly	McCann Hudson	Imlach Senior
								City win on their first ever visit to London Road as Posh's promotion push stutters. A thrilling contest goes to the wire with Lightening's brave save from George Hudson near the end. Hill switches Dwight and Grice at 1-2, and the former hits top form and the latter sets up the winner.											
31	A 24/2	TORQUAY	3,458	11 23	L 32	0-1	0-0	Pym 83 Ref: S Yates	Lightening Marsh	Kletzenbauer Bettany	Austin Allen	Nicholas Spencer	Curtis Smith	Kearns Hancock	Dwight Handley	Grice Jenkins	Satchwell Northcutt T	Hewitt Mills	Imlach Pym
								Grassless Plainmoor is a bogey ground for the Bantams, and the men who destroyed Posh fail to turn up. Only after Pym had curled a shot past an erring Lightening did the visitors start to play. In seven minutes they created three good chances and Nicholas has a 'goal' ruled out.											
32	H 2/3	LINCOLN	9,147	11 21	D 33	2-2	0-0	Kearns 60, Grice 77 Linnecor 75, 78 Ref: K Dagnall	Lightening Heath	Kletzenbauer Green	Austin Smith	Nicholas Franks	Curtis Haines	Kearns Middleton	Dwight Bannister	Grice Linnecor	Satchwell Harbertson	Allen Broadbent	Imlach Scanlon
								Lowly Imps push City all the way on a Friday night, with Linnecor's two snap-shots enough for a valuable point. Albert McCann is sorely missed as a creator and Imlach is quiet. Kearns' drive goes in off the crossbar and Grice's first goal since September is a fierce cross-shot.											
33	A 9/3	BARNSLEY	6,083	11 19	L 33	1-2	1-1	Dwight 13 Tindill 29, 50 Ref: W Robinson	Lightening Williams	Kletzenbauer Hopper	Austin Brookes	Nicholas Wood	Curtis Sharp	Kearns Houghton	Grice Smillie	Dixon Bartlett	Dwight Tindill	Allen Oliver	Imlach Ring
								Barnsley end a run of five home defeats but impressive City are unlucky. Dwight is off the mark from Grice's cross but the veteran Bert Tindill in his 550th game nets with two left-footers. Ten minutes from time in a close game Satchwell misses a sitter from Imlach's glorious cross.											
34	H 12/3	WATFORD	7,249	11 9	W 35	1-0	0-0	Dwight 82 Ref: J Cooke	Lightening Underwood	Kletzenbauer Bell	Austin Nicholas	Nicholas Catleugh	Curtis McNiece	Kearns Gregory	Grice Porter	Farmer Harmer	Dwight Chung	Allen Day	Imlach Brown
								A thrilling final twenty minutes after a dire match earlier. Farmer returns after injury against injury-struck Watford. Lightening's wonder save from Chung's bullet header sparks a counter-attack, and Grice's cross fools Underwood for Dwight to head home. Home crowds slump lower.											

#		Date	Opponent			Score	Pos	Scorers / Attendance	Lightening	Kletzenbauer	Austin	Kearns	Curtis	Allen	Grice	Hill P	Dwight		McCann	Imlach
35	H	16/3	QP RANGERS	11	L	2-3	35	McCann 75, Kletzenbauer 80 Bedford 14, 30, 83 Ref: J P-ckles 8,629 5	Drinkwater	Williams	Ingham	Keen	Rutter	Angell	McClelland	Bedford	Evans		Collins	Lazarus

QPR still have an outside chance of promotion and their fleet-footed forwards cause nightmares for Curtis and Co. They go two up with well-worked moves. After the break it's all City and McCann nets before Kletz's volley gives him a rare goal. City relax and Bedford gets his third.

| 36 | A | 23/3 | WATFORD | 10 | W | 1-0 | 37 | Dwight 82
Ref: C Kingston
5,611 9 | Underwood | Ball | Nicholas | Chung | Ryden | Gregory | Harmer | Porter | Brown | | Crisp | Bunce |

A flurry of snow and a cold night fails to deter City, who inflict the Hornets' fifth straight defeat. Lightening keeps City in the game until Bob Allen's delicious pass finds Dwight, who makes no mistake with his only chance of the game. 17-year old Bruck impresses in his second start.

| 37 | H | 30/3 | BOURNEMOUTH | 11 | L | 0-1 | 37 | Bennett 40
Ref: R Tinkler
8,654 2 | Best | Farmer | Jones | McGarry | Nelson | Standley | Spelman | Thompson | Dowsett | | Gibbs | Bennett |

City are made to pay for bad misses by Grice and Dwight when Bennett's pile-driver seals the points as the Cherries fight for promotion. After the break City pummel the visitors' goal to no avail as more chances go begging. The final Friday night game as the experiment is reviewed.

| 38 | A | 7/4 | CRYSTAL PALACE | 15 | D | 2-2 | 38 | Dwight 41, 60
Brett 1, Smillie 54
Ref: A Holland
8,438 10 | Rouse | McNichol | Little | Long | Wood | Werge | Brett | Summersby | Uphill | | Smillie | Heckman |

Away performances have improved greatly since the turn of the year, and City are close to a win. After a lapse for the 30-second opener, Lightening dazzles behind a solid defence. Byrne has left Palace for West Ham and they are weaker for it. Dwight silences the home crowd.

| 39 | A | 10/4 | GRIMSBY | 15 | L | 0-2 | 38 | Portwood 7, Rafferty 49
Ref: R Langdale
12,997 2 | Barnett | Donovan | Keeble | Cockerill | Jobling | Knights | Waite | Cullen | Portwood | | Rafferty | Jones |

Tim Ward's Grimsby have lost one game in 15 since their Christmas defeat at Coventry and are going up. Their hard defence give City nothing despite City bossing the game for long periods. The second goal looks offside but Lightening has to save Cockeril's penalty on 77 minutes.

| 40 | H | 14/4 | PORTSMOUTH | 12 | W | 2-0 | 40 | Farmer 32, 86
Ref: G Hartley
9,725 1 | Beattie | Rutter | Wilson | Brown | Snowdon | Dickinson | Barton | Gordon | Saunders | | Blackburn | Dodson |

Pompey still lead the table by five points, despite a third defeat in a row. Hill's tiny forwards are dwarfed by Pompey's defence but twice Ron Farmer nets after Dwight efforts rebound. First from the bar, then the keeper. Curtis quells the Saunders' danger and City could have had more.

| 41 | H | 16/4 | PORT VALE | 13 | L | 0-1 | 40 | Edwards 25
Ref: G Grundy
5,907 12 | Hancock | Lowe | Sproson | Miles | Nicholson | Curbishley | Llewellyn | Steele | Poole | | Longbottom | Edwards |

Steady drizzle ensures the lowest gate since 1958 and City frustrate their fans again. McCann hits the bar and Farmer twice shaves the post, but the performance is not convincing. Edwards spots Lightening off his line and floats in the winner. 'Unsuitable' Mike Grice put on transfer list.

| 42 | A | 21/4 | NORTHAMPTON | 16 | L | 1-4 | 40 | Dwight 55
Woods 25, Holton 58, 73, Lines 68
Ref: J Kelly
10,388 6 | Brodie | Foley | Woollard | Leck | Branston | Mills | Woods | Holton | Everitt | | Reid | Lines |

A first-half cloudburst creates farcical conditions and both keepers struggle in muddy goalmouths with a greasy ball. Ex-Gunner Cliff Holton invariably scores against City and, though the misses good chances, he sets a new club record with his 35th of the season as Cobblers run riot.

| 43 | H | 23/4 | BRISTOL CITY | 16 | D | 1-1 | 41 | Farmer 40
Atyeo 62
Ref: H Richards
5,965 6 | Cook | Ford | Briggs | McCall | Connor | Etheridge | Tait | Clark | Atyeo | | Williams | Noake |

Despite it being a bank holiday, another small crowd means no atmosphere. Ex-England man John Atyeo scores a tap-in for dominant Bristol and Lightening's saves prevent a defeat. No lack of effort but little guile from Hill's men, who look doomed for another bottom-half finish.

| 44 | A | 24/4 | BRISTOL CITY | 16 | L | 2-3 | 41 | Holder 47, Farmer 52
Williams 40, Clark 53, 65
Ref: A Jobling
6,674 6 | Cook | Ford | Briggs | McCall | Connor | Etheridge | Rogers | **Turner** | Clark | Imlach | **Bassett** | Noake |

Four 18-year-olds are fielded by Hill and they don't let the side down in a plucky display. Bristol's own 18-year-old, Brian Clark, is the star, benefiting from Atyeo's 'lay-offs'. Colin Holder scores after Imlach intercepts a back-pass and he could have grabbed a point near the end.

| 45 | H | 28/4 | HULL | 16 | L | 0-2 | 41 | Price 31, 95
Ref: E Norman
7,589 12 | Wesson | **Sillett** | Davidson | Garvey | Collinson | McMillan | Clarke | Price | Henderson | | King | McSeveney |

Fisher
New-boys Sillett and Humphries impress but cannot raise the team's performance, and Fisher has a very quiet afternoon. Duggie Price can't have scored two easier goals and City's small attack is snuffed out by Hull's giant defenders. The crowd pours out soon after the second goal.

| 46 | A | 30/4 | HALIFAX | 14 | W | 2-0 | 43 | Farmer 30, Dwight 67
Ref: R Leafe
2,607 18 | Wesson | Sillett | Stanley | Tilley | South | Large | Strodder | Worthington | Hopper | | Smith | Brier |

Downsborough
City finish on a winning note – the first time for seven years. It is top referee Reg Leafe's final game, and he has an easy ride as City weather Halifax's brief flurries. Holder makes both goals, a Farmer ground shot and Dwight's from a narrow angle. Brian Hill converted to a wing-half.

Home 10,256
Away 8,064
Average 8,629

LEAGUE DIVISION 3 (CUP-TIES)

Manager: Billy Frith > Jimmy Hill

SEASON 1961-62

League Cup

			F-A	H-T	Scorers, Times, and Referees	1	2	3	4	5	6	7	8	9	10	11
1	A	WORKINGTON	0-3 L	0-2		Lightening	Kletzenbauer	Austin	Nicholas	Curtis	Farmer	Myerscough	Hewitt	Dixon	Hill B	Imlach
		13/9			Commons 12, 23, Kirkup 62	Wright	Fleming	Brown	Hincheliffe	Tennant	Burkinshaw	Wilson	Timmins	Commons	McGarry	Kirkup
			4,682 4:6		Ref: W Robinson	Complacent City are hustled out of the League Cup in another drab away display. Free-transfer Mike Commons scores two opportunist goals against a weak defence. Keeper Charlie Wright makes two great saves from City's best player, Brian Hill, as City are humbled in Cumberland.										

FA Cup

			F-A	H-T	Scorers, Times, and Referees	1	2	3	4	5	6	7	8	9	10	11
1	H	GILLINGHAM	2-0 W	1-0	Satchwell 21, Hewitt 62	Lightening	Bennett	Austin	Nicholas	Curtis	Farmer	Grice	Hewitt	Hill B	Satchwell	Imlach
		4/11				Simpson	Hunt	Cockburn	Vaessen	Hughes	Farrall	Ridley	Livesey	Johnston	Waldock	Pulley
			10,628 4:22		Ref: N Hough	Gills boss Harry Barratt is a City legend but his side are no match for 10-men City after Farmer's exit with an ankle injury at 1-0. Satchwell's header and Hewitt's 35-yard thunderbolt liven up a dull game with City rarely in trouble. After Farrall is booked, the tackling gets less heated.										
2	H	KINGS LYNN	1-2 L	1-2	Hindle 28 (og)	Lightening	Bennett	Kletzenbauer	Nicholas	Curtis	Austin	Hill P	Hewitt	Dixon	Hill B	Imlach
		25/11			Johnson 33, Wright 36	Manning	Mackey	Wilson	Dunn	Hindle	Sanchez	Bacon	Lumley	Dixon	Johnson	Wright
			12,080 SL:22		Ref: F Cowen	The Southern League strugglers delight their 1,000 fans by sweeping slipshod City out. After Hindle put City ahead trying to clear, the Linnets take control. When the second-half rally fails to arrive the Linnets go through to meet Everton on merit. A first loss to non-leaguers since 1935.										

			Home						Away					
	P	W	D	L	F	A	W	D	L	F	A	Pts
1 Portsmouth	46	15	6	2	48	23	12	5	6	39	24	65
2 Grimsby	46	18	3	2	49	18	10	3	10	31	38	62
3 Bournemouth	46	14	8	1	42	18	7	9	7	27	27	59
4 QP Rangers	46	15	3	5	65	31	9	8	6	46	42	59
5 Peterborough	46	16	0	7	60	38	10	6	7	47	44	58
6 Bristol C	46	15	3	5	56	27	8	5	10	38	45	54
7 Reading	46	14	5	4	46	24	8	4	11	31	42	53
8 Northampton	46	12	6	5	52	24	8	5	10	33	33	51
9 Swindon	46	11	8	4	48	26	6	7	10	30	45	49
10 Hull	46	15	5	3	43	20	5	6	12	24	34	48
11 Bradford PA	46	13	5	5	47	27	7	2	14	33	51	47
12 Port Vale	46	12	4	7	41	23	5	7	11	24	35	45
13 Notts Co	46	14	5	4	44	23	3	4	16	23	51	43
14 COVENTRY	46	11	6	6	38	26	5	5	13	26	45	43
15 Crys Palace	46	8	8	7	50	41	6	6	11	33	39	42
16 Southend	46	10	7	6	31	26	3	9	11	26	43	42
17 Watford	46	10	9	4	37	26	4	4	15	26	48	41
18 Halifax	46	9	5	9	34	35	6	5	12	28	49	40
19 Shrewsbury	46	8	7	8	46	37	5	5	13	27	47	38
20 Barnsley	46	9	6	8	45	41	4	6	13	26	54	38
21 Torquay	46	9	4	10	48	44	6	2	15	28	56	36
22 Lincoln	46	4	10	9	31	43	5	7	11	26	44	35
23 Brentford	46	11	3	9	34	29	3	1	19	19	64	34
24 Newport	46	6	5	12	29	38	1	3	19	17	64	22
	1104	279	128	145	1064	708	145	128	279	708	1064	1104

Odds & ends

Double wins: (3) Newport, Watford, Halifax.
Double losses: (3) QP Rangers, Port Vale, Hull.

Won from behind: (1) Peterborough (a).
Lost from in front: (3) Barnsley (a), Bristol C (a), Kings Lynn FAC (h).

High spots: The form of Lightening and Curtis in defence.
Impressive early form under Jimmy Hill.
Home wins over promoted teams.

Low spots: Kings Lynn FA Cup exit.
Workington League Cup crash.
End of season home form – one win in six.

Red cards: City (0).
Red cards: Opponents (0).
Hat-tricks: (0).
Opposing hat-tricks: (1) Brian Bedford (QPR h).
Leading scorer: (12) Mike Dixon.

	Appearances				Goals		
	Lge	Sub	LC	Sub	FAC	Sub	Lge	LC	FAC	Tot
Allen, Bob	22								1	1
Austin, Frank	37		1		2					
Bassett, George	1									
Bennett, Don	21				2					
Bruck, Dietmar	6									
Curtis, George	46		1		2					
Dixon, Mike	18		1		1		12			12
Dwight, Roy	18						7			7
Farmer, Ron	26		1		1		7			7
Grice, Mike	37						6			6
Hewitt, Ron	20		1		2		7		1	8
Hill, Brian	9		1		2					
Hill, Peter	9				1		1			1
Holder, Colin	2						1			1
Humphries, Willie	1									
Imlach, Stewart	45		1		2		7			7
Kearns, Mick	26						2			2
Kletzenbauer, Frank	33		1		1		1			1
Lightening, Arthur	42		1		2					
McCann, Albert	22						3			3
Myerscough, Billy	18		1				3			3
Nicholas, Brian	24		1		2					
Satchwell, Ken	12				1		3		1	4
Sillett, John	2									
Tedds, Bill	4									
Turner, Alan	1									
Wesson, Bob	4									
(own-goals)							3		1	4
27 players used	506		11		22		64		3	67

LEAGUE DIVISION 3 — Manager: Jimmy Hill — SEASON 1962-63

No	Date		Att	Pos	Pt	F-A	H-T	Scorers, Times, and Referees	1	2	3	4	5	6	7	8	9	10	11
1	18/8	H NOTTS CO	22,832		W	2-0	0-0	Barr 76, Bly 83 Ref: F Cowen	Lightening	Sillett Edwards	Curtis Agnew	Farmer Sheridan	Curtis Gibson	Kearns Carver	Humphries Fry	**Barr** Brown	Bly Jones	Whitehouse Hateley	Laverick Tait
								The expectations are enormous for a nervy City, playing in sky blue for the first time in a league game. Thirty shots rain on County's goal and Barr scores a right-footer and sets up Bly's header to the baking crowd's relief. Sound defence seals first win over County in seven attempts.	Butler										
2	21/8	A SWINDON	14,509		L	1-4	1-3	Farmer 32 Darcy 7,14, Smith 23, Curtis 83 (og) Ref: R Smith	Lightening O'Hara	Sillett Wollen	Austin Trollope	Farmer Morgan	Curtis Owen	Kearns Woodruff	Humphries Darcy	Barr Hunt	Bly Smith	Whitehouse Atkins	Laverick Jackson
								Bert Head's exciting young team give City a nightmare time. Stand-in Darcy's goals both come from Woodruff's long throw, as City's defence freezes. Sillett is flat out injured when Jack Smith scores and Curtis's mistimed header sails in. Farmer's 25-yard volley offers only brief hope.											
3	25/8	A COLCHESTER	5,677	12 6	D	0-0	0-0	Ref: R Tinkler	Lightening Ames	Sillett Griffiths	Austin Fowler	Hill B Harris	Curtis Forbes	Kearns Hunt RM	Humphries Grice	Barr Hill R	Bly Hunt RR	Whitehouse Wright	Laverick
				3				Sillett and Brian Hill excel and Frank Austin tames the lively ex-City man Grice. City have the better of the exchanges but fail to take chances. The new forwards stutter and find Percy Ames in top form. Promoted Oysters are tamed in a much-improved display, compared with Swindon.											
4	28/8	H SWINDON	19,413	8 11	W	2-0	2-0	Whitehouse 6, Barr 24 Ref: N Matthews	Lightening O'Hara	Sillett Wollen	Austin Trollope	Hill B Morgan	Curtis Owen	Kearns Woodruff	Humphries Darcy	Barr Hunt	Bly Smith	Whitehouse Chamberlain	Laverick Jackson
				5				A promising start with two good goals fades on a wet pitch. O'Hara and Owen err for the first and Whitehouse's brainy play lets in Hugh Barr. Swindon have few chances against a solid City defence, and Lightening's reflexes save their best chance. Laverick and Bly struggle again.											
5	1/9	H SOUTHEND	17,946	11 2	L	3-4	1-1	Bly 22, 51, 56 Beesley 34, 85, 88, Woodley 64 Ref: A Jobling	**Meeson** Goy	Kletzenbauer Tharme	Austin Anderson	Kearns Bentley	Curtis Watson	Hill B Lee	Humphries Woodley	Barr Jones	Bly Beesley	Whitehouse McNeill	Dwight Kellard
				5				Lightening and McCann have gone and Laverick is dropped. Dave Meeson's debut is a nightmare as City throw away a 3-1 lead. Goy keeps the Shrimpers in the game as City have 16 first-half shots. With better service Bly finally comes good but the woeful defending costs City dear.											
6	4/9	H WATFORD	16,342	9 6	W	3-1	3-1	Kearns 17, Humphries 30, Barr 33 Harris 1 Ref: P Rhodes	Meeson Underwood	Sillett Nicholas	Kletzenbauer Meldrum	Kearns Porter	Curtis McNeice	Hill B Gregory	Humphries Howfield	Barr Larkin	Bly Fairbrother	Whitehouse Ward	Dwight Harris
				7				A much tighter defence, allied to the devastating speed and skill of Willie Humphries, give City the points. Harris's 50-second goal is a sweet left-footer from a 30-yard angle. Mick Kearns' 25-yard boomer, Humphries' fierce ground shot and Barr's cross-shot put Watford to the sword.											
7	8/9	A MILLWALL	17,936	7 4	D	3-3	2-2	Wilson 4 (og), Humphries 32, Bly 61 Terry 20, Broadfoot 30, Jones 63p Ref: J Carr	Meeson Davies	Kletzenbauer Gilchrist	Austin Brady P	Kearns Oheney	Curtis Wilson	Hill B Stocks	Humphries Broadfoot	Barr Jones	Bly Terry	Whitehouse Towers	Dwight McQuade
				8				Newly promoted Millwall are lucky to stay unbeaten after a late Whitehouse effort is ruled out for offside. Humphries' second is a deflection and an improved Meeson saves City near the end. Watched by Irish selectors, the superb Humphries scores a screamer and sets up Bly's goal.											
8	11/9	H WATFORD	10,227	11 2	L	1-6	1-2	Barr 5 Brown 14, Fraser 44, Harris 77, 87, [Ward 78, 85] Ref: K Stokes	Meeson Underwood	Kletzenbauer Bell	Austin Nicholas	Kearns Larkin	Curtis McNeice	Hill B Gregory	Humphries Howfield	Barr Fraser	Bly Brown	Whitehouse Ward	Dwight Harris
				8				Four goals in ten late minutes stun City and their fans after they looked good for a point. The defence crumbles under the home barrage and a blameless Meeson is unprotected. Curtis has his name taken and City suffer their biggest defeat for 18 months with the home wingers rampant.											
9	15/9	H SHREWSBURY	14,148	14 17	D	0-0	0-0	Ref: A Holland	Meeson Miller	Kletzenbauer Walters	Kearns Skeech	Hill B Hemsley	Curtis Morrall	Farmer Pountney	Humphries Kenning	Barr Harley	Bly Middleton	Whitehouse Rowley	Rees McLaughlin
				9				The old warhorse Arthur Rowley is one goal shy of the British scoring record but Brian Hill shackles him. On a wet afternoon, 18-year-old Ronnie Rees makes an impressive debut. Jimmy Hill blames two games a week for this lacklustre game with Hugh Barr especially off-colour.											
10	18/9	H BRADFORD PA	13,038	9 11	W	3-1	1-1	Barr 4, 58, Bly 88 Curtis 13 (og) Ref: M Faulkner	Meeson Gebbie	Kletzenbauer Walker	Kearns March	Hill B Scoular	Curtis McCalman	Bruck Williamson	Humphries Hector	Barr Spratt	Bly Green	Whitehouse Atkinson	Rees Bird
				11				Brutal Bradford's three-game winning run is ended, but not before some wild tackles. Williamson is the chief culprit, sending Humphries to hospital with a broken collar-bone. Barr is back to his best, scoring in a one-on-one with Gebbie and a header before Bly blasts the third goal.											
11	22/9	A PORT VALE	9,816	13 9	L	1-2	1-0	Barr 38 Sillett 47 (og), Grainger 66p Ref: G McCabe	Meeson Hancock	Sillett Lowe	Kearns Sproson	Hill B Ford	Curtis Nicholson	Bruck Poole	Dwight Wright	Barr Llewellyn	Bly Harkin	Whitehouse Edwards	Rees Grainger
				11				City squander the lead again to Freddie Steele's unimpressive Vale team. John Sillett slices a low cross past Meeson and the keeper bundles Edwards over after Bruck's error. Ex-England man Colin Grainger slots home the penalty. City and Vale look far from promotion candidates.											

#		Date	Opponent	Att			Pos	Score	Scorers		Meeson	Sillett	Kletzenbauer	Hill B	Curtis	Bruck	Dwight	Barr	Bly	Whitehouse	Rees
12	A	24/9	BRADFORD PA	7,664	10	15	D 12	0-0		Ref: H Wilson	Gebbie	Walker	March	Scoular	McCalman	Williamson	Hannigan	Buchanan	Green	Maxwell	Bird

A creditable draw from a hard-fought game, with Jimmy Scoular's men failing to score for the first time. The game is much cleaner than last week's, but Rees' growing reputation make him a marked man. The much-maligned Meeson and Kletz are City's stars in a better away display.

| 13 | H | 29/9 | READING | 13,429 | 9 | 19 | W 14 | 2-1 | Bly 13, Barr 57 Norton 89 | Ref: P Mitchell | Dixon | Neate | High | Walker | Spiers | Evans | Batt | Wheeler | Allen | Norton | Webb |

Humphries and Barr celebrate international selection with imperious displays against poor Reading. Despite dominating Harry Johnstone's team, City miss the chance to improve their goal-average. Bly scores when Dixon fails to hold Willie's free-kick at Barr lobs in the second.

| 14 | A | 2/10 | BRISTOL CITY | 13,422 | 10 | 6 | D 15 | 1-1 | Whitehouse 57 Derrick 11 | Ref: R Smith | Nicholls | Briggs | Thresher | Parr | Connor | Etheridge | Tait | Clark | Atyeo | Williams R | Derrick |

The Sky Blues fail to win away again but run in-form Bristol close. Curtis and Sillett marshal the dangerous John Atyeo and Jantzen Derrick well, and City have good chances. Bruck hits the underside of the bar before Whitehouse pounces when Connor's poor clearance hits Parr.

| 15 | A | 5/10 | BARNSLEY | 9,025 | 10 | 16 | L 15 | 1-2 | Barr 74 Oliver 56, Kerr 83 | Ref: R Lonsdale | Hill | Hooper | Brookes | Nicol | Winstanley | Wood | Hosie | Kerr | Leighton | Oliver | O'Hara |

On a Friday night under the Oakwell floodlights the Tykes belie their lowly status and deserve the win. Oliver's goal is untidy but Barr's header from Bly's cross gives City hope. Then Bruck fails to control a long ball and Kerr nets. Star man Dave Meeson keeps the score down.

| 16 | H | 13/10 | NORTHAMPTON | 22,163 | 13 | 7 | D 16 | 1-1 | Bly 59 Ashworth 11 | Ref: A Luty | Brodie | Foley | Woollard | Leck | Branston | Kurila | Sanders | Holton | Ashworth | Reid | Lines |

Dave Bowen's Cobblers are on the march and bring a big following. Ashworth's 13th goal of the season is a cracker. Bly scores a classic, but misses a sitter from a yard near the end after constant City pressure. A draw is fair in an end-to-end game. Curtis booked fouling Chic Brodie.

| 17 | H | 23/10 | BRISTOL CITY | 11,390 | 11 | 9 | W 18 | 4-2 | Farmer 1p, Barr 8, Bly 13, Whitehse 66 Atyeo 14, 38 | Ref: S Stoakes | Cook | Briggs | Thresher | Etheridge | Connor | Casey | Peters | Clark | Atyeo | Williams R | Derrick |

A thrilling start sees Casey handle for the first penalty since Jimmy Hill arrived, and two great headers from Humphries corners. Bristol fight back well before Whitehouse heads in a free-kick. The best game of the season ends with both teams going for goals, but City deserve the win.

| 18 | H | 27/10 | HULL | 11,821 | 12 | 16 | D 19 | 2-2 | Humphries 17, Dwight 25 Chilton 18, McSeveney 56 | Ref: J Pickles | Williams | Davidson | Garvey | Collinson | Feasey | McMillan | Clarke | Price | Chilton | Henderson | McSeveney |

After the Bristol game the fans are mystified by a poor City display. Barr's muscle pull upsets the rhythm of the team as Humphries moves to inside-forward. Chilton gives Curtis a tough time but Dwight's snap shot is the best goal. Woeful marking allows McSeveney to grab the point.

| 19 | H | 10/11 | WREXHAM | 11,366 | 10 | 14 | W 21 | 3-0 | Bly 27, 65, Whitehouse 29 | Ref: R Earper | Keelan | Jones P | McGowan | Barnes K | Fox | Jones T | Barnes R | Whitehouse | Phythian | Griffiths | Colebridge |

Another thriller, with Humphries dazzling again on a grey day. Wrexham play lovely football but Bob Wesson is in top form and keeps a second clean sheet. Bly looks a different class on the muddy pitches and blasts two past the imposing Keelan. City are four points off top spot.

| 20 | A | 17/11 | HALIFAX | 3,956 | 8 | 21 | W 23 | 4-2 | Bly 44, Humphries 56, Farmer 83, Holden 30, 74 [Rees 85] | Ref: R Windle | Knowles | Stanley | Roscoe | Tilley | South | Harrison | Priestley | Tait | Holden | Carlin | Redfern |

Wesson and Curtis are rocks as City notch their first away win. Brave Halifax deserve a half-time lead but are kept out by Wesson and swept aside after the break. Humphries torments his full-back and scores the best goal – a blistering drive from 15-yards – and sets up two others.

| 21 | A | 1/12 | BRIGHTON | 9,439 | 8 | 22 | D 24 | 2-2 | Farmer 55, Bly 88 Jennings 43, 59p | Ref: K Aston | Baker | Jest | Baxter | Bertolini | Jennings | Cassidy | Waites | Collins | Donnelly | Jackson | Goodchild |

On a rutted pitch, Curtis twists an ankle and moves to centre-forward. It is City's drabbest display for a long time and they need Ron Farmer's 35-yard goal and Bly's late effort from a cross by the brave Curtis. Brighton's penalty for Sillett's handball harsh – it was a Brighton hand!

| 22 | H | 8/12 | CARLISLE | 8,876 | 9 | 24 | W 26 | 3-2 | Humphries 22, Whitehouse 55, Bly 79 Taylor 4, Blue 87 | Ref: L Hamer | Dean | Caldwell | McBain | McConnell | Marsden | Thompson | Blue | Brayton | Livingstone | Davies | Taylor |

After 174 games in a row, George Curtis is missing, injured. On a muddy pitch Humphries is at his best, tormenting the Cumbrians and he has a hand in all the goals. Dean saves bottom of the table Carlisle from a drubbing and Archie Blue's late goal makes it an unflattering scoreline.

| 23 | A | 15/12 | NOTTS CO | 6,793 | 9 | 6 | D 27 | 1-1 | Bly 22 Astle 15 | Ref: K Seddon | Smith | Hampton | Bircumshaw | Sheridan | Gibson | Loxley | Fry | Astle | Hateley | Edwards | Tait |

£10,000 signing Hale has a quiet debut in a tough game in blustery conditions on a mudheap. City do well to contain the tallest inside trio in the division, but Jeff Astle evades Hill for a goal. Curtis blots out Hateley. Bly makes it five in five and City are unbeaten in 10 league and cup.

LEAGUE DIVISION 3 — Manager: Jimmy Hill — SEASON 1962-63

No	Date		Att	Pos	Pt	F-A	H-T	Scorers, Times, and Referees	1	2	3	4	5	6	7	8	9	10	11
24	26/12	A PETERBOROUGH	13,112	5	W 29	3-0	1-0	Bly 39, 56, Kearns 81 Ref: R Tinkler	Wesson Ronson	Sillett Whittaker	Kearns Sissons	Hill B Jackson	Curtis Hopkins	Farmer Simpson	Humphries Sheavils	Hale Horobin	Bly Hudson	Whitehouse Moulden	Rees McNamee
								City demolish the bemused leaders on a frozen pitch, with Posh old boy Bly the assassin. 1,000 City fans sing the new Sky Blue Song as City dominate the second half. Curtis contains Posh danger-man Hudson and Humphries excels again. Kearns runs 60 yards to bury a left-foot shot.											
25	29/12	H PETERBOROUGH	25,399	4 1	D 30	3-3	1-2	Bly 35, Whitehouse 78, Humphries 88 Horobin 9, 30, Moulden 59 Ref: J Parr	Wesson Ronson	Sillett Whittaker	Kearns Sissons	Hill B Jackson	Curtis Hopkins	Farmer Simpson	Humphries Sheavils	Hale Horobin	Bly Hudson	Whitehouse Moulden	Rees McNamee
								City's ground-staff work like Trojans to clear the majority of snow - the reward a massive crowd and a thrilling game. Errors give Posh the lead. At 1-3 City go for the long ball and it pays off. Whitehouse's header and Humphries' screamer from an acute angle prompts wild scenes.											
26	23/2	H BARNSLEY	12,649	4 15	W 32	2-0	1-0	Whitehouse 26, Hale 52 Ref: A Edge	Wesson Hill	Sillett Hooper	Kearns Brookes	Hill B Wood	Curtis Winstanley	Bruck Houghton	Humphries Hosie	Hale Burke	Bly Leighton	Whitehouse Kerr	Rees O'Hara
								Barnsley are the last team to beat Hill's men, but there is no repeat on a slimy surface as City emerge from the ice-age. Alan Hill keeps the score down and Wesson has a quiet day. Hale feeds Whitehouse, and then the favour is returned for the second goal, a rocket shot from Hale.											
27	26/2	H COLCHESTER	13,049	3 19	D 33	2-2	1-0	Bly 2, Humphries 49 Hunt RM 64, 80 Ref: J Bullough	Wesson Ames	Sillett Forbes	Kearns Fowler	Hill B McCrohan	Curtis Rutter	Farmer Hunt RR	Humphries Grice	Hale Hunt RM	Bly King	Whitehouse Hill	Rees Wright
								City fail to go joint top of the league as the Oysters take advantage of Hale's Achilles injury. The game had been fogged off in December and the U's had not played since. The weather is still very cold and the pitch hard and many home players look uncomfortable. 14 games unbeaten.											
28	2/3	A NORTHAMPTON	18,717	3 4	D 34	0-0	0-0	Ref: A Luty	Wesson Brodie	Sillett Foley	Kearns Everitt	Hill B Leck	Curtis Branston	Bruck Kurila	Humphries Hails	Barr Ashworth	Bly Large	Whitehouse Reid	Rees Lines
								A draw is fair in the table-topping clash on a gluepot pitch. Barr, in for the injured Hale, hits the bar and Whitehouse's goal-bound shot is deflected. Wesson saves the Cobblers' best efforts in front of the biggest crowd of the season at the County Ground, and Curtis masters Large.											
29	9/3	H QP RANGERS	15,029	3 10	W 36	4-1	2-0	Barr 38, Bly 41, 82, 88 Leary 89 Ref: K Walker	Wesson Smith	Sillett Williams	Kearns Ingham	Hill B Malcolm	Curtis Dugdale	Bruck Angell	Humphries McClelland	Barr Lazarus	Bly Leary	Whitehouse Bedford	Rees Barber
								QPR's defence somehow holds out to enormous City pressure till the last ten minutes. Humphries' penalty miss is forgotten as Bly nets a hat-trick, the second of which is the pick. Alec Stock's team have their chances before the break but are ultimately washed away in the steady rain.											
30	23/3	H CRYSTAL PALACE	17,860	4 22	W 38	1-0	1-0	Bly 15 Ref: H Hackney	Wesson Glazier	Sillett Howe	Kearns Townsend	Hill B Werge	Curtis Wood	Bruck Petchey	Humphries Allen	Barr Burridge	Bly Dowsett	Whitehouse Holton	Hale Lewis
								Bly beats his marker and hits a pile-driver from an acute angle past the superb Glazier. Struggling Palace are an uncultured bunch and have two men booked. City players want to stay fit for the Sunderland game and avoid trouble. Only ex-England man Ronnie Allen shows true class.											
31	1/4	A WREXHAM	11,357	4 6	L 38	1-5	1-2	Bly 11 (Barnes R 65, Griffiths 80/ Whitehouse 29, 74p, Metcalf 33, Ref: A Atherton	Wesson Keelan	Sillett Jones P	Kearns McGowan	Hill B Barnes K	Curtis Fox	Farmer Evans	Humphries Barnes R	Barr Griffiths	Bly Phythian	Whitehouse Whitehouse	Rees Metcalf
								Idea-less City look drained after the Man U cup-tie and are thumped by one of the best attacks in the division. Wesson saves a thrice-taken Ken Barnes penalty and Sillett clears three off the line as Wrexham rampage, backed by a loud crowd. City's 15-game unbeaten league run is over.											
32	6/4	H HALIFAX	19,656	4 24	W 40	5-4	4-0	Hudson 8, 20, 43, Bruck 36, White 60 Carlin 53, Tilley 55, Fidler 58, Tait 86p Knowles Ref: K Aston	Meeson	Sillett Strodder	Kearns Roscoe	Hill B Tilley	Curtis Stanley	Bruck Briar	Humphries Tait	Barr Harrison	**Hudson** South	Whitehouse Carlin	Rees Fidler
								Record £21,000 signing Hudson has a dream start as City rip Town apart in the first half. His finishing is deadly and Bruck's screamer is the icing on the cake. Six lack-a-daisical minutes costs City dear before Whitehouse steadies the ship. Town's late fight almost gets them a point.											
33	8/4	H MILLWALL	22,889	4 16	W 42	2-0	1-0	Hudson 9, John 86 (og) Ref: L Hamer	Wesson Davies	Sillett John	Kearns Cripps	Hill B Harper	Curtis Brady R	Bruck Anderson	Humphries Broadfoot	Barr Longbottom	Hudson Terry	Machin Jones	Rees Haverty
								Millwall play well above their station and the score flatters the Sky Blues. Hudson's early ice-cool goal is enough until John's vain attempt to keep a Hudson shot out near the end. Ernie Machin has a quietly impressive debut but Wesson is the star who keeps the sprightly visitors out.											
34	12/4	A BOURNEMOUTH	15,001	4 5	D 43	1-1	0-1	Barr 58 Bolton 5p Ref: G Roper	Wesson Best	Sillett Farmer	Kearns Jones	Hill B McGarry	Curtis Gater	Bruck Weller	Humphries Bolton	Barr Woods	Hudson Thompson	Whitehouse Singer	Rees Bumstead
								In their fifth game in 13 days a weary but battling City weather a storm. Brian Hill cannot believe it when a penalty is given after he fell on the ball. Hugh Barr levels from Hudson's low cross and near the end Whitehouse misses a good chance to end the Cherries' unbeaten home record.											

#		Date	Opponent	Result	Pos	Att	Scorers										
35	A	13/4	BRISTOL ROV	2-2	4	13,145 21 44	Bly 40, Humphries 51 Jones B 64, Williams 89 Ref: N Matthews	Wesson Million	Sillett Hilliard	Kletzenbauer Jones G	Hill B Bumpstead	Curtis Davis	Bruck Oldfield	Humphries Jarman	Bly Williams	Hudson Biggs	Machin Jones R	Dwight Muxworthy

Relegation-threatened Rovers grab a late point after two Wesson errors. Bly and Hudson play together for the only time and Terry is set up by back-to-form Humphries, who scores a rare header. The draw leaves City four points behind leaders Swindon, with three games in hand.

| 36 | H | 16/4 | BOURNEMOUTH | 1-2 | 5 | 30,289 4 44 | Whitehouse 78 Crickmore 25, 56 Ref: R Windle | Wesson Best | Sillett Farmer | Kearns Jones | Hill B McGarry | Curtis Gater | Bruck Bolton | Humphries Weller | Hudson Thompson | Hudson Singer | Whitehouse Crickmore | Rees |

A stunning defeat in front of the biggest league gate for 11 years questions City's pedigree. Cherries' player-manager Bill McGarry recalls Crickmore, who is deadly in front of goal. Rees should have had a penalty but jaded City's frenzied attacks founder on a rock-hard defence.

| 37 | H | 20/4 | BRIGHTON | 1-1 | 5 | 14,966 21 45 | Hill 58 Donnelly 2 Ref: F Cowen | Wesson McGonigal | Sillett Sanders | Kletzenbauer Burtenshaw | Hill B Bertolini | Curtis Gall | Bruck Cassidy | Farmer Webber | Rees Collins | Hudson Donnelly | Whitehouse Jackson | Hale Dillon |

City stay in the promotion race because Swindon are struggling as much. Lowly Brighton grab a vital point on a mud-heap. Brian Hill inspires a second-half rally after the early goal and is rewarded with a rare goal from 30 yards. The rally lacks conviction and City don't deserve a win.

| 38 | A | 27/4 | CARLISLE | 1-0 | 4 | 4,751 23 47 | Hudson 11 Ref: J Thacker | Wesson Dean | Sillett Caldwell | Kearns McBain | Hill B Thompson | Curtis Marsden | Bruck McConnell | Farmer Dagger | Hale Brayton | Hudson McIlmoyle | Whitehouse Oliphant | Rees Kirkup |

Curtis wishes City could win every time they play this badly. Luckless Carlisle look set to go down. Hudson heads in against a slack defence. City's rough tactics in keeping the lead win few friends. City fly to a game for the first time but are a pale shadow of the team a month ago.

| 39 | H | 29/4 | BRISTOL ROV | 5-0 | 4 | 20,387 19 49 | Rees 3, 88, Humphr's 28, 34, Hudson 87 Ref: J Parkinson | Wesson Hall | Sillett Hilliard | Kearns Jones G | Bruck Slocombe | Curtis Bradford | Farmer Oldfield | Humphries Jarmen | Hale Biggs | Hudson Ryden | Machin Jones R | Rees Muxworthy |

Promotion talk is aired again after a stunning display of wing play from Rees and Humphries. All five goals are crackers, with Willie's two both off the underside of the bar, but magician Hudson's is the classiest. Rees has two ruled out for offside and Hale crashes one against a post.

| 40 | A | 1/5 | READING | 1-4 | 4 | 9,551 21 49 | Farmer 63† Travers 3, Webb 21, 88, 89 Ref: J Finney | Wesson Wilkie | Sillett Walker | Kearns Meldrum | Hill B Evans | Curtis Spiers | Farmer Travers | Humphries Wheeler | Hale Norton | Hudson Allen | Whitehouse Streeves | Rees Webb |

Lowly Reading are flattered by the scoreline as once again Duggie Webb haunts City. Travers' shot bounces down from the underside of the bar and is only given by a linesman, and Webb's second looks well offside. City offer little, apart from the foul on Humphries for the penalty.

| 41 | H | 4/5 | PORT VALE | 0-0 | 4 | 18,307 6 49 | Richards 77 Ref: R Smith | Wesson Hancock K | Sillett Whalley | Kletzenbauer Sproson | Bruck Steele | Curtis Nicholson | Hill B Miles | Humphries Rowland | Barr Poole | Hudson Richards | Machin Hancock B | Rees Edwards |

The final home game is a big let-down and a third home loss makes promotion look impossible. Vale have now beaten all the top four sides in recent weeks. City miss an incredible five chances in fifteen first-half minutes. After Richards' soft goal, uninspiring City fail to lift their game.

| 42 | A | 7/5 | HULL | 0-2 | 4 | 5,255 7 49 | Cummins 69, Collinson 87 Ref: K Tuck | Wesson Williams | Sillett Davidson | Kletzenbauer Garvey | Hill B Collinson | Curtis Feasey | Farmer McMillan | Humphries Clarke | Hale Simpkin | Hudson Chilton | Machin Cummins | Dwight McSeveney |

After an uninspiring first half, the game improves but City's forwards don't. The decision to freeze out Bly looks increasingly wrong, with Hudson struggling against a big stopper. The normally solid defence looks tired as ex-Eire international Cummins booms in a 25-yarder.

| 43 | A | 11/5 | SOUTHEND | 1-1 | 5 | 9,275 7 50 | Costello 33 (og) Smith 7 Ref: D Smith | Wesson Gay | Kletzenbauer Costello | Kearns Neal | Bruck Bentley | Curtis Watson | Bruck Bradbury | Hudson Woodley | Dwight Jones | Hudson Smith | Farmer Burridge | Rees McKinven |

After three losses in a row, Hill, for the first time sets out to defend in depth. The plan backfires after 50 seconds when Kearns misjudges a back-pass. Hudson forces Lou Costello to fire into his own net but City show little adventure. The point ends a run of four losses at Roots Hall.

| 44 | A | 15/5 | CRYSTAL PALACE | 0-0 | 4 | 12,672 13 51 | Ref: J Osborne | Wesson Glazier | Sillett Howe | Barr Wood | Hill B Townsend | Curtis Long | Bruck Holton | Humphries Werge | Hale Patchey | Dwight Dowsett | Hudson Burridge | Rees Allen |

A fair result with chances at both ends. Hudson twice heads against the post and Dwight hits wood too as City attack more. Wesson keeps City secure in the last quarter with a great save from Burridge. Third place and £500 prize money looks possible. Plans unveiled for a new stand.

| 45 | A | 20/5 | SHREWSBURY | 1-2 | 6 | 4,695 15 51 | Farmer 5†p Clarke 23 Gregson 75 Ref: L Tirebuck | Wesson Beel | Sillett Walters | Kearns Skeech | Barr Harley | Curtis Dolby | Bruck Pountney | Humphries Gregson | Dwight Middleton | Hudson Clarke | Farmer Nixon | Rees French |

Another mediocre first half on a wet and windy night is followed by a lively second period. Debutant keeper Beel rugby-tackles Hudson for the spot-kick. All the players agree that Gregson's shot goes through a hole in the net and into the goal but the ref allows it. Hill fumes at the end.

| 46 | A | 22/5 | QP RANGERS | 3-1 | 4 | 3,261 13 53 | Rees 71, Sillett 74, Hale 83p Collins 77 Ref: T Reynolds | Wesson Springett | Sillett Angell | Kletzenbauer Ingham | Kearns Malcolm | Curtis Williams | Bruck Taylor | Humphries Lazarus | Hale Keen | Hudson Bedford | Machin Collins | Rees Barber |

A tiny crowd rattles around White City in the R's final game of a ten-month trial. Tony Ingham's 548th and final game ends in the R's seventh home loss. Sillett's first City goal is a booming free-kick and 17-year-old Peter Springett is beaten from the spot after Humphries is fouled.

Home Average 17,098
Away 9,968

LEAGUE DIVISION 3 (CUP-TIES)   Manager: Jimmy Hill   SEASON 1962-63

League Cup

				F-A	H-T	Scorers, Times, and Referees	1	2	3	4	5	6	7	8	9	10	11
2	H	SWANSEA	W	3-2	1-2	Whitehouse 16, Bly 49, Rees 55	Meeson	Sillett	Kletzenbauer	Hill B	Curtis	Bruck	Humphries	Barr	Bly	Whitehouse	Rees
	26/9	10,321 2:15				Meeson 14 (og), Webster 23	Dwyer	Hughes	Griffiths	Davies	Nurse	Saunders	Jones	Thomas	Webster	Williams	Morgans
						Ref: H Richards											
						City reach the third round for the first time in their second game in three days. Meeson fumbles in a Jones cross and is well beaten by ex-Busby Babe Webster. After the break City boss the game and Bly sweeps in after Bruck's shot comes off a post before Rees' 25-yard shot fizzes in.											
3	A	PORTSMOUTH	L	1-5	1-4	Laverick 38 (Gordon 39, Sillett 46 (og))	Meeson	Sillett	Kletzenbauer	Kearns	Curtis	Satchwell	Farmer	Bly	Whitehouse	Laverick
	17/10	8,685 2:13				Dodson 11, Saunders 22p, 25,	Milkins	Gunter	Wilson	Harris	Snowdon	Dickinson	Barton	Gordon	Saunders	McCann	Dodson
						Ref: D Smith											
						Pompey are struggling in Division Two but destroy injury-hit City with a dazzling display. Ex-City man McCann has a blinder, as do the wing men. Laverick's lob apart, City offer little and although the penalty is harsh it is one-way traffic. Sillett's deflection for the own-goal is deadly.											

FA Cup

				F-A	H-T	Scorers, Times, and Referees	1	2	3	4	5	6	7	8	9	10	11
1	H	BOURNEMOUTH	W	1-0	1-0	Whitehouse 9	Wesson	Sillett	Kearns	Hill B	Curtis	Farmer	Humphries	Barr	Bly	Whitehouse	Dwight
	3/11	14,499 7				Ref: G McCabe	Best	Farmer	Jones	Bolton	McGarry	Standley	Bumstead	Archer	Dowsett	Singer	Crickmore
						A blood and thunder cup-tie with two fine young keepers to the fore. 19-year-old David Best and 22-year-old Bob Wesson pull of numerous great saves. Whitehouse whips in to score from a back-pass. The Cherries fight to the end and Wesson's clawing leap stops Singer's stinger.											
2	A	MILLWALL	D	0-0	0-0		Wesson	Sillett	Kearns	Hill B	Curtis	Farmer	Humphries	Barr	Bly	Whitehouse	Rees
	24/11	14,633 18				Ref: F Cowen	Davies	John	Gilchrist	Obeney	Brady R	Wilson	Broadfoot	Jones	Terry	Anderson	Haverty
						Superb defending earns City a replay against a lively but unsubtle Millwall. The Sky Blues soak up intense pressure but nearly win it. Davies up-ends Bly well inside the area but the ref gives a free-kick outside the area. From the free-kick Jimmy Whitehouse's headed goal is ruled out.											
2R	H	MILLWALL	W	2-1	2-0	Barr 24, Whitehouse 27	Wesson	Sillett	Kearns	Hill B	Curtis	Farmer	Humphries	Barr	Dwight	Whitehouse	Rees
	27/11	22,434 18				Jones 49p	Davies	John	Gilchrist	Obeney	Brady R	Wilson	Spiers	Jones	Terry	Anderson	Haverty
						Ref: F Cowen											
						Millwall come to defend in depth but a superb individual Barr goal and the impressive Whitehouse's diving header force them out. Curtis's reckless challenge is punished with a penalty. Millwall briefly threaten and the result is in doubt till the end. A record £3,816 taken at the gate.											
3	A	LINCOLN	W	5-1	3-0	Whitehouse 1, Jackson 13 (og), Barr 44,	Wesson	Sillett	Kearns	Hill B	Curtis	Bruck	Humphries	Barr	Bly	Whitehouse	Rees
	6/3	7,440 4:15				Punter 76 [Bly 66, Farmer 75]	Carling	Jones	Smith	Middleton	Jackson	Franks	Bannister	Campbell	Punter	Linnecor	Scanlon
						Ref: J Pickles											
						At the sixteenth attempt the game finally goes ahead 60 days late and Whitehouse nets after 15 seconds. The game is over by half-time as slick City rout the Imps. Lincoln briefly briefly after the break before a Bly thunderbolt and a cool Farmer wrap up the win to the joy of 700 City fans.											
4	A	PORTSMOUTH	D	1-1	0-1	Hale 85	Wesson	Sillett	Kearns	Hill B	Curtis	Bruck	Humphries	Hale	Bly	Whitehouse	Rees
	13/3	11,482 2:12				Saunders 10	Milkins	Gunter	Wilson	Harris	Snowdon	Dickinson	Yeo	Gordon	Saunders	McCann	Dodson
						Ref: A Sturgeon											
						Never-say-die City recover from Saunders' fluke goal to dominate their higher status opponents and miss a hatful of chances. Hale's screamer sparks a dramatic finale, with Milkins' agile save keeping Whitehouse's goal-bound shot out. The princely Hale is back and in brilliant form.											
4R	H	PORTSMOUTH	D	2-2 aet	2-0	Whitehouse 3, 44	Wesson	Sillett	Kearns	Hill B	Curtis	Farmer	Humphries	Hale	Bly	Whitehouse	Rees
	16/3	25,642 2:12				McCann 58, Saunders 74	Shearing	Gunter	Dickinson	Campbell	Snowdon	Harris	Yeo	Gordon	Saunders	McCann	Dodson
						Ref: A Sturgeon											
						Pompey are let off the hook after a one-sided first half. Whitehouse mesmerises George Smith's men with a vicious shot and deft header, but ex-City man Albie McCann scores one and makes the other. Fruitless extra-time means a third tie at Tottenham. Record receipts of £4,454.											
4 RR	N	PORTSMOUTH	W	2-1	2-1	Bly 21, Whitehouse 37	Wesson	Sillett	Kearns	Hill B	Curtis	Bruck	Humphries	Barr	Bly	Whitehouse	Rees
	19/3	15,867 2:13				Saunders 13	Milkins	Gunter	Wilson	Harris	Snowdon	Dickinson	Barton	Gordon	Saunders	McCann	Neil
		(at White Hart Ln)				Ref: A Sturgeon											
						City deservedly make it 21 unbeaten League and FA Cup games after recovering from Saunders' early rocket. The immaculate Brian Hill again blots out the threat of Gordon. Bly nets his 25th goal and his deft header creates the winner. The Sky Blue Song is deafening throughout.											

5	H	SUNDERLAND	4	W	2:1	0-1	Bruck 82, Curtis 85			
	25/3		40,487	2:1			Crossan 33			
							Ref: G McCabe			
QF	H	MANCHESTER U	4	L	1:3	1-1	Bly 5			
	30/3		44,000	1:17			Charlton 27, 49, Quixall 72			
							Ref: E Crawford			

Wesson	Sillett	Kearns	Hill B	Curtis	Humphries	Bruck	Barr	Bly	Whitehouse	Rees
Montgomery	Nelson	Ashurst	Anderson	Hurley	Davison	McNab	Herd	Sharkey	Crossan	Mulhall

Amazing scenes as City reach the last eight for the first time since 1910. The second division leaders are in charge till half-time and have the breaks when City are on top after the break. A memorable last ten minutes. Bruck's 30-yard lob sails in and Curtis' header seals a famous win.

Wesson	Sillett	Kearns	Hill B	Curtis	Humphries	Bruck	Barr	Bly	Whitehouse	Rees
Gregg	Brennan	Dunne	Crerand	Foulkes	Setters	Stiles	Quixall	Herd	Law	Charlton

Another post-war record crowd and £8,600 in receipts as Busby's men end the great cup run. City boss the early play and almost go 2-0 up but United regroup and Charlton takes over. City don't have the luck, Bly hitting the bar and Humphries' goal ruled out, but United go through.

	P	W	D	L	Home F	A	W	D	L	Away F	A	Pts
1 Northampton	46	16	6	1	64	19	4	9	10	45	41	62
2 Swindon	46	18	2	3	60	22	4	12	7	27	34	58
3 Port Vale	46	16	4	3	47	25	7	4	12	25	33	54
4 COVENTRY	46	14	6	3	54	28	4	11	8	29	41	53
5 Bournemouth	46	11	12	0	39	16	7	4	12	24	30	52
6 Peterborough	46	11	5	7	48	33	9	6	8	45	42	51
7 Notts Co	46	15	3	5	46	29	4	10	9	27	45	51
8 Southend	46	11	7	5	38	24	8	5	10	37	53	50
9 Wrexham	46	14	6	3	54	27	6	3	14	30	56	49
10 Hull	46	12	6	5	40	22	7	4	12	34	47	48
11 Crys Palace	46	10	7	6	38	22	7	6	10	30	36	47
12 Colchester	46	11	6	6	41	35	6	5	11	32	58	47
13 QP Rangers	46	9	8	6	44	36	8	5	10	41	40	45
14 Bristol C	46	10	9	4	54	38	6	4	13	46	54	45
15 Shrewsbury	46	13	4	6	57	41	3	8	12	26	40	44
16 Millwall	46	11	6	6	50	32	4	7	12	32	55	43
17 Watford	46	12	3	8	55	40	5	5	13	27	45	42
18 Barnsley	46	12	6	5	39	28	3	5	15	24	46	41
19 Bristol Rov	46	11	8	4	45	29	4	3	16	25	59	41
20 Reading	46	13	4	6	51	30	3	4	16	23	48	40
21 Bradford PA	46	10	9	4	43	36	5	3	16	36	61	40
22 Brighton	46	7	6	10	28	38	5	5	13	30	46	36
23 Carlisle	46	12	4	7	41	37	1	7	15	17	20	52	35
24 Halifax	46	8	3	12	41	51	1	5	17	23	55	30
	1104	287	138	127	1117	738	127	136	287	738	1117	1104

Odds & ends

Double wins: (3) Halifax, Carlisle, QPR.
Double losses: (1) Port Vale.

Won from behind: (6) Watford (h), Halifax (a), Carlisle (h), Swansea LC (h), Portsmouth FAC (h), Sunderland FAC (h).
Lost from in front: (4) Watford (a), Port Vale (a), Wrexham (a), Man U FAC (h).

High spots: FA Cup run to quarter-finals.
Unbeaten run of 23 games (15 in the league).
Goalscoring feats of Terry Bly.
Win at Peterborough.
Hudson's debut hat-trick.

Low spots: Slump after FA Cup exit.
Home defeats to Southend and Bournemouth.
Poor away form.

Red cards: (0).
Red cards opponents: (0).
Hat-tricks: (3) Bly (Southend h), Bly (QPR h), Hudson (Halifax h).
Opposing hat-tricks: (2) Beasley (Southend h), Webb (Reading a).
Leading scorer: (29) Terry Bly.

	Appearances				Goals			
	Lge	Sub	LC	Sub	FAC	Sub	Lge	LC	FAC	Tot
Austin, Frank	8								
Barr, Hugh	34	1	2		7		12	2		14
Bly, Terry	32		2		8		25	1	3	29
Bruck, Dietmar	24	2	2		4		1			2
Curtis, George	45	2	2		9		1		1	1
Dwight, Roy	13				2		1			1
Farmer, Ron	22		1		5		6			7
Hale, Ken	15				2		2		1	7
Hill, Brian	37				9		1			3
Hudson, George	15	1					6			1
Humphries, Willie	41	1	1		9		10			6
Kearns, Mick	36	1	1		9		2			10
Kletzenbauer, Frank	19	2								2
Laverick, Bobby	4	1						1		1
Lightening, Arthur	4									
Machin, Ernie	6									
Meeson, Dave	15	2								
Rees, Ronnie	33	1	1		8		4		1	5
Satchwell, Ken			1							
Sillett, John	38	2	2		9		1			1
Tedds, Bill	1									
Wesson, Bob	27				9					
Whitehouse, Jimmy	37		2		9					
(own-goals)							9	1	6	16
							3		1	4
(23 players used)	506		22		99		83	4	16	103

LEAGUE DIVISION 3 — Manager: Jimmy Hill — SEASON 1963-64

No	Date	H/A	Opponent	Att	Pos	Pt	F-A	H-T	Scorers, Times, and Referees	1	2	3	4	5	6	7	8	9	10	11
1	24/8	H	CRYSTAL PALACE	26,037		W	5-1	1-1	Machin 44, Farmer 61p, 84p, 87, Burridge 43 [Hudson 80] Ref: J Carr	Wesson	Sillett	Kearns	Hill	Curtis	Farmer	Humphries	Hale	Hudson	Machin	Rees
										Glazier	Howe	Townsend	Long	Wood	Petchey	Werge	Holton	Dowsett	Burridge	Allen
									For the second year running Palace use strong-arm tactics but they back-fire disastrously. Late goals flatter City and the first penalty is harsh. Machin's header levels Burridge's 25-yarder, and Farmer's 35-yard free-kick goes in via a post. Despite conceding five, Bill Glazier impresses.											
2	29/8	A	NOTTS CO	18,669		W	3-0	1-0	Hudson 21, 46, Humphries 51 Ref: A Sparling	Wesson	Sillett	Kearns	Hill	Curtis	Farmer	Humphries	Hale	Hudson	Machin	Rees
										Smith	Edwards	Bircumshaw	Sheridan	Gibson	Loxley	Povey	Astle	Bly	Tait	Barber
									City romp home in front of their 3,000 fans with Hudson winning the duel between him and Terry Bly. Terry is easily contained by Curtis, and Hudson scores two opportunist goals, the second from a sublime header. Humphries' shot is off the post and 'The Hud' misses more chances.											
3	31/8	A	WALSALL	17,440	1	W	3-0	0-0	Hudson 57, Rees 59, Farmer 76 Ref: A Jones	Wesson	Kletzenbauer	Kearns	Hill	Curtis	Farmer	Humphries	Hale	Hudson	Machin	Rees
					23					White	Palin	Sharples	Dudley	McPherson	Howells	Meek	Hodgkisson	Newton	Matthews	Fell
									Relegated Walsall start well and upset City. The storm is weathered and, roared on by 5,000 fans, City destroy the Saddlers after the break. Hudson blasts in after Hill's header is parried, Rees buries Hill's cross and Farmer hits a 30-yard screamer as the Sky Blue Song booms out.											
4	7/9	H	READING	24,992	1	D	0-0	0-0	Ref: K Dagnall	Wesson	Sillett	Kearns	Hill	Curtis	Farmer	Humphries	Hale	Hudson	Machin	Rees
					20					Dixon	Neate	Meldrum	Evans	Spiers	Thornhill	Morris	Wheeler	Kerr	Shreeves	Jones
									On a wet day City lose their 100% record with a poor display. Reading are not overawed, contain City's weak efforts and almost catch them on the break away with Bob Wesson having to pull off a diving save. Kerr's late 'goal' is ruled out for offside after Hudson's header goes wide.											
5	10/9	H	NOTTS CO	27,796	1	W	2-0	0-0	Humphries 74, Hudson 88 Ref: H Richards	Wesson	Sillett	Kearns	Hill	Curtis	Farmer	Humphries	Hale	Hudson	Machin	Rees
					24					Butler	Hampton	Bircumshaw	Edwards	Gibson	Carver	Povey	Jones	Bly	Astle	Flower
									Keeper Butler keeps Eddie Lowe's team in the game but City finally break through County's massed defence by switching tactics to the long ball. Hudson is the hero, again outshining the sole striker Bly, making the first goal and heading home after good work by Ken Hale and Rees.											
6	14/9	A	LUTON	14,511	1	W	3-1	2-0	Barr 2, Humphries 6, 65 Daniel 56p Ref: N Burtenshaw	Wesson	Sillett	Kearns	Hill	Curtis	Farmer	Humphries	Hale	Barr	Machin	Rees
					19					Baynham	Daniel	McBain	McGuffie	Fincham	Bramwell	Walden	Turner	Fairchild	Pacey	Weir
									Almost half the crowd are City fans and they give great vocal support. Relegated Luton are put to the sword early on with 'Yogi' Barr netting with his second touch. Ron Baynham keeps the score down but is beaten by Humphries' diving header. Wesson trips Fairchild for the penalty.											
7	17/9	H	CREWE	29,571	1	W	5-1	2-0	Hale 28, Hudson 30, 51, Keery 54 (og), King 87 [Machin 73] Ref: B Setchell	Wesson	Sillett	Kearns	Hill	Curtis	Farmer	Humphries	Hale	Hudson	Machin	Rees
					17					Hickson	Whelan	Leigh	Keery	Barnes	Riggs	Wheatley	Shepherd	Lord	King	Smith
									Promoted Crewe are the latest victims of slick City. Machin, Hale and Hudson are immense and 'The Hud' scores two and makes Machin's header but misses a hat-trick when Whelan clears a header off the line. Keery heads an own-goal and Riggs' penalty is well saved by Wesson.											
8	21/9	A	HULL	12,315	1	L	1-2	0-1	Hale 46 Ref: K Howley	Wesson	Sillett	Kearns	Hill	Curtis	Farmer	Humphries	Hale	Hudson	Machin	Rees
					12					Swan	Davidson	Butler	Sharpe	Milner	MacMillan	Clarke	Henderson	Chilton	Simpkin	McSeveney
									The unbeaten run ends in an unsatisfactory way. Hull give City a tough first half but Hale's angled shot levels things. With City on top, George Curtis is adjudged to have handled but most judges think it was a header outside the area. Mystery too over Hudson's earlier disallowed 'goal'.											
9	28/9	H	MANSFIELD	22,994	2	L	0-3	0-1	Tyrer 4, Coates 62, Wagstaff 73 Ref: W Faulkner	Wesson	Sillett	Kearns	Hill	Curtis	Farmer	Humphries	Hale	Hudson	Whitehouse	Rees
					8					Treharne	Toon	Humble	Chapman S	Gill	Morris	Boner	Coates	Wagstaff	Hollett	Tyrer
									Promoted Mansfield spring a big shock as City again fail to break down a packed defence. The injured Machin is missed and a limping Kearns is a passenger and the Stags grab their few chances. Keeper Treharne has a blinder but City are a pale shadow and it's a sharp reminder for all.											
10	2/10	A	CREWE	7,583	3	D	2-2	1-0	Hudson 44, Hale 86 Lord 65, Dillon 75 Ref: K Norman	Wesson	Sillett	Kearns	Hill	Curtis	Farmer	Humphries	Hale	Hudson	Machin	Rees
					21					Hickson	Whelan	Leigh	Keery	Ewing	Riggs	Shepherd	Tait	Lord	King	Dillon
									After bossing the first half City relax and are hustled out of their game by a gutsy Crewe display. Lord causes panic in City ranks and gives Curtis a hard ride. City recover their poise just in time for Hale to drive home after Hudson's flick on from a free-kick. A draw is a fair result.											
11	5/10	A	BRENTFORD	15,829	3	W	3-2	1-0	Farmer 32p, Hudson 70, Rees 85 Dick 76, McAdams 89 Ref: M Fussey	Wesson	Sillett	Kearns	Hill	Curtis	Farmer	Humphries	Hale	Hudson	Machin	Rees
					13					Ryecraft	Coote	Jones	Smith	Scott	Crowe	Block	Brooks	McAdams	Dick	Hales
									City are unlucky not to win this thriller 5-1 in what Derrick Robins describes as 'the best away display in 10 years'. Scott up-ends Humphries for the penalty. Hudson nets after fine work by Machin and Farmer. Rees turns in a Machin corner as the Sky Blues have 27 shots on target.											

182

#	H/A	Date	W/D/L	Score	Att / Pos	Scorers / Ref	Wesson	Sillett	Kearns	Hill	Curtis	Farmer	Humphries	Hale	Hudson	Machin	Rees
12	H	8/10	W	2-1	23,884 / 17 / 18	Hale 8, Hudson 34 / Hooper 82 / Ref: H Hackney	Gibson	Ford	Briggs	Parr	Connor	Low	Derrick	Clark	Atyeo	Williams	Hooper
						The late goal flatters Bristol, with poor finishing and a good keeper key facto's. City fail to drive home their superiority and fans have a nail-biting finish. Hale pounces on a loose ball at a corner before the dazzling Hudson lashes in after Hale's long cross bounces off Gibson's chest.											
13	H	12/10	W	3-0	23,881 / 22 / 20	Hale 50, Hudson 62, Rees 65 / Ref: P Eye	Wesson	Fleet	Holland	Lambert	Fox	Jones T	Myerscough	Phythian	Hudson	Metcalf	Mitten Bent
						Willie Humphries is absent on international duty but two goals from stand-in Mitten's inswinging corners relieve City's first-half nerves. Hale scrambles in the first and Rees heads home another. In between, the hard-working Hudson slips the off-side trap and nets John Mitten's cross.											
14	A	15/10	W	1-0	13,582 / 17 / 22	Hale 4 / Ref: J Finney	Gibson	Briggs	Thresher	Parr	Connor	Low	Derrick	Clark	Atyeo	Williams	Hooper
						Hale's early shot deflects off a defender to give City a lucky lead but they are rarely troubled by the home side. Gibson is the much busier keeper as Hill's men get applauded for some good play. Later, as Bristol rally, the defence holds firm and Wesson has only one save to make.											
15	A	19/10	L	1-2	7,189 / 12 / 22	Humphries 86 / Hunt 12, Grice 32 / Ref: S Stoakes	Wesson	Forbes	Woods	McCrohan	Rutter	Docherty	Grice	Hunt RR	King	Stark	Wright
						An off-colour display is punished by a lively Oysters' team who defend their lead like an away team. City's out of touch forwards cannot break them down and even Curtis's move up-front fails to change the game. Ex-City man Mike Grice hits a screamer that stuns the 1,500 City fans.											
16	H	22/10	W	8-1	27,344 / 3 / 24	Harley 2 (og), Hudson 33, 71, Barr 44, 80, [Rees 46, 69, 87] / Brodie 3 / Ref: D Brady	Wesson	Wright	Turner	Harley	Dolby	Hemsley	Gregson	Ross	Clarke	Brodie	Middleton Rees
						After an even first half, everything clicks for a slick Sky Blues. 18-year-old Eeel errs for two of the goals as his defence lose their heads with a flurry of fouls. Machin fails to net but is the star in a compelling rout of a far poor Town, as City score eight for the first time in 30 years.											
17	H	26/10	D	2-2	25,928 / 12 / 25	Machin 3, Hudson 32 / Harris 78, 84 / Ref: K Walker	Jennings	Bell	Nicholas	Crisp	Mancini	Cateugh	Spelman	Larkin	Livesey	Oliver	Harris
						Anti-climax after the Shrewsbury game. City threaten to notch another big score but Machin's serious knee injury just after the break upsets the flow. The Hornets revive and almost win it at the death, missing three golden chances. City look fragile at the back, with Brian Hill missed.											
18	A	30/10	D	0-0	13,669 / 5 / 26	/ Ref: R Egan	Boswell	Wright	Turner	Harley	Dolby	Hemsley	Gregson	Ross	Clarke	Gould	Middleton
						Luck deserts the Shrews again in a match they dominate. Injury-hit Sky Blue have to defend all night as Arthur Rowley's team seek revenge. Rowley himself hits a post and Middleton has a 'goal' ruled out, but Wesson holds firm. 3,000 City fans brave the wet to cheer their heroes.											
19	A	2/11	W	2-1	12,003 / 18 / 28	Hale 22, Rees 57 / Bradbury 61p / Ref: R Spittle	Rhodes	Costello	Neal	Kletzenbauer	Watson	Bradbury	Slater	Smith	Conway	Beesley	Woodley
						City fly to Southend and fly out with two points despite a late battering from the Shrimpers. A deserved win for 2,000 City fans, with the sharp Hale heading in and a Hudson-inspired Rees goal. Curtis rides the crowd with his strong tackles but Ron Farmer floors Smith for the penalty.											
20	H	9/11	W	3-2	29,633 / 16 / 30	Hale 26, 51, Hudson 41 / Cooper 16, Dougan 21 / Ref: R Harper	Duff	Singleton	Sissons	Cooper	Rankmore	Pearce	Moulden	Horobin	Smith	Dougan	Senior
						An ugly first half ends with captains Curtis and Dougan being lectured by the ref. The Doog inspires Posh's fine start but Wesson errs for both goals. Hale-inspired City fight back with three scrappy goals but look tired in the closing stages. Wesson atones by saving Moulden's rocket.											
21	H	23/11	W	4-2	23,901 / 14 / 32	Humphries 44, Hudson 70, 81, Hale 71 / Mabbutt 38, Brown 80 / Ref: J Cattlin	Hall	Hillard	Jones G	Stone	Bradford	Mabbutt	Jarman	Brown	Biggs	Hamilton	Jenkins
						Bert Tann's Rovers give City a close game in the Cup rehearsal and the opportunist Hudson is the difference. Humphries looks tired after a midweek international at Wembley but scores with a boomer. Rovers lack a finisher. The gate is down but still the fifth largest in the League.											
22	A	30/11	W	6-3	10,897 / 16 / 34	Hudson 34, 53, 59, Humph 41, Hale 56, Bedford 11, 78, Keen 79 [Rees 70] / Ref: N Matthews	Springett	Brady P	Angell	Malcolm	Brady R	Keen	Lazarus	Leary	Bedford	Collins	McQuade
						QPR bosses Alec Stock says City are best Div 3 side he's ever seen and Loncon press wax lyrically about Hill's men. Willie and the Hud star but it's a team effort in the mud. The sublime Hudson terrorises Brady and makes it three hat-tricks in 15 days. 2,000 City fans roar then on.											
23	A	14/12	D	1-1	18,942 / 3 / 35	Humphries 77 / Stephenson 23 / Ref: J Lowry	Glazier	Sewell	Howe	Petchey	Wood	Stephenson	Kellard	Whitehouse	Birch	Burridge	Allen
						Captain Curtis's leg needs seven stitches but he returns to inspire a fight-back. In an ugly game Howe is booked for three vicious tackles on Humphries, who recovers to score a screamer. In a thrilling finale Hudson almost grabs a goal before Wesson robs Allen with a diving save.											

LEAGUE DIVISION 3 — Manager: Jimmy Hill — SEASON 1963-64

184

No	Date		Att	Pos	Pt	F-A	H-T	Scorers, Times, and Referees	1	2	3	4	5	6	7	8	9	10	11
24	H 21/12	WALSALL	19,563	1	15	W 1-0	0-0	Hale 55 Ref: W Haynes	Wesson White	Sillett Roper	Kearns Sharples	Hill Palin	Curtis McPherson	Farmer Wills	Humphries Meek	Whitehouse Matthews	Hudson Newton	Hale Hodkisson	Rees Foster
					37			On a rock-hard icy pitch City show their pedigree and deservedly go six points clear at the top. Caretaker-boss Alf Wood comes with a blanket defence but the skills of Hudson and Hale unlock the door and the score flatters the Saddlers. Ex-City man Newton muffs their best chance.											
25	A 26/12	BARNSLEY	12,502	1	20	D 1-1	1-0	Whitehouse 38 O'Hara 72p Ref: A Sparling	Wesson Hill	Sillett Hopper	Kearns Brookes	Hill Wood	Curtis Winstanley	Farmer Houghton	Humphries Sheavills	Whitehouse Kerr	Hudson Leighton	Hale Byrne	Rees O'Hara
					38			3,000 City fans and the players are fuming at the controversial penalty for handball. City's goal is a delightful move involving Humphries and Ken Hale but City fade after the break. Barnsley play the long-ball in the mud and are rewarded. City's first point in eight visits to Oakwell.											
26	H 28/12	BARNSLEY	26,922	1	20	W 3-1	1-0	Hudson 23, 86, Hale 89 Byrne 49 Ref: C Duxbury	Wesson Williamson	Sillett Hopper	Kearns Brookes	Hill Wood	Curtis Winstanley	Farmer Houghton	Rees Sheavills	Hale Cochrane	Hudson Leighton	Bruck Byrne	Mitten O'Hara
					40			City leave it late to finish off Johnny Steele's plucky team. Bad shooting and brave keeping keeps the score down as City have 30 shots to seven. The imperious Hudson nets a diving header and a crisp shot from Sillett's run but has two ruled out. Hale bulldozes through for his goal.											
27	H 3/1	MILLWALL	27,487	1	21	W 3-0	2-0	Rees 12, Humphries 23, Farmer 64p Ref: J Parkinson	Wesson Stepney	Kletzenbauer Gilchrist	Kearns Finnegan	Hill Anderson	Curtis Snowdon	Farmer Wilson	Humphries McLaughlin	Whitehouse Towend	Hudson Haverty	Hale Terry	Rees Jones
					42			Hudson plays this Friday night game with a groin strain and could have scored three. He heads down for Ronnie Rees' opener and his goal-bound shot is handled by Anderson for the penalty. Billy Gray's Lions offer little and are unable to stop the Sky Blues going eight points clear.											
28	A 11/1	READING	17,102	1	6	D 2-2	2-0	Whitehouse 17, 18 Kerr 76, Thornhill 83 Ref: J Cooke	Wesson Wilkie	Sillett Walker	Kletzenbauer Meldrum	Hill Evans	Curtis Spiers	Farmer Thornhill	Humphries Wheeler	Whitehouse Kerr	Barr Tindall	Hale Allen	Rees Jones
					43			A stomach bug affects City's players and several are less than 100% fit. Ex-Reading man Whitehouse's goals look set to break a 55-year bogey at Elm Park, but a spirited revival pegs back the Sky Blues. Jimmy's second goal seems to have hit a post but the linesman confirms the goal.											
29	H 18/1	LUTON	20,921	1	24	D 3-3	2-3	Rees 26, Farmer 33, Kletzenbauer 88 McKechnie 6, 9, Turner 41 Ref: J Pickles	Wesson Baynham	Kearns McBain	Kletzenbauer Bramwell	Hill Morton	Curtis Fincham	Farmer Lownds	Humphries Turner	Whitehouse McKechnie	Barr O'Rourke	Hale Reid	Rees Walden
					44			Kletz saves the 14-match unbeaten run with a stunning late goal as the Hatters tear up the form book and almost get a first away win. Bill Harvey's men wear canvas boots on an icy pitch and dance rings round a slow City defence. Ron Farmer's thunderous volley is the best goal.											
30	A 22/1	OLDHAM	20,008	1	2	L 0-2	0-1	Ledger 17, Whitaker 79 Ref: R Harper	Wesson Bollands	Kletzenbauer Branagan	Kearns Taylor	Hill Frizzell	Curtis Williams	Farmer Sievewright	Humphries Johnstone	Machin Ledger	Barr Bowie	Hale Colquhoun	Rees Whitaker
					44			Ernie Machin's premature return ends in further injury as City lose for the first time since October. The injured Sillett and Hudson are sorely missed in an exciting, close evening tussle. The Curtis-Ledger battle is fascinating but the Oldham man scores one goal and makes the other.											
31	H 1/2	HULL	23,476	1	9	D 2-2	1-0	Farmer 36p, Rees 80 Davidson 52, Chilton 73p Ref:	Wesson Williams	Sillett Davidson	Kearns Butler	Hill Collinson	Curtis Feasey	Farmer MacMillan	Humphries Clarke	Whitehouse Wilkinson	Barr Chilton	Hale Henderson	Rees McSeveney
					45			More chances squandered and another late goal saves City. Farmer coolly nets from the spot after Humphries is tripped. Cliff Britton's team are gritty but City let them off the hook. Lead cut to five points.											
32	A 8/2	MANSFIELD	16,755	1	10	L 2-3	1-1	Hill 28, Farmer 87p Chapman R 36, 71, Hall 64 Ref: G Grundy	Wesson Treharne	Sillett Jones	Kearns Humble	Hill Chapman S	Curtis Gill	Farmer Morris	Humphries Hall	Whitehouse Govan	Hudson Wagstaff	Hale Chapman R	Rees Scanlon
					45			Poor finishing is damaging the promotion hopes as the Stags complete the double. City are the better team but Tommy Cummings' team are ruthless in front of goal, with Ken Wagstaffe superb. 5,000 City fans see chances galore spurned but Rees' disallowed 'goal' at 1-1 looks good.											
33	H 15/2	BRENTFORD	22,775	1	17	D 2-2	1-1	Crowe 26 (og), Hale 54 Dick 2, Ward 47 Ref: J Cattlin	Wesson Brodie	Sillett Jones	Kletzenbauer Thomson	Hill Higginson	Curtis Scott	Farmer Crowe	Humphries Lazarus	Barr Ward	Newton McAdams	Hale Dick	Rees Block
					46			The lead is cut to two points after a third home draw in a row. New boy Newton hits the post and causes problems but it's a shoddy team display against an average Bees team. Matt Crowe deflects Ron Farmer's shot and Hale heads in a free-kick. Even Curtis looks shaky today.											
34	A 22/2	WREXHAM	9,847	1	23	D 1-1	0-0	Newton 67 Jones P 83 Ref: W Crossley	Meeson Fleet	Sillett Robertson	Kletzenbauer Holland	Hill Barnes	Curtis Fox	Kearns Jones P	Farmer Mayers	Newton Myerscough	Gould McMillan	Hale Phythian	Rees Colbridge
					47			Seven games without a win after Hill adopts negative tactics to keep out Ken Barnes' struggling team. Wesson is dropped for Dave Meeson and Gould stands in for 'The Hud'. A breakaway by Hill creates Newton's own goal but still City defend and are punished by Jones' thumper.											

#	H/A	Date	Opponent	W/D/L	Score	Pos	Scorers	Att	1	2	3	4	5	6	7	8	9	10	11	Opp 1	Opp 2	Opp 3	Opp 4	Opp 5	Opp 6	Opp 7	Opp 8	Opp 9	Opp 10	Opp 11	Report
35	H	29/2	BOURNEMOUTH	D	2-2	48	Newton 18, Hill 26, Crickmore 38, Woods 80 Ref: R Egan	24,955	Meeson	Best	Farmer	Kearns	Keith	Hill	Groves	Curtis	Gater	Farmer	Bolton	Humphries	Bumstead	Newton	Woods	Hudson	Coughlin	Hale	O'Neill	Rees	Crickmore			David Best's superb form keeps a rejuvenated City at bay. 35 shots rain in on the Cherries' goal and City throw away a two-goal lead. Hudson, back from injury, but is not at his best. Brian Hill's 25-yard left-foot shot deserves to win the game but Crickmore's goal is five yards offside.
36	A	7/3	WATFORD	D	1-1	49	Hale 56 Oliver 74 Ref: M Fussey	23,410	Meeson	Jennings	Bell	Kearns	Jones	Hill	Crisp	Curtis	Chung	Farmer	Welbourne	Humphries	Fraser	Newton	McAnearney	Hudson	Livesey	Hale	Oliver	Rees	Harris			Watford's largest post-war crowd provide a cup-tie atmosphere with 6,000 City fans in vocal form. Both centre-halves have blinders. Young Irish 'keeper Pat Jennings saves brilliantly from Humphries and Rees as City pile on the heat. Meeson is beaten by a soft goal for a fair result.
37	H	13/3	SOUTHEND	L	2-5	49	Farmer 54p, Hudson 68 (Woodley 78) Gilfillan 10, Farmer 30 (og), Beesley 32, 63, 83 Ref: J Mitchell	28,887	Meeson	Boy	Costello	Kearns	King	Hill	Bentley	Curtis	Watson	Farmer	Bradbury	Humphries	Woodley	Newton	Gilfillan	Hudson	Conway	Hale	Beesley	Rees	McKinven			A tenth game without a win means City lose the top spot on Friday the 13th. City concede five at home for the first time since the war. Two goals are defensive errors (Meeson and Hill) and two are breakaways as City chase the game. Farmer is fouled for the penalty. Hill must act.
38	A	21/3	BOURNEMOUTH	L	1-2	49	Rees 38 Bumstead 10, 77 Ref: T Dawes	16,085	Meeson	Best	Farmer	Kearns	Keith	Hill	Groves	Curtis	Gater	Farmer	Bolton	Humphries	Bumstead	Hale	Woods	Hudson	Coughlin	Smith	O'Neill	Rees	Coxon			New signings Smith and Kirby make little impression for a jittery Sky Blues. Meeson saves Coughlin's early spot-kick after Kearns handles, but errs for Bumstead's headed winner. Humphries is axed but the attack is lop-sided. Again Best is in great form and saves Kirby's best shot.
39	H	28/3	OLDHAM	W	4-1	51	Kirby 5, 69, 88, Newton 8 Craig 77 Ref: J Lowry	23,516	Wesson	Bollands	Branagan	Hill	McGinn	Bruck	McCall	Curtis	Williams	Farmer	Sievewright	Humphries	Ledger	Newton	Bowie	Hudson	Lister	Smith	Craig	Rees	Colquhoun			Kirby's three headers on his home debut end the 11-game winless run but it's not very convincing. Hudson, Hale and Meeson are dropped and new left-back Hill crosses for the first two goals, with Humphries crossing for the last two. Oldham have slumped since January and offer little.
40	A	30/3	PORT VALE	W	1-0	52	Wilson 3 (og) Steele 86 Ref: H Wilson	17,567	Wesson	Hancock	Whalley	Kearns	Wilson	Bruck	Poole	Curtis	Nicholson	Farmer	Sproson	Humphries	Bingham	Hale	Mudie	Smith	Richards	Smith	Steele	Rees	Smith R			City look calmer at last but decide to defend in depth after the break. A breakaway goal punishes their cautiousness in a rough and tumble game. Hill is superb against Irish cap Bingham, and Curtis snuffs out the wily Richards. Rees' shot hits a post and deflects off poor Wilson.
41	H	31/3	PORT VALE	D	1-1	53	Kirby 63 Smith R 57 Ref: E Norman	29,641	Wesson	Hancock	Whalley	Kearns	Wilson	Bruck	Rawlings	Curtis	Nicholson	Farmer	Sproson	Mitten	Bingham	Newton	Mudie	Smith	Harkin	Kirby	Steele	Rees	Smith R			Possession counts for nothing against an iron defence as City pound away without success. Freddie Steele's men put nine men behind the ball and frustrate City. Wesson, harassed by Harkin, lets Smith's lob go under the bar. Kirby's clinical finish from Bruck's cross restores parity.
42	A	4/4	BRISTOL ROV	W	1-0	55	Hale 46 Ref: J Pickles	12,006	Wesson	Hall	Hillard	Kearns	Jones G	Bruck	Mabbutt	Curtis	Stone	Farmer	Munro	Humphries	Frude	Hale	Biggs	Smith	Brown	Kirby	Jones R				City notch a first away win since November at wet and windy Eastville. A gutsy team display earns the points but the last 30 minutes are nerve-racking for the 3,000 fans. Hale's goal comes 13 seconds into the second half after Munro slips to let him in. Smith later hits the bar.
43	H	11/4	QP RANGERS	W	4-2	57	Humphries 4, Rees 17, Farmer 72p, Collins 12, 23 (Kirby 85) Smith F	Brady P	Angell	Ref: S Kayley	27,384	Wesson	Sillett	Brady P	Angell	Kearns	Hill	Malcolm	Curtis	Brady R	Farmer	Gibbs	Humphries	Collins	Hale	Bedford	Smith	Leary	Kirby	Keen	Rees	McLeod	Just as another draw seems likely Kirby is up-ended for Farmer's eighth penalty of the season. City go top as Palace are beaten but it is a stuttering display against negative R's. Humphries scores after Kirby's miskick, Rees' goal is a boomer and Kirby heads home Hale's corner.
44	A	18/4	MILLWALL	D	0-0	58	Ref: K Howley	22,443	Wesson	Stepney	Gilchrist	Kearns	John	Hill	Anderson	Curtis	Leedham	Farmer	Wilson	Humphries	Senior	Hale	Whitehouse	Newton	Terry	Smith	Townend	Rees	Curran			8,000 City fans watch a dour physical tussle with little football played. Farmer's 43rd-minute penalty miss is his first after 12 successful ones. He changes his direction and Stepney is fooled but the shot hits the post. Millwall have few chances against a George Curtis-inspired defence.
45	A	20/4	PETERBOROUGH	L	0-2	58	Thompson 33, Dougan 70 Ref: A Sparling	26,307	Wesson	Duff	Singleton	Kearns	Wright	Hill	Rankmore	Curtis	Rutter	Farmer	Jackson	Humphries	Thompson	Newton	Moulden	Hudson	Dougan	Smith	Smith	Rees	McNamee			A Posh record league crowd, including 12,000 from Coventry, see City's promotion hopes dented in the rain. After a good start, with Newton hitting a post, City play second fiddle. Thompson scores a debut goal and Dougan's goal is top class. With luck Posh could have scored more.
46	H	25/4	COLCHESTER	W	1-0	60	Hudson 24 Ref: H Richards	36,901	Wesson	Ames	Forbes	Kearns	Fowler	Hill	McCrohan	Curtis	Rutter	Farmer	Docherty	Humphries	Grice	Hudson	Hill	Kirby	King	Smith	Stark	Rees	Wright			Hudson, the prodigal son, is recalled and nets the only goal from a Rees cross. With Palace and Watford losing, C'ty are champions by 0.17 of a goal. Colchester offer little and City waste chances. A delirious crowd, the biggest league gate since 1949 is the largest of the day in England.

Home 26,017 Away 15,511 Average

LEAGUE DIVISION 3 (CUP-TIES) Manager: Jimmy Hill SEASON 1963-64

League Cup

			F-A	H-T	Scorers, Times, and Referees	1	2	3	4	5	6	7	8	9	10	11
1	A	LUTON	W 4-3	2:2	Machin 15, Rees 36, Sillett 69, Hill 71	Wesson	Sillett	Kearns	Hill	Curtis	Bruck	Humphries	Hale	Hudson	Machin	Rees
		3,821 22			Salisbury 41, 76, Fincham 43p	Baynham	Morton	Bramwell	Pacey	Fincham	Lownds	Fairchild	Salisbury	McKechnie	Riddick	Weir
					Ref: G Roper											

Much-changed Hatters give City a closer game than 11 days previously, but cannot stop a first-ever away win in the League Cup. City concede a penalty for the fourth game in a row. Baynham is beaten by long-range efforts after the break and City always look more likely winners.

2	A	ROTHERHAM	L 2-4	1-1	Humphries 32, Hudson 46	Wesson	Sillett	Kletzenbauer	Bruck	Curtis	Farmer	Humphries	Hale	Hudson	Whitehouse	Rees
		7,826 2:16			Bennett 14, 85, Houghton 54, 81	Ironside	Carver	Morgan	Lambert	Madden	Jackson	Lyons	Bennett	Tiler	Houghton	Butler
					Ref: G Grundy											

A third away game in six days and a virile Rotherham's stamina tells in the final stages, with City down to ten men. City twice lead, through Humphries' freak corner and Hudson's lightening strike, but crowd hero Albert Bennett looks a star in the making and punishes the Sky Blues.

FA Cup

1	A	TROWBRIDGE	W 6-1	3-0	Huds'n 24, 26, 60, Kearns 44, Rees 57,	Wesson	Sillett	Kearns	Hill	Curtis	Farmer	Humphries	Barr	Hudson	Hale	Rees
		6,524 SLt:13			Skeen 88 [Prosser 77 (og)]	Holland	Prosser	Lancaster	Meehan	Morris	Tavener	Skeen	Head	Meacock	Noake	Thompson
					Ref: N Matthews											

A comfortable win over Southern League part-timers, with City in control for 90 minutes. The score could have been doubled but City spare them embarrassment. At the end City's players applaud the plucky losers off. The deadly Hudson's second, a header, is the pick of the goals.

2	H	BRISTOL ROV	L 1-2	0-2	Hale 87	Wesson	Sillett	Kearns	Hill	Curtis	Farmer	Humphries	Barr	Hudson	Hale	Rees
		26,248 13			Bradford 6, Jarman 44	Hall	Hillard	Jones G	Oldfield	Davis	Mabbutt	Jarman	Brown	Biggs	Hamilton	Bradford
					Ref: G McCabe											

Bristol deservedly get revenge for the league defeat with a crisp and well-drilled defence. City have 22 shots to Rovers' eight, but 36-year-old ex-England man Geoff Bradford and Gloucester cricketer Harold Jarman are match-winners. Hill is disappointed but promotion is the priority.

	P	W	D	L	Home F	A	W	D	L	Away F	A	Pts	Odds & ends
1 COVENTRY	46	14	7	2	62	32	8	9	6	36	29	60	Double wins: (5) Notts Co, Walsall, Bristol C, QP Rangers, Bristol R.
2 Crys Palace	46	17	4	2	38	14	6	10	7	35	37	60	Double losses: (1) Mansfield.
3 Watford	46	16	6	1	57	28	7	6	10	22	31	58	
4 Bournemouth	46	17	4	2	47	15	7	4	12	32	43	56	Won from behind: (4) Palace (h), Peterborough (h), Bristol R (h), QPR (a).
5 Bristol C	46	13	7	3	52	24	6	8	9	32	40	55	Lost from in front: (2) Mansfield (a), Rotherham LC (a).
6 Reading	46	15	5	3	49	26	6	5	12	30	36	52	
7 Mansfield	46	15	8	0	51	20	5	3	15	25	42	51	High spots: Promotion on the final day.
8 Hull	46	11	9	3	45	27	5	8	10	28	41	49	Pre-January form (14 games without defeat).
9 Oldham	46	13	3	7	44	35	7	5	11	29	35	48	Massive home crowds and away followings.
10 Peterborough	46	13	6	4	52	27	5	5	13	23	43	47	Shrewsbury home win (8-1).
11 Shrewsbury	46	13	6	4	43	19	5	5	13	30	61	47	Hudson's pre-January scoring record (26 goals).
12 Bristol R	46	9	6	8	52	34	10	2	11	39	45	46	
13 Port Vale	46	13	6	4	35	13	3	8	12	18	36	46	Low points: Cup defeats.
14 Southend	46	9	10	4	42	26	6	6	11	35	52	45	Southend debacle on Friday 13th.
15 QP Rangers	46	13	4	6	34	34	5	5	13	29	44	45	Post-Christmas slump (11 games without a win).
16 Brentford	46	11	4	8	54	36	4	10	9	33	44	44	Machin's knee injury.
17 Colchester	46	10	8	5	45	26	2	11	10	25	42	43	Defeat at Peterborough in penultimate game.
18 Luton	46	12	2	9	42	41	4	8	11	22	39	42	
19 Walsall	46	7	9	7	34	35	6	5	12	25	41	40	
20 Barnsley	46	9	9	5	34	29	3	6	14	34	55	39	
21 Millwall	46	9	4	10	33	29	5	6	12	20	38	38	Red cards: (0).
22 Crewe	46	10	5	8	29	26	1	7	15	21	51	34	Red cards opponents: (0).
23 Wrexham	46	9	4	10	50	42	4	2	17	25	65	32	Hat-tricks: (5) Farmer (Palace h), Rees (Shrewsbury h), Hudson (QPR a), Kirby (Oldham h), Hudson (Trowbridge FAC a).
24 Notts Co	46	7	8	8	29	26	2	1	20	16	66	27	Opposing hat-tricks: (0).
	1104	285	144	123	1066	664	123	144	285	664	1066	1104	Leading scorer: (28) George Hudson.

	Appearances Lge	Sub	LC	Sub	FAC	Sub	Goals Lge	LC	FAC	Tot
Barr, Hugh	13						3			3
Bruck, Dietmar	10		2			2				
Curtis, George	46		2		2					
Farmer, Ron	44		1		2		11			11
Gould, Bobby	2									
Hale, Ken	39		2		2		16		1	17
Hill, Brian	40		1		2		2	1		3
Hudson, George	32		2		2		24	1	3	28
Humphries, Willie	40		2		2		10	1		11
Kearns, Mick	42		1		2					1
Kirby, George	9						5			5
Kletzenbauer, Frank	9		1				1			1
Machin, Ernie	17		1				3		1	4
Meeson, Dave	5									
Mitten, John	4									
Newton, Graham	8						3			3
Rees, Ronnie	46		2		2		13	1	1	15
Sillett, John	41		2		2			1		1
Smith, John	9									
Wesson, Bob	41		2		2					
Whitehouse, Jimmy	9		1				3			3
(own-goals)							4		1	5
21 players used	506		22		22		98	6	7	111

LEAGUE DIVISION 2 — Manager: Jimmy Hill — SEASON 1964-65

No	Date		Att	Pos	Pt	F-A	H-T	Scorers, Times, and Referees	1	2	3	4	5	6	7	8	9	10	11
1	H 22/8	PLYMOUTH	34,650	W	2	2-0	0-0	Farmer 57p, Smith 63 Ref: J Mitchell	Wesson	Hill	Kearns	Smith	Curtis	Farmer	Humphries	Hale	Hudson	Kirby	Rees
									McLaren	Book	Cobb	Williams	Wyatt	Newman	Jackson	Sanderson	Lord	Treblicock	Jennings

Defensive Argyle stay in the game thanks to McLaren's saves before Cobb handles near the post. Farmer's slide-rule penalty. Sillett's lumbago means there is a late switch and new wing-half John Smith scores from Kirby's knock-down. On a hot day City let Malcolm Allison's side off.

| 2 | A 25/8 | IPSWICH | 17,252 | W | 4 | 3-1 | 1-1 | Rees 8, Humphries 59, Hale 60
Blackwood 7
Ref: B Setchell | Wesson | Hill | Kearns | Smith | Curtis | Farmer | Humphries | Hale | Hudson | Kirby | Rees |
| | | | | | | | | | Bailey | Davin | McNeil | Baxter | Nelson | Bolton | Broadfoot | Blackwood | Baker | Leadbitter | Brogan |

Jackie Milburn's relegated team are surprised by the division's new boys. Wearing black armbands for City director G H Smart, they bounce back from Bob Wesson's error to finish clinically. Rees scores the first and sets up the superb Hale's goal. Ipswich are restricted to long shots.

| 3 | A 29/8 | BOLTON | 14,891 | W | 6 | 3-1 | 2-0 | Lee 15 (og), Kirby 33, 71
Davies 49
Ref: R Windle | Wesson | Hill | Kearns | Smith | Curtis | Farmer | Humphries | Hale | Hudson | Kirby | Rees |
| | | | | | | | | | Hopkinson | Hartle | Hatton | Rimmer | Edwards | Lennard | Lee | Fry | Davies | Bromley | Taylor |

City's first ever visit to Burnden Park is a hard-fought win. Bolton's young forwards chase ceaselessly but Lee doesn't look where he puts his back-pass. Kirby wins the heading duel with Wyn Davies and scores two headers. 4,000 City fans cheer as City dominate the last half-hour.

| 4 | H 1/9 | IPSWICH | 37,782 | W | 8 | 5-3 | 2-1 | Kirby 25, 33, Hale 64, 65, Hudson 75
Baker 21, Hegan 74, Brogan 77
Ref: R Tinkler | Wesson | Hill | Kearns | Smith | Curtis | Farmer | Humphries | Hale | Hudson | Kirby | Rees |
| | | | | | | | | | Bailey | Davin | Bolton | Baxter | Nelson | Blackwood | Broadfoot | Hegan | Baker | Colrain | Brogan |

A thrilling win maintains the 100% record in a game of 54 shots (36 by City). Baker's lob is followed by two Kirby headers before Hale tucks two shots past Bailey. The fans want 'the old five' and City, attacking in force, are caught on the break before Kirby nods down for 'the Hud'.

| 5 | H 5/9 | MIDDLESBROUGH | 36,086 | W | 10 | 3-0 | 1-0 | Humphries 37, Kirby 52, Hudson 85
Ref: L Hamer | Wesson | Hill | Kearns | Smith | Curtis | Farmer | Humphries | Hale | Hudson | Kirby | Rees |
| | | | | | | | | | Connachan | Gates | Jones | Townsend | Nurse | Orritt | Kaye | Gibson | Horsfield | Irvine | Braithwaite |

Boro's strong-arm tactics fail to stop them losing their unbeaten record to the Sky Blues. Raich Carter's men are angry, as Rees holds down the keeper for the first goal, but have no complaints at Kirby's header and Hudson's cheeky third. The woodwork saves Boro three more times.

| 6 | A 9/9 | DERBY | 32,720 | L | 10 | 1-2 | 0-1 | Bowers 14, Thomas 80
Parry 89 (og)
Ref: H Richards | Wesson | Hill | Kearns | Smith | Curtis | Farmer | Humphries | Hale | Hudson | Kirby | Rees |
| | | | | | | | | | Matthews | Barrowclough | Ferguson | Webster | Young | Parry | Hughes | Thomas | Burton | Durban | Bowers |

The gates are locked as Tim Ward's team inflict a first defeat on the Sky Blues. City dominate ten-man Rams (Bowers is limping for an hour) for long periods but poor shooting and the veteran ex-City Reg Matthews keeps them out. Even the roar of 10,000 fans fail to lift Hill's men.

| 7 | A 12/9 | NEWCASTLE | 37,481 | L | 10 | 0-2 | 0-0 | Taylor 52, Thomas 61
Ref: E Crawford | Wesson | Hill | Kearns | Smith | Curtis | Farmer | Humphries | Hale | Hudson | Kirby | Rees |
| | | | | | | | | | Marshall | Craig | Clark | Anderson | McGrath | Moncur | Hockey | Hilley | Thomas | McGarry | Taylor |

Despite Hill's early hamstring injury, City comfortably hold Joe Harvey's talented but dirty team until Taylor's 'banana' shot. Things become ugly and Ron McGarry is sent off for punching Ron Farmer. Thomas bludgeons the ball and Kearns into the net but the ref allows the goal.

| 8 | H 15/9 | DERBY | 38,278 | L | 10 | 0-2 | 0-0 | Thomas 55, Durban 72
Ref: K Dagnall | Wesson | Hill | Kearns | Smith | Curtis | Farmer | Humphries | Hale | Hudson | Kirby | Rees |
| | | | | | | | | | Matthews | Richardson | Ferguson | Webster | Young | Parry | Hughes | Thomas | Burton | Durban | Cleevely |

City have 26 shots, but captain for the night Matthews has to make few saves. A cool Derby defence master a frantic City and take their few chances against a weakened defence. The second biggest post-war league crowd pay record receipts of £6,000. The Sky Blue bubble has burst.

| 9 | H 19/9 | NORTHAMPTON | 30,069 | L | 10 | 0-1 | 0-0 | Robson 76
Ref: G McCabe | Wesson | Sillett | Kearns | Bruck | Curtis | Farmer | Humphries | Hale | Kirby | Smith | Rees |
| | | | | | | | | | Harvey | Foley | Everitt | Leck | Branston | Kiernan | Walden | Hunt | Livesey | Etheridge | Robson |

Wesson's careless throw creates the goal for the defensive Cobblers. Dave Bowen's team give little away and the Sky Blues forwards' lack confidence. Smith and Hale are poor and, despite Kirby's gallant efforts and a loud crowd, it's four losses in a row for the first time in 7 years.

| 10 | A 26/9 | SOUTHAMPTON | 22,196 | L | 10 | 1-4 | 0-2 | Curtis 82
Paine 4, 78, O'Brien 18, Burnside 65
Ref: D Smith | Meeson | Sillett | Kearns | Bruck | Curtis | Farmer | Rees | Hale | Hudson | Machin | Mitten |
| | | | | | | | | | Hollowbread | Williams | Hollywood | Wimshurst | Knapp | Huxford | Paine | O'Brien | Chivers | Burnside | Sydenham |

City have not won at the Dell since 1939 and the run of losses is the worst since 1926. City have plenty of the play and shots but the ruthless Saints rip City's defence apart with their speedy wingers to the fore. On his 300th game Curtis contains Under 23 cap Chivers and heads a goal.

188

#	H/A	Opponent	Date	Att			W/D/L	Pos	Score	Scorers											Report
11	A	SWANSEA	29/9	12,794	9	D	1-1	15	11	Rees 10 Todd 89 Ref: J Finley	Meeson Briggs	Tedds Hughes	Kearns Ward	Bruck Thomas	Curtis Johnson	Farmer Williams	Rees Evans	Smith Draper	Hudson Todd	Machin McLaughlin	Mitten Harris	The rot ends, thanks to local boy Rees' powerful early shot which raises the roof at the Vetch. Defensive City hang on until the death when Meeson misses a corner and Todd's overhead flick drops in. Curtis and Kearns are dual centre-halves and swallow up the Swans' long balls.
12	H	HUDDERSFIELD	3/10	26,994	13	L	2-3	20	11	Hudson 33, Farmer 42p Cod'ton 17p, Lewis 44, Bald'stone 76 Wood Ref: G Fartley	Meeson Wood	Tedds Parker	Kearns McNab	Bruck Holden	Curtis Coddington	Farmer Dinsdale	Humphries McHale	Smith Lewis	Hudson Stokes	Machin Balderstone	Mitten Massie	Struggling Town gain only their second win against a poor City lacking in confidence. Bruck's muscle injury means he is a passenger on the wing. Coddington takes a 20-yard run before a softly hit penalty rolls in. Lewis fouls back-to-form Humphries, but the inside men are too deep.
13	H	SWINDON	10/10	25,216	10 17	W	3-2	13	Machin 13, Hudson 26, Hale 79 Skeen 27 Hunt 38p Ref: K Seddon	Meeson Oakley	Sillett Dawson	Hill Trollope	Kearns Morgan	Curtis McPherson	Farmer Smart	Humphries Leggett	Smith Hunt	Hudson Summerbee	Machin Skeen	Rees Rogers	Hill's return gives the defence a lift and a better-balanced team give Bert Head's young Swindon a pounding. City's first win in eight would have been bigger but for the brave Oakley. Ernie Hunt's slick cross sets up Skeen, but Hale scores the winner after Rees is denied a penalty.
14	A	PORTSMOUTH	17/10	14,621	10 6	W	2-0	15	Gould 15, Rees 37 Ref: G Powell	Glazier Milkins	Sillett Cordjohn	Hill Lunniss	Kearns Lewis	Curtis Dickinson	Farmer Harris	Humphries McClelland	Hale Portwood	Hudson Tindall	Gould McCann	Rees Barton	Britain's most expensive goalkeeper debuts and pulls off four brilliant saves to break Pompey's hearts. Rees sets up Gould's flicked goal and slams in a pile-driver. City's defence looks secure after that, with John Sillett heading off the line when Glazier was beaten by Tindall's shot.
15	H	MANCHESTER C	24/10	28,693	10 14	D	2-2	16	Gould 43 Hudson 44 Curtis 11 (og), Young 86 Ref: R Harper	Glazier Ogley	Farmer Becuzzi	Hill Gomersall	Kearns Kennedy	Curtis Gratrix	Farmer Oakes	Humphries Young	Hale Gray	Hudson Murray	Gould Kevan	Rees Wagstaffe	City rue missed chances by Hudson and Gould, when Neil Young coolly levels near the end. Glazier misses a cross and Murray's header hits a post and Curtis. Humphries crosses for Gould's diving header and Hudson's firm finish. A fair result in a game between two average sides.
16	A	CHARLTON	31/10	16,418	10 12	L	0-3	16	Firmani 12, Matthews 72, Kennedy 83 Ref: J P'ckles	Glazier Rose	Farmer Miller	Burckitt Stocks	Smith Bailey	Curtis Hewie	Farmer Kinsey	Humphries Matthews	Hale Kennedy	Hudson Firmani	Machin Edwards	Rees Glover	3,000 City fans are left disappointed with a poor display, with the forwards lacking any thrust. City miss three early chances before Firmani's opener and but for Glazier the score would have been worse. Mike Bailey is a driving force for Frank Hill's Addicks, and looks England-class.
17	H	LEYTON ORIENT	7/11	24,416	12 13	D	1-1	17	Hale 89p Dunmore 7 Ref: J Lowry	Glazier Pinner	Sillett Hollow	Kearns Webb	Bruck Ward	Curtis Nelson	Farmer Lea	Humphries Price	Smith Gregory	Hudson Phillips	Gould Dunmore	Machin MacDonald	Dunmore is totally unmarked for his header as City struggle in the first half and Glazier bravely saves from Gregory. Humphries limps through the second half but City improve. Lea pulls down Machin but Hale's spot-kick is saved. The ref orders a retake and Hale nets. Hudson is axed.
18	A	BURY	13/11	6,366	13 12	L	**0-5**	17	Yard 1, i8, Bell 52, 67, Alston 89 Ref: R Windle	Glazier Harker	Sillett Threlfall	Kearns Leech	Smith Turner	Curtis Bunner	Farmer Atherton	Humphries Clarton	Smith Alston	Hudson Yard	Machin Bell	Mitten Parry	A disastrous wet night in Bury ends in humiliation. Yard's second goal is a wild cross that curls past bemused Glazier. Then the ref's legs turn City's attack into a home breakaway for Bell's first, a diving header. Alston's goal is a stunning 25-yarder. City have played worse and drawn.
19	H	CRYSTAL PALACE	21/11	24,145	13 7	D	0-0	18	Ref: E Norman	Glazier Millington	Burckitt Long	Kearns Howe	Farmer Whitehouse	Curtis Stephenson	Farmer Wood	Rees Imlach	Hale Smith K	Hudson Holton	Hale Werge	Mitten Kellard	Both teams are down to ten men for the last 25 minutes as Tony Millington cuts his face and Farmer pulls a muscle. Stand-in keeper Brian Whitehouse is beaten twice but saved by the post. Lucky Palace survive but at least new England Under 23 cap Bill Glazier is back to his best.
20	A	NORWICH	28/11	18,098	15 4	L	0-1	18	Mannion 79 Ref: R Aldous	Glazier Keelan	Burckitt Kelly	Harris Mullett	Smith Lucas	Curtis Butler	Farmer Alcock	Rees Heath	Hale Bolland	Hudson Davies	Rees Bryceland	Mitten Mannion	It is 7½ hours since an outfield goal and things look a bit desperate. Hale is unlucky to have his 'goal' disallowed for offside. The quick Allan Harris looks a good signing, but the experiment with Rees at number 10 fails. In a dour game the Canaries don't look promotion candidates.
21	H	ROTHERHAM	5/12	20,029	18 11	L	3-5	18	Hudson 60, Keyworth 77, Hale 89 Galley 1', 32, 69, Ben't 15, Butler 47 Morritt Ref: L Callaghan	Burckitt Wilcockson	Harris Clish	Bruck Lambert	Smith Madden	Kearns Jackson	Humphries Lyons	Hale Bennett	Hudson Galley	Hudson Houghton	Keyworth Butler	Rees	The well-drilled and slick Millers take up where Leicester left off to end a black week for City. The injured Curtis is sorely missed as John Galley scores a debut hat-trick and gives Kearns the runaround. Keyworth heads in on his debut, but Danny Williams' team have eased off.

LEAGUE DIVISION 2 — Manager: Jimmy Hill — SEASON 1964-65

No	Date	Att	Pos	Pt	F-A	H-T	1	2	3	4	5	6	7	8	9	10	11
22 A PLYMOUTH 12/12	13,892	12	W	20	3-2	3-2	Glazier	Sillett	Harris	Bruck	Curtis	Kearns	Humphries	Machin	Keyworth	Hudson	Rees
		5					McLaren	Book	Reeves	Neale	Newman	Jackson	Jones	Trebilcock	Lord	Sanderson	Jennings

Scorers: Machin 7, Keyworth 32, Bruck 40
Trebilcock 16, Jones 25
Ref: R Paine

Curtis returns to inspire the Sky Blues to end Argyle's unbeaten home record. Back-to-form Hudson is involved in all three goals and City defend like dervishes after the break. Glazier errs for the second goal but is dazzling later as Malcolm Allison's men bombard City till the end.

| 23 H BOLTON 19/12 | 23,387 | 15 | D | 21 | 0-0 | 0-0 | Glazier | Sillett | Harris | Bruck | Curtis | Kearns | Humphries | Machin | Keyworth | Hudson | Rees |
| | | 4 | | | | | Hopkinson | Hartle | Farrimond | Rimmer | Edwards | Hatton | Lee | Hill | Davies | Bromley | Taylor |

Ref: J Cooke

City tame the best attack in the division but the ref allows the game to become an ugly battle. City's wingers are out of touch and Hudson off-colour. Lee is lucky not to be sent off for cynical fouls on Rees and Harris. Curtis and Wyn Davies' ding-dong battle ends with honours even.

| 24 A PRESTON 26/12 | 22,215 | 17 | L | 21 | 2-3 | 1-1 | Glazier | Sillett | Hill | Bruck | Curtis | Kearns | Humphries | Machin | Hudson | Hudson | Rees |
| | | 9 | | | | | Barton | Ross | Smith | Kendall | Singleton | Davidson | Wilson | Godfrey | Dawson | Spavin | Holden |

Scorers: Hudson 39, 69
Wilson 28, Kendall 50, 82
Ref: V James

2,000 City fans brave the severe cold and see a drama on an icy pitch. A half-pace Kendall is the difference, rifling in the first and heading the winner. City are unlucky with some decisions, chiefly Machin's disallowed goal, but Kearns boobs for the first. Humphries misses late chance.

| 25 H PRESTON 28/12 | 22,667 | 13 | W | 23 | 3-0 | 2-0 | Glazier | Sillett | Hill | Bruck | Curtis | Kearns | Humphries | Machin | Hudson | Hale | Rees |
| | | 10 | | | | | Barton | Ross | Smith | Davidson | Singleton | Cranston | Wilson | Godfrey | Dawson | Spavin | Holden |

Scorers: Hudson 5, Hudson 40, Humphries 50
Ref: J Finney

A masterful display on a snowbound pitch with a scoreline that flatters PNE. With Kendall injured, the visitors are thrashed and barely have a shot. The irresistible Hudson sets up Machin's header from a long clearance before cheekily chipping Barton and then makes Humphries' goal.

| 26 A MIDDLESBROUGH 2/1 | 15,714 | 11 | W | 25 | 3-2 | 1-1 | Glazier | Sillett | Hill | Bruck | Curtis | Kearns | Humphries | Machin | Hudson | Hale | Rees |
| | | 14 | | | | | Connachan | Chapman | Jones | Townsend | Nurse | Spraggon | Kaye | Gibson | Irvine | Masson | Ratcliffe |

Scorers: Machin 25, Hale 68, Hudson 88
Gibson 31, Nurse 86
Ref: A Luty

Nurse's late goal looks to have saved a point until Hudson controls the ball superbly and drills home the winner. On an icy pitch, a Boro error is punished by Machin and local boy Hale raps in the second. Hero Glazier is beaten by a Gibbo special and Nurse's deflected shot off Curtis.

| 27 H NEWCASTLE 16/1 | 28,032 | 8 | W | 27 | 5-4 | 4-1 | Glazier | Hill | Harris | Bruck | Curtis | Kearns | Humphries | Gould | Hudson | Hale | Rees |
| | | 1 | | | | | Marshall | Craig | Clark | Anderson | McGrath | Iley | Hockey | Hilley | McGarry | Cummings | Suddick |

Scorers: M'll 8 (og), Gould 16, Hale 19p, Hud'40,
Hilley 31,79, McGarry 75, 87 (Rees 66)
Ref: W Crossley

Both teams defy the wind and mud to put on a memorable show. 2,000 away fans see their team's revival just fail, although the inspirational Iley's free-kick goes close at the death. City are magical for the first hour and deserve the win. Humphries' corner is palmed in by Marshall.

| 28 A NORTHAMPTON 23/1 | 18,741 | 8 | D | 28 | 1-1 | 0-1 | Wesson | Hill | Harris | Bruck | Curtis | Kearns | Humphries | Hale | Hudson | Clements | Rees |
| | | 2 | | | | | Harvey | Foley | Everitt | Leck | Branston | Kiernan | Lines | Martin | Brown | Leek | Robson |

Scorers: Clements 73
Leek 33
Ref: R Egan

Dave Bowen's team's charge to Division 1 is slowed by a gritty City display. The mighty Curtis and Co keep the Cobblers at bay before the break, with Wesson, in for burn victim Glazier, superb. A deserved point thanks to Clements' debut goal, which sends 7,000 fans delirious.

| 29 H SOUTHAMPTON 6/2 | 25,298 | 9 | D | 29 | 1-1 | 0-0 | Glazier | Hill | Harris | Bruck | Curtis | Kearns | Humphries | Hale | Hudson | Clements | Rees |
| | | 7 | | | | | Hollowbread | Williams | Traynor | Wimshurst | Paton | Huxford | Paine | O'Brien | Chivers | Melia | Sydenham |

Scorers: Clements 78
O'Brien 53
Ref: D Smith

Despite needing a late goal to draw, City deserve to beat Ted Bates' defensive Saints. Harris masters the tricky international Paine but it's Terry's cross that O'Brien hammers in. On a muddy pitch, Clements scores again with a left-footer from Hill's job. Machin out for the season.

| 30 A HUDDERSFIELD 13/2 | 13,042 | 10 | L | 29 | 1-2 | 1-2 | Glazier | Hill | Harris | Bruck | Curtis | Kearns | Humphries | Hale | Hudson! | Clements | Rees |
| | | 16 | | | | | Wood | McNab | Meagan | Nicholson | Coddington | Dinsdale | McHale | Massie | Leighton | Quigley | O'Grady |

Scorers: Clements 37
Massie 9, McHale 22
Ref: J Parkinson

Hudson is the first sending off in over four years. Just before the break he retaliates to Dinsdale's foul by flooring the Town defender. 10-man City fight hard and Ray Wood tips Ken Hale's shot round the post at the death. The awesome Glazier keeps Town at bay, but the result is fair.

| 31 A SWINDON 20/2 | 14,053 | 12 | L | 29 | 1-4 | 0-3 | Glazier | Hill | Harris | Bruck | Curtis | Kearns | Rees | Gould | Hudson | Hunt | Clements |
| | | 16 | | | | | Hicks | Dawson | Trollope | Smart | McPherson | Atherton | Summerbee | Hunt | Brown | Atkins | Rogers |

Scorers: Hudson 75 (Dawson 54)
Rogers 8, 44, Summerbee 39,
Ref: G Davis

Lowly Swindon give City a drubbing which, but for Glazier, would have been a lot worse. Hunt and Rogers also hit the woodwork, the live-wire Rogers denied a hat-trick. City get slim respite from the non-stop attacks and have few chances. Brian Hill limps through the latter stages.

#	H/A	Opponent	Date	W/L	Score	HT	Pos	Att												Scorers / Ref	Report
32	H	PORTSMOUTH	27/2	L	1-2	1-2	14	22,181	Glazier Milkins	Hill Wilson	Harris Lunniss	Bruck Gordon	Curtis Dickinson	Kearns Harris	Humphries McClelland	Smith Lewis	Hudson Hiron	Clements Edwards	Rees Barton	Rees 20, Hiron 22, 25, Ref: F Cwen	City have 20 shots at Pompey's goal but most of them are from long distance and are no trouble. Rees' header is quickly cancelled out by Hiron's header and shot, as he leads Curtis a merry dance. Pompey defend in depth, and 38-year old Jimmy Dickinson marks Hudson well.
33	A	ROTHERHAM	6/3	W	2-0	0-0	12	7,741 14 31	Glazier Morritt	Sillett Carver	Harris Clish	Farmer Lambert	Curtis Madden	Hill Hardy	Rees Lyons	Hudson Bennett	Keyworth Galley	Hale Hellawell	Clements Casper	Hudson 74, Clements 77, Ref: L Hamer	City's reshuffled side banish relegation thoughts by becoming only the third side to win at Millmoor and avenge the earlier defeat. Curtis has Galley taped, and Hill does a superb job on Newcastle-bound Bennett. The home raids are soaked up and a quick one-two grabs the points.
34	H	CHARLTON	13/3	W	2-0	1-0	10	21,621 22 33	Glazier Rose	Sillett Bonds	Harris Hewie	Farmer Snedden	Curtis Haydock	Hill Tocknell	Rees Kennedy	Hudson Matthews	Keyworth Firmani	Hale Glover	Clements Kinsey	Rees 23, Clements 54, Ref: K Walker	Even with Sillett hobbling on the wing, City are too good for a poor Charlton, who badly miss Mike Bailey. The Addicks are let off the hook but succumb to a Hale-created goal and Clements' swivel and finish from a corner. Flu-victim Keyworth struggles as Hale blows hot and cold.
35	H	BURY	27/3	W	2-1	2-0	10	18,777 15 35	Glazier Harker	Sillett Gallagher	Harris Eastham	Farmer Turner	Curtis Bunner	Hill Leech	Rees Alston	Gould Griffin	Keyworth Yard	Hale Bell	Clements Durrant	Clements 15, Keyworth 20, Griffin 77, Ref: D Brady	Despite missing three good chances, City gain revenge for their Gigg Lane debacle. Out-of-touch Gould, in for suspended Hudson is the main culprit. Clements is the star again and scores a screamer. Keyworth's header from Hill's long punt catches Harker offguard. Bury finish strong.
36	A	CRYSTAL PALACE	3/4	D	2-2	2-1	12	15,900 8 36	Glazier Jackson	Sillett Howe	Harris Fuller	Farmer Long	Curtis Holton	Hill Stephenson	Rees Woods	Hale Dowsett	Hudson Whitehouse	Hale Horobin	Mitten Holsgrove	Clements 16, Mitten 40, Holsgrove 12, Woods 82, Ref: R Tinkler	An impressive display, with John Mitten playing out of his skin, deserves both points. Only Jackson's saves and Hudson's bad misses reprieve Dick Graham's physical team. New Irish cap Clements thumps in another cracker and Hudson's whipped cross is met at close range by Mitten.
37	H	NORWICH	10/4	W	3-0	2-0	10	22,552 6 38	Glazier Barnard	Sillett Stringer	Harris Mullett	Farmer Lucas	Curtis Butler	Hill Sutton	Rees Heath	Hale Bryceland	Hudson Allcock	Clements Davies	Mitten Punton	Hudson 16, Clements 23, Rees 47, Ref: S Stoakes	The Canaries start with a slim chance of promotion but fail to impress. Hudson and Rees are back in form. George's shot goes in off both posts but he deserves more goals. Cool Clem scores again and Rees' effort screams in before City ease off and give the fine young Barnard a rest.
38	A	MANCHESTER C	17/4	D	1-1	1-1	10	10,804 12 39	Glazier Ogley	Sillett Bacuzzi	Harris Gomersall	Farmer Doyle	Curtis Kennedy	Hill Oakes	Rees Connor	Hale Crossan	Hudson Wood	Clements Pardoe	Mitten Young	Hale 44, Connor 21, Ref: J Thacker	After 41 minutes Glazier breaks his leg in an accidental clash with Pardoe, and Rees takes over in goal. Brave Ronnie and a solid defence keep the managerless Blues at bay after Hale's shot goes in off a post for City's first ever goal at Maine Road. 1,000 fans roar City to a great point.
39	A	CARDIFF	19/4	L	1-3	1-2	10	11,330 14 39	Wesson Wilson	Kearns Rodrigues	Harris Baker	Farmer Williams	Curtis Murray	Hill Hole	Rees Johnston	Smith Allchurch	Hudson Charles J	Clements King	Mitten Lewis	Farmer 44, King 28, Allchurch 38, 52, Ref: G Martin	A first defeat in six is down to a rare poor defensive display. Kearns has a nightmare against Lewis but King is the architect, with 'old' stars Ivor Allchurch and John Charles playing key roles. Stand-in Wesson is at fault for the third and his flap leaves Allchurch with an easy goal.
40	H	CARDIFF	20/4	L	0-2	0-1	10	23,881 13 39	Wesson Wilson	Sillett Rodrigues	Harris Baker	Bruck Williams	Curtis Murray	Hill Hole	Rees Johnston	Gould Allchurch	Turner Charles J	Hale King	Clements Lewis	Lewis 6, Hole 47, Ref: J Cattlin	JH makes six changes in vain as City rarely look like scoring. Lewis's corner curls past bemused Sillett and Wesson. Curtis keeps John Charles mainly quiet but the old warhorse does set up Hole's cool finish. Gould and Turner find things hard up front as experience tells over youth.
41	H	SWANSEA	24/4	W	3-0	2-0	10	23,683 22 41	Wesson Black	Sillett Evans	Harris Hughes	Farmer Johnson	Curtis Jones	Hill Davies	Farmer Humphries	Hudson McGuigan	Keyworth Kirby	Smith Todd	Clements McLaughlin	Hudson 27, 38, Clements 88, Ref: J Bullough	Humphries and Kirby make swift returns but cannot stop Trevor Morris's team being relegated after 16 years in Division 2. Curtis wins the much-hyped duel with a lack-lustre George Kirby. The menacing Hudson is the star, ruthlessly scoring two and chipping for Clements' header.
42	A	LEYTON ORIENT	28/4	W	3-1	2-0	10	6,355 19 43	Wesson Davies	Sillett Webb	Harris Worrell	Farmer Sorrell	Curtis Nelson	Hill Harris	Rees McGeorge	Turner Metchick	Hudson Gregory	Smith Scott	Clements Elwood	Hudson 8, 37, 60, Scott 71, Ref: T Dawes	An impressive end-of-season display against Dave Sexton's inept O's, who have just avoided relegation. Hudson heads in Clements' cross then slides in Rees' cross. Clements has a hand in all three goals and his fierce shot is blocked for George to seal his hat-trick. Curtis is a rock again.

Home Average 26,621 Away 16,384

LEAGUE DIVISION 2 (CUP-TIES)   Manager: Jimmy Hill   SEASON 1964-65

League Cup

2 H IPSWICH   6   W   4-1   0-0   14,778   22
Scorers, Times, and Referees: Mitten 71, Hudson 73, 87, Rees 77, Colrain 52. Ref: A Jones

1	2	3	4	5	6	7	8	9	10	11
Meeson	Sillett	Kearns	Bruck	Curtis	Farmer	Rees	Newton	Hudson	Machin	Mitten
Bailey	Carberry	McNeil	Blackwood	Bolton	Thrower	Broadfoot	Hegan	Colrain	Leadbetter	Brogan

New Welsh cap Rees is clapped onto the field by both teams and is the architect of City's late win. He is involved in the first three goals scoring a screamer, his shot came off the post for Mitten and teeing up 'The Hud'. Ipswich are still winless. Ernie Machin returns after injury.

3 H MANSFIELD   10   W   3-2   2-2   12,387   3:7
Scorers: Hale 30, Gould 37, Rees 70, Wagstaff 26, Scanlon 36. Ref: J Mitchell

1	2	3	4	5	6	7	8	9	10	11
Meeson	Sillett	Hill	Smith	Curtis	Kearns	Humphries	Hale	Hudson	Gould	Rees
Treharne	Poynton	Hall B	Hall I	Gill	Morris	Tyrer	Wagstaff	Cooper	Gavan	Scanlon

City reach the last 16 for the first time, in a game riddled with errors. It's revenge over the Stags for the double defeat last season, but they need luck to overcome a Wagstaff-inspired team. Gould scores on his home debut and Hudson looks back to his best. Gill's mistake lets in Rees.

4 H SUNDERLAND   12   W   4-2   4-0   19,227   1:20
Scorers: Hudson 15, 38, Hale 31, 32, O'Hare 58, 78. Ref: J Parkinson

1	2	3	4	5	6	7	8	9	10	11
Wesson	Sillett	Kearns	Smith	Curtis	Bruck	Rees	Hale	Hudson	Machin	Mitten
Montgomery	Nelson	Ashurst	Harvey	Rooks	McNab	Usher	Crossan	O'Hara	Herd	Mulhall

The Makems have lost every away game this season and the score-line flatters them. They are run ragged by impressive City who score four well-taken goals, with Hudson's two the best. City ease off and allow O'Hare to profit from slack defending, but the result is never in doubt.

5 H LEICESTER   15   L   1-8   0-3   27,443   1:11
Scorers: Hudson 63 (Gibson 52, Norman 55, 87) St'w 2, 89, Hod'n 8, 81, Curtis 44 (og), Banks. Ref: C Duxbury

1	2	3	4	5	6	7	8	9	10	11
Wesson	Tedds	Burckitt	Kearns	Curtis	Smith	Humphries	Barr	Hudson	Hale	Rees
Banks	Sjoberg	Norman	Roberts	King	McDermott	Hodgson	Cross	Goodfellow	Gibson	Stringfellow

Curtis aggravates a ligament injury slicing in the third goal and is taken off. Leicester have all the luck and ruthlessly expose ten-man City to inflict a record home defeat on City. Every mistake is punished and Wesson has a nightmare. Hudson's overhead kick is the pick of the goals.

FA Cup

3 A ASTON VILLA   11   L   0-3   0-1   47,656   1:21
Scorers: Hateley 13, 66, MacLeod 83. Ref: K Dagnall

1	2	3	4	5	6	7	8	9	10	11
Glazier	Sillett	Harris	Bruck	Curtis	Kearns	Humphries	Hill	Hudson	Machin	Rees
Withers	Lee	Aitken	Wylie	Sleeuwenh'k	Pountney	Baker	Stobart	Hateley	Woosnam	MacLeod

Villa are rarely in trouble against lack-lustre City. 20,000 away fans see Hill's gamble in dropping Hale for Brian Hill backfire, and the gap between the two divisions is clear. Machin's miss near the break is crucial and Tony Hateley's goals are classy. Glazier keeps the score down.

	P	W	D	L	Home F	A	W	D	L	Away F	A	Pts	Odds & ends
1 Newcastle	42	16	4	1	50	16	8	5	8	31	29	57	Double wins: (3) Ipswich, Plymouth, Middlesbrough.
2 Northampton	42	14	7	0	37	16	6	9	6	29	34	56	Double losses: (3) Derby, Huddersfield, Cardiff.
3 Bolton	42	13	6	2	46	17	7	4	10	34	41	50	
4 Southampton	42	12	6	3	49	25	5	8	8	34	38	48	Won from behind: (5) Ipswich (a), Ipswich (h), Plymouth (a),
5 Ipswich	42	11	7	3	48	30	4	10	7	26	37	47	Ipswich LC (h), Mansfield LC (h)
6 Norwich	42	15	4	2	47	21	5	3	13	14	36	47	Lost from in front: (2) Huddersfield (h), Portsmouth (h).
7 Crys Palace	42	11	6	4	37	24	5	7	9	18	27	45	
8 Huddersfield	42	12	4	5	28	15	5	6	10	25	36	44	High spots: Five-game winning start.
9 Derby	42	11	5	5	48	35	5	6	10	36	44	43	Strong finish to season.
10 COVENTRY	42	10	5	6	41	29	7	4	10	31	41	43	Clements' emergence after Christmas.
11 Manchester C	42	12	3	6	40	24	4	6	11	23	38	41	League Cup run to quarter-final.
12 Preston	42	11	8	2	46	29	3	5	13	30	52	41	Thrilling win over champions Newcastle.
13 Cardiff	42	10	7	4	43	25	3	7	11	21	32	40	Form of goalkeeper Bill Glazier.
14 Rotherham	42	10	7	4	39	25	4	5	12	31	44	40	
15 Plymouth	42	10	7	4	36	30	6	1	14	27	51	40	Low spots: Two wins in 16-game run in the autumn.
16 Bury	42	9	4	8	36	30	5	6	10	24	36	38	League Cup debacle against Leicester.
17 Middlesbro	42	8	5	8	40	31	5	4	12	30	45	38	FA Cup loss at Villa Park.
18 Charlton	42	8	5	8	35	34	5	4	12	29	41	35	
19 Leyton Orient	42	10	4	7	36	34	2	7	12	14	38	35	
20 Portsmouth	42	11	4	6	36	22	1	6	14	20	55	34	
21 Swindon	42	12	3	6	43	30	2	2	17	20	51	33	Red cards: George Hudson (Huddersfield a).
22 Swansea	42	9	7	5	40	29	2	3	16	22	55	32	Red cards opponents: McGarry (Newcastle a).
	924	245	118	99	901	569	99	118	245	569	901	924	Hat-tricks: (1) George Hudson (Leyton Orient a).
													Opposing hat-tricks: (1) John Galley (Rotherham h).
													Leading scorer: (24) George Hudson.

	Appearances Lge	Sub	LC	Sub	FAC	Sub	Goals Lge	LC	FAC	Tot
Barr, Hugh			1							
Bruck, Dietmar	18		2							
Burckitt, John	5		1							
Clements, Dave	15									
Curtis, George	41		4		1					
Farmer, Ron	25		1							
Glazier, Bill	24				1					
Gould, Bobby	8	1					3	1		4
Hale, Ken	32		3				9		3	12
Harris, Allan	20				1					
Hill, Brian	28	1		1						
Hudson, George	38	4	4	1			19	5		24
Humphries, Willie	27	2		1			3			3
Kearns, Mick	36	4								
Keyworth, Ken	7						3			3
Kirby, George	9						5			5
Machin, Ernie	14	2		1			4			4
Meeson, Dave	4	2								
Mitten, John	10	2					1	1		2
Newton, Graham		1								
Rees, Ronnie	41	4		1			7	2		9
Sillett, John	17	3		1						
Smith, John	24	3								
Tedds, Bill	3	1								
Turner, Alan	2									
Wesson, Bob	14		2							
(own-goals)							3			3
26 players used	462	44		11			72	12		84

LEAGUE DIVISION 2 — Manager: Jimmy Hill — SEASON 1965-66

No	H/A	Date	Opponent	Att	Pos	Pt	W/D/L	F-A	H-T	1	2	3	4	5	6	7	8	9	10	11	12 sub used
1	H	21/8	WOLVERHAMPTON	36,771			W	2-1	0-0	Wesson	Kearns	Harris	Farmer	Curtis	Hill	Rees	Hale	Hudson	Machin	Clements	
										MacLaren	Knighton	Thomson	Flowers	Woodfield	Miller	Wharton	Woodruff	McIlmoyle	Knowles	Wagstaffe	

Scorers: Hudson 79, 84; McIlmoyle 58. Ref: L Hamer.

Relegated Wolves playing in Division 2 for the first time since 1932 are unlucky to lose a dour game of few chances. Hudson heads over Dave MacLaren from a narrow angle and then sidefoots home from Clements' pull-back. On the first day of the new substitute rules, neither is used.

| 2 | A | 24/8 | BURY | 7,564 | | 3 | D | 1-1 | 1-0 | Wesson | Kearns | Harris | Farmer | Curtis | Hill | Rees | Hale | Hudson | Machin | Clements | |
| | | | | | | | | | | Harker | Bray | Eastham | Turner | Clunie | Colquhoun | Henderson* | Maltby | Pointer | Bell | Alston | Griffin |

Scorers: Hudson 42; Eastham 74. Ref: H Hackney.

Ronnie Rees goes in goal for 10 mins after Wesson dislocates a finger and keeps Bert Head's Shakers out. On a wet, windy night City, with the wind, lead after Hudson intercepts a back-pass. Wesson is unsighted for the equaliser which goes through a forest of legs. A solid team display.

| 3 | A | 28/8 | ROTHERHAM | 11,134 | 5 | 4 | D | 1-1 | 1-1 | Wesson | Kearns | Harris | Farmer | Curtis | Hill | Rees | Hale | Hudson | Machin | Clements | |
| | | | | | 12 | | | | | Morritt | Wilcockson | Clish | Hardy | Madden | Tiler | Lyons | Chappell | Galley | Williams | Pring | |

Scorers: Hudson 23; Chappell 29. Ref: S Kayley.

City break the Miller's weak offside trap for Hudson to score from Farmer's nod-on. Promising youngster Chappell heads in Pring's cross. In a game of few chances, Wesson saves well from Clish, and Rees and Hill go close. Brian Hill has one of his finest games, never losing a tackle.

| 4 | H | 31/8 | BURY | 28,296 | 2 | 6 | W | 1-0 | 0-0 | Wesson | Kearns | Harris | Farmer | Curtis | Hill | Rees | Hale | Hudson | Machin | Clements | |
| | | | | | 13 | | | | | Harker | Bray | Eastham | Colquhoun | Clunie | Lindsay | Griffin | Maltby | Pointer | Bell | Parry | |

Scorers: Clements 87. Ref: R Harper.

City's lack-lustre attack cannot break down an average Bury side. The solid-looking defence is rarely troubled but Hale and Machin are struggling. A slick move wins the game with Rees crossing for Clements' header. Former England men, Ray's Parry and Pointer are kept quiet.

| 5 | H | 4/9 | MANCHESTER C | 29,467 | 5 | 7 | D | 3-3 | 2-1 | Wesson | Kearns | Harris | Farmer* | Curtis | Hill | Rees | Hale | Hudson | Machin | Clements | Bruck |
| | | | | | 6 | | | | | Dowd | Cheetham | Connor | Gray | Kennedy | Oakes | Summerbee | Crossan | Murray | Pardoe | Young | |

Scorers: Farmer 9p, Clements 39, Hudson 59; Young 23, 63, Murray 56. Ref: E Crawford.

Bruck becomes City's first sub when Crossan's elbow breaks Farmer's cheekbone. Mercer's skilful men contribute to a cracker. Machin is sandwiched for the penalty. Kearns at fault for Murray's tap-in and Dowd misses a corner for Clem's header. The dazzling Rees almost wins it.

| 6 | A | 8/9 | SOUTHAMPTON | 19,870 | 9 | 7 | L | 0-1 | 0-0 | Wesson | Kearns | Harris | Bruck | Curtis | Hill | Rees | Hale | Hudson | Machin | Clements | |
| | | | | | 2 | | | | | Hollowbr'd* | Williams | Hollywood | Walker | Knapp | Huxford | Paine | O'Brien | Chivers | Melia | Sydenham | Wimshurst |

Scorers: Chivers 61. Ref: E Wallace.

City fail to end the Dell bogey stretching back to 1939, despite Huxford being in goal for an hour after Hollowbread's injury. City dominate the first half but let Saints off the hook. After the break, Ted Bates' men are on top. Terry Paine sets up the goal from John Sydenham's corner.

| 7 | A | 11/9 | BRISTOL CITY | 19,887 | 8 | 8 | D | 1-1 | 0-1 | Wesson | Kearns | Harris | Bruck | Curtis | Hill | Rees | Hale | Hudson | Machin | Clements | |
| | | | | | 2 | | | | | Gibson | Showell | Briggs | Drury | Connor | Low | Peters | Sharpe | Bush* | Clarke | Hooper | Derrick |

Scorers: Connor 63 (og); Bush 17. Ref: H Richards.

Fred Ford's promoted Bristol are unbeaten but the result flatters them. City are on top for long periods but have no cutting edge. Terry Bush's shot through a crowd goes in off the post. Jack Connor hammers into his own net trying to clear his lines. Hudson and Rees are well marked.

| 8 | H | 14/9 | SOUTHAMPTON | 29,969 | 2 | 10 | W | 5-1 | 1-0 | Wesson | Kearns | Harris | Bruck | Curtis | Hill | Rees | Hale | Hudson | Machin | Clements | Smith |
| | | | | | 1 | | | | | Godfrey | Jones | Williams | Walker | Knapp | Huxford | Paine | Turner* | Dean | Melia | Sydenham | |

Scorers: Hudson 32, Bruck 53, Clements 72, Paine 89 [Machin 78, Kearns 88p]. Ref: J Mitchell.

Despite not being at their best, City thrash the leaders. Two goals are classics. Hudson bamboozles Knapp before heading home, and Bruck's goal is a thunderbolt. The third and fourth are poorly defended before Jones' hand stops Hudson's pass reaching Clements. Saints cut up rough.

| 9 | H | 18/9 | CRYSTAL PALACE | 25,211 | 6 | 10 | L | 0-1 | 0-1 | Wesson | Kearns | Harris | Bruck | Curtis | Hill | Rees | Smith | Hudson | Machin | Clements | |
| | | | | | 4 | | | | | Jackson | Whitehouse | Long | Yard | Stephenson | Bannister | Woods | Smith | Wood | Burnside | Kellard | |

Scorers: Smith 2. Ref: R Pritchard.

Palace defend their early lead like dervishes and frustrate Hill's men. Wood, a centre-half, wears No 9 shirt and is an extra defender. City lack a cutting edge but John Jackson has a blinder in goal. Bob Wesson has little to do all afternoon but Hudson and Rees are only seen in flashes.

| 10 | H | 25/9 | CARLISLE | 20,746 | 4 | 12 | W | 3-2 | 2-1 | Wesson | Kearns | Farmer | McConnell* | Curtis | Hill | Rees | Gould | Hudson | Machin | Mitten | |
| | | | | | 11 | | | | | Dean | Gallagher | Caldwell | Passmoor | Harland | Blain | Evans | Livingstone | Balderstone | Simpson | |

Scorers: Hudson 15, Gould 44, Farmer 54p; Balderstone 2, 89. Ref: J Parkinson.

Rees is the star in a good win over promoted Carlisle. He crosses for Hudson's bullet header and is felled by Passmoor for the penalty. Gould has two efforts ruled out. In pouring rain the cricketer Balderstone snaps two opportunist goals but the scoreline flatters Alan Ashman's team.

#	H/A Date	P	W/D/L	Score	Pos	Scorers / Ref	Attendance	Wesson	Harris	Farmer	Curtis	Hill	Rees	Gould	Hudson	Machin	Mitten				
11	A CARDIFF 6/10	2	W	2-1	15 14	Curtis 44, Rees 87 Williams 55 Ref: E Wallace	12,469	Wesson John	Kearns Rodrigues	Harris Baker	Farmer Coldrick*	Curtis Murray	Hill Hole	Rees Johnston	Gould King	Hudson Williams	Machin Harkin	Mitten Lewis		Sum erhayes		
	City wear red and white stripes to aid the historic first CCTV coverage of a game. Rees, playing here again four days after his Welsh cap v England, wins it with a scorching left-footer. Curtis' bullet header is reward for a strong first half, and Cardiff's fight-back is foiled by Wesson.																				
12	A PRESTON 9/10	3	D	0-0	7 15	Ref: H Wilson	19,672	Wesson Kelly	Kearns Ross	Harris Donnelly	Farmer Lawton	Curtis Cranston	Hill Kendall	Rees Wilson	Roberts Godfrey	Hudson Dawson	Machin* Spavin	Clements Veal*		Gould Ashworth		
	On the day the Sky Blue Special runs for the first time, the defence take the honours. In a physical game Machin is subbed with a thigh knock and Gould is booked for a foul on Cranston. The attack is poor, with Hudson and Rees below par and Roberts is denied by a brave Kelly save.																				
13	H CHARLTON 16/10	2	W	2-0	13 17	Hudson 26, Roberts 36, 46 Campbell 87 Ref: C Cooke	25,884	Wesson Rose	Kearns Bonds	Harris Hewie	Farmer Bailey	Curtis Haydock	Hill Kinsey*	Rees Matthews	Hale Campbell	Hudson Saunders	Roberts Peacock	Clements Kenning		Snedden		
	Son of City legend Ted Roberts, Dudley scores twice on his home debut despite being concussed. His first is from close range, the second a towering header. Hudson's load looks lighter with Roberts' goals and Wesson is brilliant again. City fail to make their domination tell again.																				
14	A PLYMOUTH 23/10	2	W	2-1	14 19	Roberts 31, Hudson 54 Trebilcock 36 Ref: A Weller	14,914	Wesson Leiper	Kearns Book	Harris Baird	Farmer Williams	Curtis Nelson	Hill* Hore	Rees Jones	Hale Piper	Hudson Lord	Roberts Trebilcock	Clements Jennings		Machin		
	Despite Book's man-for-man marking, Roberts' thunderbolt puts City ahead after great work by Rees and Hudson. Wesson is slow off his line and Trebilcock picks his spot. Leiper fails to hold Curtis' free-kick and Hudson pounces. Argyle are unlucky not to draw but City hold firm.																				
15	H PORTSMOUTH 30/10	1	W	3-2	6 21	Hudson 47, Roberts 61, Farmer 89p McLelland 25, Barton 76 Ref: F Nicholson	25,349	Wesson Armstrong	Kearns Lewis	Harris Wilson	Farmer Gordon	Curtis Harris	Hill Campbell	Rees McClelland	Hale Hiron	Hudson Edwards	Roberts McCann	Clements Barton				
	Farmer atones for his error in letting in Barton by netting a last minute spot-kick to send City top on goal-average. Pompey are livid after Rees' shot hits Campbell's arm and are the better team for much of the game. Hudson nets in his 100th league game, but Roberts struggles for once.																				
16	A BOLTON 6/11	3	L	2-4	11 21	Curtis 6, Rees 88 Bromley 21, Davies 34, 75, Butler 89 Ref: K Howley	13,499	Wesson Hopkinson	Kearns Hartle	Harris Farrimond	Farmer Rimmer	Curtis Napier	Hill Hatton	Rees Butler	Hale Hill	Hudson Davies	Machin Bromley	Clements Taylor				
	The scouts are watching Wyn Davies and he gives them food for thought scoring two and making the fourth. Wesson spills a cross for his first, then he heads home despite Curtis' pressure and chips over for Butler. Freddie Hill teases City, who play second fiddle to a good Bolton side.																				
17	H IPSWICH 13/11	3	W	2-1	15 23	Farmer 5p, Roberts 13, Gould 59 Brogan 11 Ref: H Richards	23,195	Wesson Hancock	Kearns Davin	Harris Smith	Farmer Lea	Curtis Baxter	Hill McNeil	Denton Broadfoot	Roberts* Hegan	Gould Brogan	Machin Treacy	Rees Spearitt		Hale		
	Hill's gamble on a young attack pays off. Peter Denton impresses and is fouled for the penalty. Dudley Roberts limps off after a bad tackle, soon after a fine header from Rees' cross. Hale crosses for Gould but dominant City fail to take Bill McGarry's depleted side to the cleaners.																				
18	A BIRMINGHAM 20/11	1	W	1-0	21 25	Farmer 61p Ref: K Stokes	25,953	Wesson Herriot	Kearns Green	Harris Martin	Farmer Wylie	Curtis Foster	Hill Page	Denton Hocker	Gould Vowden	Hudson Thomson	Machin Darrell	Rees* Thwaites				
	City win the first 'derby' for 13 years and Joe Mallet's relegated Blues are in deep trouble. An ugly game of 47 free-kicks and little football is settled by a penalty after Green and Martin's sandwich on Gould. 10,000 away fans cause traffic chaos and many miss the first half-hour.																				
19	H LEYTON ORIENT 27/11	2	D	1-1	22 26	Hudson 33 Gregory 72 Ref: J Carr	20,086	Wesson Rouse	Kearns Webb	Harris Went	Farmer Sorrell	Curtis Ferry	Hill Allen	Rees Musgrave	Hale Gregory	Hudson Flatt	Machir Smith	Rees Worrell				
	Not for the first time, City fail to break down a packed defence. Ex-City man John Smith skippers the O's to a famous point but they are a poor side. Hudson scores a header from Rees' chip despite being played out of position. Bob Wesson is punished for one lapse when he spills a shot.																				
20	A MIDDLESBROUGH 4/12	2	D	0-0	19 27	Farmer 77 Irvine 58 Ref: K Dagnall	12,024	Wesson Connachan* Gates	Kearns Jones	Harris Anderson	Farmer Rooks	Curtis Spraggon	Hill Ratcliffe	Denton McMordie	Hudson Irvine	Gould Gibson	Machin Holliday	Sillett Orritt				
	After 65 mins Connachan breaks an arm in a clash with Hudson and Orritt goes in goal. Irvine beats Curtis in a chase to score. Farmer atones for a miss by heading home Gould's cross but City lack a finishing touch. Hill, who has signed a new 5-year contract, is scouting for a striker.																				
21	H HUDDERSFIELD 11/12	3	L	0-3	1 27	Nicholson 33, Gilliver 49, Curtis 73 (og) Ref: H Davies	27,735	Wesson Oldfield	Sillett Atkins	Harris McNab	Farmer Nicholson	Curtis Coddington	Hill Meagan	Rees* McHale	Hudson Gilliver	Machin Leighton	Clements Quigley	Gould Veal*		Weston		
	Hill is looking for a new striker after Town pour scorn on City's promotion credentials. PM Harold Wilson sees his impressive team go three points clear. The defence back off Nicholson, who buries his shot. Wesson errs for the second and Kevin McHale's fierce shot flies off Curtis.																				

LEAGUE DIVISION 2 — Manager: Jimmy Hill — SEASON 1965-66

No	Date		Att	Pos	Pt	F-A	H-T	Scorers, Times, and Referees	1	2	3	4	5	6	7	8	9	10	11	12 sub used
22	27/12	A NORWICH	27,203	3 *9*	D 28	1-1	0-0	Pointer 75 / *Davies 62* / Ref: R Aldous	Wesson *Keelan*	Sillett *Stringer*	Harris *Mullett*	Farmer *Sutton*	Curtis *Sharpe*	Kearns *Allcock*	Rees *Anderson*	**Pointer** *Heath*	Hudson *Davies*	Machin *Bryceland*	Clements *Punton*	On an icy pitch Christmas Eve signing Ray Pointer lashes home after Hudson's deflected shot. Highly rated crowd hero Ron Davies eludes Curtis only once and nets. Ron Ashman's Canaries are unbeaten in ten games but City finish the stronger with a morale-boosting festive point.
23	28/12	H NORWICH	24,888	2 *9*	W 30	2-0	0-0	Mitten 53, Rees 80 / Ref: W Crossley	Wesson *Keelan*	Sillett *Stringer*	Kearns *Mullett*	Bruck *Hill*	Curtis *Sharpe*	Farmer *Allcock*	Rees *Anderson*	Pointer *Heath*	Hudson *Davies*	Machin *Bryceland*	Mitten *Punton*	With Huddersfield losing to Blues the gap is two points. On a frozen surface City deserve a bigger win for an excellent attacking performance. Norwich's unbeaten run goes up in smoke as Mitten strokes home Rees' cross and Pointer's cross is headed down by Hudson for Rees' shot.
24	1/1	H PRESTON	26,818	2 *11*	W 32	5-1	4-1	Pointer 4, 6, 44, Curtis 19, Hudson 58 / *Godfrey 40* / Ref: A Sparling	Wesson *Barton*	Roberts *Ross*	Kearns *Smith*	Bruck *Kendall*	Curtis *Singleton*	Farmer *Lapot*	Rees *Hannigan*	Pointer *Wilson*	Hudson *Dawson**	Machin *Spavin*	Mitten *Lee Godfrey*	Ruthless City pull level with Huddersfield with a stunning first half. With no full-backs fit, Roberts steps in and does a sterling job. Hudson's diving header from Mitten's cross is the best goal but Pointer gets the standing ovation with a bullet header and two clinical rebounds of posts.
25	8/1	A IPSWICH	13,054	4 *16*	L 32	0-1	0-0	*Hegan 67* / Ref: R Spittle	Wesson *Hancock*	Kearns *Davin*	Harris *McNeil*	Bruck *Harper*	Curtis *Baxter*	Farmer *Lea*	Rees *Bragan*	Pointer *Hegan*	Hudson *Baker*	Machin *Walsh*	Mitten *Kellard*	City disappoint in East Anglia, falling to Hegan's snap-shot which gives Wesson no chance. Both sides have good claims for 'goals' ruled out. Curtis' header looks over the line, as does Hegan's earlier shot. Pointer is roughed up by Lea, and Baxter and Harper protect a quiet Hancock.
26	15/1	H PLYMOUTH	21,363	4 *20*	W 34	5-1	1-1	Rees 32, Williams 66 (og), Bickle 14 [Farmer 68, 75p, Bruck 88] / Ref: M Fussey	Wesson *Leiper*	Kearns *Book*	Harris *Baird*	Bruck *Williams*	Curtis *Nelson*	Farmer *Newman*	Rees *Jennings*	Pointer *Brimacombe*	Hudson *Bickle*	Machin *Piper*	Mitten *Reeves*	City master the snowy surface and Derek Ufton's defensive Argyle. Rees' header cancels Bickle's fierce shot. Mitten's driven cross is going wide until Williams' intervention. Farmer's pile-driver bounces out off a stanchion and Pointer wins a penalty before Bruck's long-range shot.
27	29/1	A WOLVERHAMPTON	44,718	2 *4*	W 36	1-0	1-0	Pointer 37 / Ref: K Dagnall	Wesson *MacLaren*	Sillett *Wilson*	Harris *Thomson*	Bruck *Flowers*	Curtis *Woodfield*	Farmer *Holsgrove*	Rees *Wharton*	Pointer *Hunt*	Hudson *McIlmoyle*	Machin *Woodruff*	Mitten *Wagstaffe*	The biggest Molineux crowd for four years is boosted by 15,000 from Coventry. City's cast-iron defence soaks up the early pressure before Pointer guides home Sillett's long free-kick. Wolves' spirit is broken by a superb team display and Rees is unlucky not to win a late penalty.
28	5/2	H ROTHERHAM	24,932	3 *9*	D 37	2-2	1-1	Mitten 20, Pointer 89 / *Galley 63, Lyons 72* / Ref: K Seddon	Wesson *Jones*	Sillett *Wilcockson*	Harris *Clish*	Bruck *Rabjohn*	Curtis *Hasleden*	Farmer *Tiler*	Rees *Lyons*	Pointer *Chappell*	Hudson *Galley*	Machin* *Casper*	Mitten *Pring*	Roberts
																				Stale beer after the Molineux champagne. Pointer's late scrambled goal rescues a point after a woeful second-half performance. Hudson's goal drought continues and Wesson is beaten by John Galley's 35-yard shot too late. Lyons scrappy goal seems to have won it for Jack Mansell's men.
29	19/2	A MANCHESTER C	40,190	3 *1*	L 37	0-1	0-1	*Crossan 2* / Ref: R Harper	Wesson *Dowd*	Kearns *Kennedy*	Harris *Bacuzzi*	Bruck *Doyle*	Curtis *Heslop*	Farmer *Oakes*	Rees *Summerbee*	Pointer *Crossan*	Hudson *Pardoe*	Roberts *Connor*	Clements *Young*	Mercer's men win a closely fought promotion clash in the mud but Johnny Crossan looks offside from Mike Doyle's pass. Coventry miss good chances, with Machin's stand-in Dudley Roberts the biggest culprit. The defence is solid but the attack is stuttering, with Hudson anonymous.
30	26/2	H BRISTOL CITY	30,089	3 *6*	D 38	2-2	1-1	Pointer 23, Hudson 75 / *Atyeo 21, 72* / Ref: R Egan	Wesson *Gibson*	Kearns *Ford*	Harris *Briggs*	Bruck *Drury*	Curtis *Showell*	Farmer *Parr*	Rees *Savino*	Pointer *Clark*	Hudson *Atyeo*	Machin *Low*	Clements *Peters*	Sloppy City let Bristol off the hook with another poor second-half showing. Wesson fails to stop the evergreen Atyeo's soft shot and misses Low's cross for his header. Pointer's ceaseless running is not matched by Hudson's lazy-looking style but the legend lashes home the leveller.
31	12/3	A CRYSTAL PALACE	15,715	3 *8*	W 40	1-0	0-0	Rees 52 / Ref: J Cattlin	Wesson *Jackson*	Kearns *Sewell*	Harris *Howe*	Farmer *Long*	Curtis *Payne*	Harris *Bannister*	Denton *Yard*	Gould *Kember*	Pointer *Burnside*	Machin *Smith*	Rees *Imlach*	Palace lose at home for only the second time but Jackson lets Rees' shot go under him to avenge the home defeat. Hill is under pressure to replace Hudson before the deadline. A solid performance against out-of-sorts Palace who, other than Imlach's crosses, rarely trouble Wesson.

#		Date	Opponent	H/A	Res	Score	Att	Pos	Scorers / Ref	Wesson	Kearns	Harris	Farmer	Curtis	Hill	Rees	Gould	Pointer	Machin		Clements		Notes
32	A	18/3	CARLISLE		D	2-2	13,167	3 17 41	Pointer 6, Gould 58 Carlin 4, Wilson 50 Ref: J Thacker	Wesson Dean	Kearns Gallagher	Harris Caldwell	Farmer McConnell	Curtis Passmoor	Hill Harland	Rees Welsh	Gould Wilson	Pointer Livingstone	Machin Carlin		Clements Balderstone		City win a hard-earned point on a Friday night in Cumbria. Gould sets up Pointer, who reciprocates for the second equaliser, but Wilson's diving header is the best goal. Alan Ashman's team have a great home record but City could have won. Rees is booked for the fourth time.
33	H	26/3	CARDIFF		W	3-1	20,296	3 17 43	Denton 3, Farmer 15p, Machin 87 Andrews 70 Ref: F Cowan	Wesson John	Kearns Carver	Harris Ferguson	Farmer Williams	Curtis Coldrick	Bruck Hole	Denton Farrell	Gould Andrews	Pointer Toshack	Machin Johnstor		Rees King		A game of two halves, with City losing the plot after a good first half. Cardiff, however, cannot capitalise, with Andrews missing two good chances. Peter Denton's cross is punched in by John, then he is felled for the spot-kick. Machin's goal is from a cleverly worked free-kick.
34	H	2/4	BOLTON		D	2-2	19,461	3 12 44	Gould 44, Rees 81 Lee 17, Taylor 59 Ref: D Smith	Wesson Hopkinson	Kearns Rimmer	Harris Cooper	Farmer Beech	Curtis Napier	Bruck Lennard	Denton Lee	Gould Bromley	Pointer Davies	Machin Hill		Rees Taylor		City are hanging onto the coat-tails of Man City and Huddersfield, but crowds are poor. Wesson has an off day and lets in Taylor's soft shot. Gould is on fire and his fierce shot is too hot for 'Hoppy', but many are off-colour. Rees' stunning left-footer bounces back off the stanchion.
35	A	9/4	PORTSMOUTH		L	0-2	19,216	4 15 44	Portwood 25, McClelland 65 Ref: G Davis	Wesson Milkins	Kearns Wilson	Harris Tindall	Farmer Gordon	Curtis Haydock	Bruck Lewis	Denton McClelland	Gould Portwood	Pointer* Hiron	Machin Edwards		Rees McCann		After beating Huddersfield three days earlier, Pompey get a second big scalp with Brian Lewis the star. City only wake up after Wesson drops McClelland's corner into the net, but with Pointer off injured and Rees sick from the flight down, the attack stutters. Wesson breaks his nose.
36	A	11/4	DERBY		L	0-1	21,745	4 9 44	Durban 82 Ref: K Walker	Glazier Matthews	Kearns Richardson	Harris Daniel	Bruck Webster	Curtis Saxton	Bruck Waller	Rees Hughes	Farmer Thomas	Pointer Buxton	Machin Durban		Clements Hodgson		Glazier is back after almost a year and pulls off stunning saves to keep Derby out. Gould and Clements miss good chances. In a game of 60 fouls, lucky Derby get a free-kick for dangerous kicking by Bruck. Durban's dipping free-kick fools everyone. City deserve a draw in the mud.
37	H	12/4	DERBY		W	3-2	25,380	4 9 46	Machin 3, Kearns 13p, Curtis 85 Thomas 33, Kearns 88 (og) Ref: G Howell	Glazier Matthews	Kearns Richardson	Harris Daniel	Bruck Webster	Curtis Saxton	Bruck Waller	Rees Hughes	Gould Thomas	Roberts Buxton	Machin Durban		Mitten Hodgson		Stuttering City are still in the hunt. Derby impress again and look worth a point after recovering from an early battering, but ex-City man Reg Matthews dallies at a corner and Curtis heads in. Penalty-king Farmer is missing, but his deputy Mick Kearns scores when Machin is fouled.
38	H	16/4	BIRMINGHAM		W	4-3	27,111	4 10 48	P'ter 6, Machin 39, Rees 70, C'tis 80 Jackson 43, Vowden 47, Fenton 89 Herriot Ref: J Carr	Glazier Herriot	Kearns Martin	Harris Fraser	Bruck Wylie	Curtis Foster	Bruck Beard	Rees Jackson	Gould Vincent	Pointer Fenton	Machin Vowden		Mitten Hockey		Stan Cullis has revived the Blues and they give City a hard game. With rivals slipping, City are level with second-placed Huddersfield. Pointer is back with a slick goal but Curtis is a never-say-die hero, setting up for Rees and scoring himself. Gould never gives up and deserves a goal.
39	A	23/4	LEYTON ORIENT		D	1-1	5,800	3 22 49	Mitten 16 Metchick 5 Ref: V James	Glazier Rouse	Kearns Jones	Harris Worrell	Bruck Allen	Curtis Ferry	Bruck Sorrell	Rees Price	Gould O'Brien*	Pointer Flatt	Machin Gregory		Mitten Metchick	Went	Relegated Orient score from their only shot and City are kicking themselves for a dropped point. Orient are hasty in subbing O'Brien on 24 minutes, as Flatt is injured and limps on the wing. Still City cannot score against a woeful team. Glazier is late going for Metchick's drive.
40	A	26/4	CHARLTON		L	0-2	15,169	3 18 49	Glover 18, Kenning 55 Ref: L Callaghan	Glazier Wright	Kearns Bonds	Harris Kinsey	Bruck Burridge	Curtis King	Bruck Tacknell	Rees Kenning	Gould* Matthews	Pointer Holton	Machin Saunders		Mitten Glover*	Farmer Campbell	Promotion hopes look dashed in a game relayed back to 11,000 at Highfield Road. Hamstring victim Gould is subbed early on but then Pointer and Rees are crocked. Bob Stokoe's Charlton are helped by a Glazier error for the second, but are worth the win over a tired and drained City.
41	H	30/4	MIDDLESBROUGH		W	2-1	19,747	3 20 51	Roberts -4, Pointer 17 Gibson 6 Ref: J Cattlin	Glazier Appleby	Kearns Butler	Harris Jones	Bruck Horner	Curtis Smith	Bruck Davidson	Denton Downing	Pointer Gibson	Roberts Irvine	Machin McMordie		Clements Lawson		City are left with a slim hope of promotion but brave Boro look set to go down. The injured Rees and Gould are missed, but with only the classy Ian Gibson showing for the visitors, City deserve the win. Roberts heads in before Ray Pointer pounces. Curtis' headers deserve a goal.
42	A	7/5	HUDDERSFIELD		W	2-0	24,997	2 4 53	Pointer 40, Gould 71 Ref: F Cowen	Glazier Oldfield	Kearns Atkins	Harris McNab	Bruck Nicholson	Curtis Coddington	Farmer Meagan	Rees McHale	Machin Gilliver	Gould Leighton	Pointe Smith		Clements Massie		3,000 City fans celebrate as if they are promoted but Southampton can pip them. If only City could have played like this at Derby, Charlton or Orient! City, playing in all-white, win through Pointer's ruthless finish off Machin's corner and Gould's cool lob after Atkins' poor back-pass.

Home 25,370 Away 18,950 Average

LEAGUE DIVISION 2 (CUP-TIES) — Manager: Jimmy Hill — SEASON 1965-66

League Cup

		Att	F-A	H-T	1	2	3	4	5	6	7	8	9	10	11	12 sub used
2 A LEYTON ORIENT 22/9	6 W	5,326	3-0	3-0	Wesson	Kearns	Harris	Farmer	Curtis	Hill	Rees	Smith	Hudson	Machin	Mitten	
					Rouse	Webb	Worrell	Went	Ferry	Sorrell	McGeorge	Gregory	Flatt	Allen	Metchick	

Scorers: Hudson 7, Harris 12, Machin 32
Ref: G Martin

City cruise into Round 3 against woeful Orient. Dave Sexton has a promising young team but little experience. Hudson heads in Rees' cross before Harris's 35-yard lob beats a distracted Rouse for a joke goal. Machin's goal ends the game as a contest. City ease up and miss chances.

| 3 A MANCHESTER C 13/10 | 3 W | 18,213 | 3-2 | 1-1 | Wesson | Dowd | Harris | Farmer | Curtis | Hill | Rees | Hale | Hudson | Roberts | Clements | |
| | | | 4 | | | Kennedy | Sear | Cheetham | Heslop | Oakes | Summerbee | Crossan | Pardoe | Brand | Young | |

Scorers: Hudson 5, Clem'ts 60, Oakes 89 (og), Pardoe 21, Crossan 72
Ref: R Windle

Oakes' misdirected back-pass sends City through after a thriller. Hudson's classy lob sets the scene. Breathless City then weather a first-half storm, with Young starring. Clements' low shot makes it 2-1 before Crossan equalises. Harris and Summerbee have a bitter ding-dong battle.

| 4 H WEST BROM 3/11 | 1 D | 38,476 | 1-1 | 1-1 | Wesson | Kearns | Harris | Farmer | Curtis | Hill | Machin | Hale | Hudson | Roberts | Rees | |
| | | | 1:6 | | Sheppard | Cram | Fairfax | Lovett | Jones | Fraser | Brown | Crawford | Kaye | Hope | Clark | |

Scorers: Hale 18, Kaye 42
Ref: L Callaghan

The second largest crowd in the competition's history watches a thriller. Sheppard twice blocks shots but Hale chips over him. Classy Albion level with a swift break and John Kaye's shot goes in off Curtis' heel. City never let Albion settle but the Baggies have the best chances to win.

| 4R A WEST BROM 10/11 | 3 L | 31,956 | 1-6 | 1-2 | Wesson | Kearns | Harris | Farmer | Curtis | Hill | Rees | Hale | Hudson | Machin | Clark | |
| | | | 1:4 | | Sheppard | Cram | Fairfax | Lovett | Jones | Fraser | Brown | Astle | Kaye | Hope | Clark | |

Scorers: Machin 27 [Fraser 62, 65] Astle 1, 58, 76, Brown 40
Ref: E Crawford

At 1-2, City look capable of drawing level but Jeff Astle's stunning headed second opens the floodgates and the scoreline flatters Albion. Two of the goals are deflections that give Wesson no chance. 7,000 City fans cheer valiantly but class tells. Albion will go on to win the trophy.

FA Cup

| 3 A SWINDON 22/1 | 4 W | 20,200 | 2-1 | 1-0 | Wesson | Kearns | Harris | Bruck | Curtis | Farmer | Rees | Pointer | Hudson | Machin | Mitten | |
| | | | 3:7 | | Downsboro' | Dawson | Trollope | Morgan | Nurse | Richardson | Henderson | Smart | East | Brown | Rogers | |

Scorers: Trollope 8 (og), Rees 81, Brown 68
Ref: L Callaghan

Ice and pools of water make it a treacherous surface but both teams adapt and put on a spectacle. Swindon are unlucky not to draw with Rogers losing his footing when through in the 2nd minute and hitting the bar near the end. Brown's goal is a Kearns error, but Rees' grounder is true.

| 4 A CREWE 12/2 | 3 D | 10,040 | 1-1 | 0-1 | Wesson | Mailey | Harris | Bruck | Curtis | Hill | Rees | Pointer | Hudson | Farmer | Clements | |
| | | | 4:17 | | Mailey | Whelan | Leigh | Bradshaw | Barnes | Gannon | Gowans | Kane | Sandiford | King | Wheatley | |

Scorers: Rees 88, Curtis 9 (og)
Ref: J Carr

Ernie Tagg's brave Crewe are two minutes from a big shock when Rees scores a deserved equaliser. Crewe harry and hustle City in the first half and Peter Kane's shot goes in off Curtis' face. City dominate after the break but Mailey is the hero. Increased prices keep the crowd low.

| 4R H CREWE 14/2 | 3 W | 27,820 | 4-1 | 2-1 | Wesson | Mailey | Harris | Bruck | Curtis | Hill | Denton | Pointer | Hudson | Farmer | Clements | 72p |
| | | | 4:18 | | Mailey | Whelan | Leigh | Bradshaw | Stott | Bodell | Gannon | Kane | Sandiford | King | Wheatley | |

Scorers: Clem'ts 4, Hudson 37, 88, Farmer 72p, Sandiford 14p
Ref: J Carr

Four players are booked and the captains lectured by a fussy ref as City make heavy weather of Crewe. Mailey flicks Clements' corner into the net. Hudson gets a kick in the mouth heading his first, but dribbles through a ruck of players for his second. Bodell handles Clements cross.

| 5 A EVERTON 5/3 | 3 L | 60,350 | 0-3 | 0-1 | Wesson | Kearns | Harris | Bruck | Curtis | Hill | Machin | Farmer | Pointer | Gould | Rees | |
| | | | 1:9 | | West | Brown | Wilson | Gabriel | Labone | Harris | Scott | Young | Pickering | Harvey | Temple | |

Scorers: Young 13, Temple 69, Pickering 87
Ref: R Tinkler

City, with Hudson and Hale gone, put out a defensive line-up which fails. Both sides change kit but neither plays well. City are on top after the break but Derek Temple's scrappy goal ends the contest. Wesson and Curtis' mix-up gifts a third to Everton, who will go on to win the Cup.

		P	W	D	L	F	A	W	D	L	F	A	Pts
						Home					Away		
1	Manchester C	42	14	7	0	40	14	8	5	8	36	30	59
2	Southampton	42	13	4	4	51	25	9	6	6	34	31	54
3	COVENTRY	42	14	5	2	54	31	6	8	7	19	22	53
4	Huddersfield	42	12	7	2	35	12	7	6	8	27	24	51
5	Bristol C	42	9	10	2	27	15	8	7	6	36	33	51
6	Wolves	42	15	4	2	52	18	5	6	10	35	43	50
7	Rotherham	42	12	6	3	48	29	4	8	9	27	45	46
8	Derby	42	13	2	6	48	31	3	9	9	23	37	43
9	Bolton	42	12	2	7	43	25	4	7	10	19	34	41
10	Birmingham	42	10	6	5	41	29	6	3	12	29	46	41
11	Crys Palace	42	11	7	3	29	16	3	6	12	18	36	41
12	Portsmouth	42	13	4	4	47	26	3	4	14	27	52	40
13	Norwich	42	8	7	6	33	27	4	8	9	19	25	39
14	Carlisle	42	16	2	3	43	19	1	3	17	17	44	39
15	Ipswich	42	12	6	3	38	23	3	3	15	20	43	39
16	Charlton	42	10	6	5	39	29	2	8	11	22	41	38
17	Preston	42	7	10	4	37	23	4	5	12	25	47	37
18	Plymouth	42	7	8	6	37	26	5	5	11	17	37	37
19	Bury	42	12	5	4	45	25	2	2	17	17	51	35
20	Cardiff	42	10	3	8	37	35	2	7	12	34	56	34
21	Middlesbro	42	8	8	5	36	28	2	5	14	22	58	33
22	Leyton Orient	42	3	9	9	19	36	2	4	15	19	44	23
		924	241	128	93	879	542	93	128	241	542	879	924

Odds & ends

Double wins: (4) Wolves, Cardiff, Plymouth, Birmingham.
Double losses: (0).

Won from behind: (5) Wolves (h), Carlisle (h), Portsmouth (h), Plymouth (h), Middlesbrough (h).
Lost from in front: (1) Bolton (a).

High spots: Away wins at Wolves and Huddersfield.
League Cup draw with West Brom.
Form of Curtis, Hill and Rees.
Farmer's eight successful penalty-kicks
Solid home form – most goals in the division.
Pointer's scoring run.

Low spots: Cup exits at West Brom and Everton.
Crucial Easter defeats at Portsmouth and Derby.
Poor scoring record away from home.

Red cards: none.
Red cards opponents: none.

Hat-tricks: (1) Ray Pointer (Preston h).
Opposing hat-tricks: (1) Jeff Astle (WBA LC a).
Leading scorer: (17) George Hudson.

	Appearances						Goals			
	Lge	Sub	LC	Sub	FAC	Sub	Lge	LC	FAC	Tot
Bruck, Dietmar	22	1			4		2			2
Clements, Dave	22	1	1		2		3	1	1	5
Curtis, George	42		4		4		5			5
Denton, Peter	9				1		1			1
Farmer, Ron	34	1	4		4		9		1	10
Glazier, Bill	7									
Gould, Bobby	17	2			1		5			5
Hale, Ken	12	1	3					1		1
Harris, Allan	40		4		4					
Hill, Brian	22		4		3			1		1
Hudson, George	28		4		3		13	2	2	17
Kearns, Mick	40		4		4		2			2
Machin, Ernie	38	1	3		2		4	2		6
Mitten, John	12		1		1		3			3
Pointer, Ray	19				4		11			11
Rees, Ronnie	41		4		3		7		2	9
Roberts, Dudley	10	1	3				6			6
Sillett, John	10	1	1							
Smith, John	1		1							
Turner, Alan	1									
Wesson, Bob	35		4		4					
(own-goals)							2	1	1	4
21 players used	462	10	44		44		73	8	7	88

LEAGUE DIVISION 2 — Manager: Jimmy Hill — SEASON 1966-67

No	Date		Att	Pos	Pt	F-A	H-T	1	2	3	4	5	6	7	8	9	10	11	12 sub used
1	20/8	H HULL	27,933		W	1-0	0-0	Glazier	Kearns	Bruck	Hill	Curtis	Farmer	**Key**	Gibson	Gould	Pointer	Rees	
					2			McKechnie	Davidson!	Butler D	Jarvis	Milner	Simpkin	Henderson	Wagstaff	Chilton	Houghton	Butler I	
	Bruck 48																		
	Ref: F Cowen							In blistering heat, Bruck's 35-yard ground-shot creeps past a surprised Hull new-boy McKechnie. Newly promoted Tigers' potent strike-force is tamed but City have to defend well near the end. Davidson off for hitting Gould. Machin is injured but Ian Gibson is the new fans' hero.											
2	24/8	A PLYMOUTH	16,061		L	2-4	2-2	Glazier	Kearns	Bruck	Hill	Curtis	Farmer	Rees	Gibson	Gould	Pointer*	Clements	
					2			Leiper	Rounsevell	Baird	Piper	Nelson	Newman	Jones	Neale	Bickle	Reynolds	Jennings	Mitten
	Gould 24, Pointer 44							A bad night for the defence and Glazier especially. Bill is at fault for at least two goals and the other two are 30-yard shots that he fails to stop. After Leiper carries outside the area, Gibson's free-kick is volleyed in by Pointer. City fail to press home their superiority and Bickle pounces.											
	Piper 5, Jones 9, Bickle 78, 88																		
	Ref: P Rhodes																		
3	27/8	A PORTSMOUTH	16,297	7	W	2-0	1-0	Glazier	Kearns	Bruck	Hill	Curtis	Farmer	Rees	Gibson	Gould	Pointer	Clements	
				15	4			Milkins	Pack	Tindall	Gordon	Haydock	Harris	Barton*	McCann	Hiron	Lewis	Kellard	McClelland
	Clements 25, Gould 46							Pompey are reeling from a 4-5 defeat to Birmingham and are no match for a fresher Gibson-inspired City. Classy Gibbo makes both goals, a Clements' header and Gould's vicious shot. Curtis muffs two chances for a rout. Glazier shows his class but Rees and Pointer are off-form.											
	Ref: H Davies																		
4	30/8	H PLYMOUTH	20,343	5	W	1-0	1-0	Glazier	Kearns	Bruck	Hill	Curtis	Farmer	Rees	Gibson	Gould	Pointer	Clements	
				7	6			Leiper	Rounsevell	Baird	Piper	Nelson	Newman	Jones	Neale	Bickle	Reynolds	Jennings	
	Pointer 37							City are lucky to beat a polished Argyle side. Pointer volleys home on the horizontal as he falls, but the expected goal rush doesn't come. Bill Glazier redeems himself with several fine saves and with Ian Gibson marked by Piper only the effervescent Gould troubles Derek Ufton's side.											
	Ref: D Wells																		
5	3/9	H BIRMINGHAM	36,400	5	D	1-1	0-0	Glazier	Kearns	Bruck	Hill	Curtis	Farmer	Rees	Gibson	Gould	Machin	Clements	
				1	7			Herriot	Martin	Green	Wylie*	Foster	Beard	Thomson	Bridges	Vowden	Murray	Fenton	
	Gould 58							Missed chances cost City a point but they end defensive Blues' 100% record. The persistent Gould is on fire with numerous goal-attempts and scores a stunning goal. Cullis's men net with their only second-half chance. Hockey is sent off for fouling Ron Farmer after an earlier booking.											
	Vowden 73																		
	Ref: F Nicholson																		
6	5/9	A MILLWALL	15,766	5	L	0-1	0-0	Glazier	Kearns	Bruck	Hill	Curtis	Farmer	Rees	Gibson	Gould	Machin	Pointer	
				10	7			Leslie	Gilchrist	McCullough	Jones	Snowden	Wilson	Broadfoot	Dunphy	Julians	Neil	Rowan	
	Broadfoot 65							Promoted Millwall with the support of a vociferous crowd have not lost at home in 49 matches. Their physical play hampers City's football but Lawrie Leslie is the hero saving from Gould and Pointer. Joe Broadfoot scores from 35 yards and Ron Farmer's similar shot goes past the post.											
	Ref: D Smith																		
7	10/9	A NORWICH	13,454	7	D	1-1	0-0	Glazier	Kearns	Bruck	Hill	Curtis	Farmer	Rees	Gibson	Gould	Machin	Clements	
				19	8			Keelan	Stringer	Black*	Lucas	Sharpe	Mullett	Anderson	Bryceland	Bolland	Curran	Punton	Sutton
	Gould 63							Rees skins debutant Alan Black to cross for Gould's header and a deserved draw. It takes Curran's strong header from a long free-kick to rouse a sluggish and defensive Sky Blues. Lack of goals is Hill's problem with Rees and Gibbo out of form again. 600 away fans cheer the rare goal.											
	Curran 49																		
	Ref: A Weller																		
8	17/9	H BRISTOL CITY	21,140	5	W	1-0	0-0	Glazier	Kearns	Bruck	Hill	Curtis	Farmer	Rees	Gibson	Gould	Pointer	Clements	
				20	10			Gibson	Ford	Briggs	Parr	Connor	Low	Peters	Clark	Down	Sharpe	Hartley	Mitten
	Kearns 65p							Only five sides have scored fewer than City. With Farmer off with concussion after a clash with Clark, Kearns gets away with a poor spot-kick after Low's handball. Boring Bristol come for a point and their best chance is headed out by Bruck. Hill rejects job with newly-formed NASL.											
	Ref: H Richards																		
9	24/9	H BURY	22,076	4	W	3-0	1-0	Glazier	Kearns	Bruck	Hill	Curtis	Clements	Key	**Tudor**	Gould	Gibson	Rees	
				12	12			Ramsbottom	Leech	Eastham	Turner	Colquhoun	Parry	Lowes	Maltby	Aimson	Owen	Claxton	
	Gould 5, Clements 61, Gibson 76							The game is decided on the hour. The division's top scorer Owen's 'goal' is ruled out for hands. Bury are incensed but City net within seconds with Clements' thunderous shot. Gould heads home with power and Gibson's wicked shot comes down off the bar but looks well over the line.											
	Ref: J Osbourne																		
10	1/10	A PRESTON	13,681	8	L	2-3	1-2	Glazier	Kearns	Bruck	Hill	Curtis	Clements	Key	Tudor	Gould	Gibson	Rees	
				11	12			Kelly	Ross	Smith	Spavin	Singleton	Cranston	Wilson	Hannigan	Dawson	Lawton	Lee	
	Tudor 40, Curtis 54							City come from 0-2 to level but throw away the initiative and settle for a point. The referee could have given two penalties apiece but only punishes Kearns' trip on Lee. Tudor clips in his first goal and Curtis heads in to level, but City are out of luck with two shots hitting wood.											
	Dawson 2p, Hannigan 27, Wilson 59																		
	Ref: N Callender																		

#	H/A	Opponent	Date	Res	Pos	Pts	Att	Scorers	Glazier	Kearns	Bruck*	Hill	Clements	Curtis	Machin	Pointer	Gould	Gibson	Rees	Key	Report
11	A	CARLISLE	8/10	0-1	10	10	10,885	Clements 77	Glazier Ross	Kearns Neill	Bruck* Caldwell	Hill McConnell	Clements Garbutt	Curtis Passmoor	Machin Welsh	Pointer Carlin	Gould Wilson	Gibson Baldersione	Rees Hartle	Key	Wilson 30, Garbutt 64. Ref: G Kew. A disjointed City fall in Cumberland. Curtis is punished for a rare error by Wilson, and Neil's cross is swept home by Garbutt. Clements is pushed forward at 0-2 and hits four stunning shots, and one goes in off a post. Gould and Rees miss good chances and Gibson looks off-colour.
12	H	BLACKBURN	15/10	2-0	8	12	21,017	Tudor 7, Gould 19	Glazier Barton	Kearns Newton	Hill Joyce	Clements Clayton	Curtis Holt	Machin Ferguson	Key Connelly	Gould McEvoy	Tudor Douglas	Mitten Harrison	Ref: W Holian	Relegated Rovers have several former England men and current cap Keith Newton but are no match for lively City Farmer and Machin are back and help City defend their early lead. City are now four points behind leaders Hull. Hill denies rumours of Johnny Haynes' signing.
13	A	BOLTON	22/10	1-1	8	14	14,669	Machin 77	Glazier Hopkinson	Kearns Hatton D	Hill Cooper	Clements Rimmer	Curtis Napier	Machin Bromley	Rees Lee	Gould Byrom	Tudor Lennard	Mitten Taylor	Ref: R Windle	Byrom 86. An excellent second-half display deserves both points. City's pressure is rewarded when local boy Machin slides in after good work by Mitten. Bromley sets up Byrom who is in for Davies, sold to Newcastle this week. Tudor has four chances but is foiled by ex-England man Hopkinson.
14	H	CHARLTON	29/10	1-0	6	15	19,888	Gould 10	Glazier Wright	Kearns Bonds	Hill* Kinsey	Clements Reeves	Curtis King	Machin Appleton	Rees Kenning	Gould Saunders	Tudor Campbell	Mitten Glover	Coop	Ref: V Batty	Another scrappy home win, thanks to a good defensive display but it's not pretty. A nervous last ten minutes are wasted by the average visitors whose star man is keeper Wright who saves well from Rees and Gould. Kearns celebrates his 300th league game by keeping Len Glover quiet.
15	A	DERBY	5/11	2-1	5	17	22,949	Tudor 3, Machin 66	Glazier Matthews	Kearns Richardson	Bruck Daniel	Farmer Webster	Curtis Waller*	Machin Saxton	Rees Hughes	Gould Hector	Tudor Buxton	Machin Durban	Mitten Hodgson	Thomas	Hodgson 90. Ref: F Cowen. City put on one of their best displays of the season to notch a first-ever win at Derby. £40,000 Kevin Hector is bossed by Clements, and Farmer is superb. Derby have few chances and lose for the first time in seven. But for sloppy shooting and Matthews, it would have been a bigger win.
16	H	CRYSTAL PALACE	12/11	1-2	6	17	23,035	Gould 28	Glazier Jackson J	Kearns Howe	Bruck Bannister	Farmer Payne	Curtis Stephenson	Machin Wood	Rees Robertson	Gould Kember	Tudor Woodruff	Mitten Jackson C	Ref: S Kayley		Jackson C 6, Kember 60. In a thriller, captain for the day Glazier is at fault for both goals. Mitten misses a sitter and Jackson pulls off some great stops. Woodruff's long throw creates the second goal for the best Palace side for years. Gould's opportunism gets him a goal and he also hits the bar near the end.
17	A	HUDDERSFIELD	19/11	1-3	7	17	15,192	Tudor 39	Glazier Parkin	Kearns Cattlin	Bruck Nicholson	Farmer Coddington	Curtis Meagan	Machin Hellawell	Rees* Rudge	Gould Leighton	Tudor Dobson	Mitten Hill	Coop	Ref: K Dagnall	Dobson 60, Leighton 64, Meagan 88 Oldfield. Non-stop Town pressure earns a deserved victory. Gould guides Mitten's long cross into the path of Tudor. Mike Hellawell's pace sets up the equaliser before Glazier fails to hold a shot and Tony Leighton pounces. The third, a dipper, catches the otherwise brilliant Glazier off his line.
18	H	CARDIFF	26/11	3-2	6	19	19,682	Tudor 25, Gibson 46, 55	Thomas Wilson	Kearns Coldrick	Coop Ferguson	Farmer Williams	Curtis Murray	Clements Harris	Key Farrell	Gibson Toshack	Tudor Brown	Machin Johnston	Rees Bird	Glover	Toshack 97, 88. Ref: K Seddon. With the top six all losing, City gain ground but should have had a scoring spree. Cardiff may be poor but the returning Gibson shows Hill what he has been missing with a one-man show and a sublime second goal. Gould misses a hatful and Wilson gifts two. City relax at the end.
19	A	WOLVERHAMPTON	3/12	3-1	4	23	27,232	Gibson 7, Key 73, Rees 32	Glazier Davies	Kearns Wilson	Bruck Thomson	Farmer Bailey	Curtis Woodfield	Clements Flowers	Gould Wharton	Machin Hunt	Gould McIlmoyle	Tudor* Burnside	Rees Wagstaffe		Burnside 50. Ref: N Burtenshaw. On a snow-covered pitch, City take a battering for an hour after Gibbo's snap goal. Burnside's header looks ominous but heroic defensive play, with Bill Glazier at his best and two cross-shots, knock Wolves off top spot. A famous victory and three in a row over Ronnie Allen's team.
20	H	IPSWICH	9/12	5-0	3	25	25,724	Gould 4, 15, 33, Key, Gibson	Glazier Hancock	Kearns McNeil	Bruck Houghton	Farmer Harper D	Curtis Baxter	Clements Lea	Key Spearritt	Gould Hegan	Machin* Crawford	Gibson Baker	Rees Brogan	Morrissey	Ref: I Jones. On a wet Friday night the scoreline does not flatter City, who rip the leaders apart. Gibson is at the heart of everything and scores a memorable chipped goal over seven defenders. Gould and Rees are on fire and the former deserves his three goals, a tap-in, a vicious drive and a header.
21	A	HULL	17/12	0-1	4	25	26,577	Key 46, Tudor 76	Glazier Swan	Kearns Davidson	Bruck Butler D	Farmer Jarvis	Curtis Milner	Clements Simpkin	Key Henderson	Machin Wagstaff	Gould Chilton	Tudor Wilkinson	Rees Butler I		Butler I 9, 88. Ref: L Hamer. City's defence has the upper hand against the best attack in the division. Cliff Britton's team have scored 48 and put six past Palace but leave their equaliser, a mis-hit, late. Curtis and Clements master Chilton and Wagstaff, and injured Gibbo is not missed. Key's goal is a deflection.

LEAGUE DIVISION 2 — Manager: Jimmy Hill — SEASON 1966-67

No	Date		Att	Pos	Pt	F-A	H-T	Scorers, Times, and Referees	1	2	3	4	5	6	7	8	9	10	11	12 sub used
22	H ROTHERHAM 26/12		31,619	2	W 16	4-2 28	2-2	Gould 7, 65, Gibson 24, Farmer 77p Massey 33, Williams 39 Ref: L Callaghan	Glazier Hill*	Kearns Wilcockson	Bruck Clish	Farmer Rabjohn	Curtis Haselden	Clements Tiler	Key Massey	Machin Williams	Gould Galley	Gibson* Chappell	Rees Harrity	Hill Pring
								A big holiday crowd see an incident-packed match, and City deservedly win. Bobby Gould is again the hero with a tap-in, a thunderous shot which breaks Alan Hill's finger, and he is fouled for the penalty. Gibson limps off and Galley goes in goal, but is sadly attacked by a City fan.												
23	A ROTHERHAM 27/12		13,301	2	D 15	1-1 29	0-	Clements 90 Massey 71 Ref: G Cooke	Glazier Jones	Kearns Wilcockson	Bruck Clish	Hill Rabjohn	Curtis Haselden	Clements Tiler	Key Massey	Machin Williams	Gould Galley	Farmer Chappell	Rees Pring	
								The Millers carry a grudge from the previous day and rough City up. Curtis and co defend desperately but with great heart. City's players are convinced that Massey handles for the goal. When it looks all over, Clements levels in the 92nd minute with a shot through a crowd of players.												
24	H PORTSMOUTH 31/12		24,981	2	W 12	5-1 31	2-0	Tudor 19, Gould 42, Machin 46, [Mitten 52, Key 55] Hiron 64 Ref: P Bye	Glazier Milkins	Kearns Pack	Bruck Tindall	Farmer Gordon	Curtis Radcliffe	Clements Harris	Key Lewis	Machin McCann	Gould Hiron	Tudor Edwards	Mitten Kellard	
								Pompey arrive with the best away record in the division, depart humbled and lucky to have got off with five. 17 goals in four home games have lit up City's season. Tudor, Machin and Key score headers, Gould profits from Milkins' bad kick, and Mitten's cool flick tops a great display.												
25	A BIRMINGHAM 7/1		36,316	1	D 12	1-1 32	0-1	Machin 52 Curtis 23 (og) Ref: W Crossley	Glazier Herriot	Kearns Murray	Bruck Green	Farmer Thomson	Curtis Sharples	Clements Beard	Key Hockey	Machin Leggat	Gould Bullock	Tudor Vowden	Mitten Bridges	
								10,000 City fans boost Blues' biggest crowd for two years as City go top for the first time, on a wet pitch. Clements' low cross when a shot looks on leaves Machin with an easy finish against a confused defence.												
26	H NORWICH 14/1		27,354	1	W 21	2-1 34	0-0	Farmer 58, Machin 89 Sheffield 85 Ref: H Davies	Glazier Keelan	Kearns Stringer	Bruck Mullett	Farmer Lucas	Curtis Brown	Clements Allcock	Key Kenning	Machin Bolland	Gould Sheffield	Gibson Curran	Rees Anderson	
								City struggle to beat lowly but gallant Norwich, for whom Keelan is in top form. Ron Farmer's free-kick skids off the goalmouth sand. Curran has an offside goal ruled out. Sheffield's close-range header is trumped when Farmer's cross is set up by Gould for the outstanding Machin.												
27	A BRISTOL CITY 21/1		21,600	1	D 18	2-2 35	2-2	Curtis 14, Bruck 36 Crowe 11, Bush 18 Ref: G Roper	Glazier Gibson	Kearns Ford	Bruck Briggs	Farmer Parr	Curtis Connor	Clements Low	Key Derrick	Machin Crowe	Gould Bush	Gibson Quigley	Rees Peters	
								Unconvincing City extend their unbeaten run to ten after falling behind again. Bristol score from two errors, with Crowe unmarked to volley in and dithering Clements robbed by Bush. Curtis' bullet header from a free-kick and Bruck's vicious shot restores parity. City hang on at the end.												
28	H BURY 4/2		9,871	1	W 19	1-0 37	0-0	Rees 79 Ref: P Partridge	Glazier Harker	Kearns Colquhoun	Bruck Eastham	Farmer Turner	Curtis Waldron	Clements Lindsay	Key* Lowes	Machin Jones	Gould Aimson	Tudor Owen	Rees Parry	Gould Lee
								It's like a home match, with 2,500 travelling fans. The axed Gould is on at half-time for the injured Key and has an offside 'goal' ruled out. Brian Lewis makes a quiet debut and sits back after Lawton's goal. After constant attacking, Machin heads in Gibson's cross in a fine move to send the crowd wild.												
29	H PRESTON 11/2		29,047	1	W 7	2-1 39	0-1	Machin 80, Gould 86 Lawton 25 Ref: B Homewood	Glazier Kelly	Kearns Ross	Bruck Smith	Farmer Lawton	Curtis Singleton	Clements Kendall	Lewis Hannigan	Machin Godfrey	Gould Greenhalgh	Gibson Spavin*	Rees Wilson	
								Late goals are stock-in-trade for City and Gould justifies his recall sliding home from Farmer's slide-rule pass. Jimmy Milne's team use rough-arm tactics and sit back after Lawton's goal.												
30	A CHARLTON 18/2		17,914	1	W 16	2-1 41	0-0	Gould 50, 89 Myers 89 Ref: P Bye	Glazier Wright	Kearns Bonds	Bruck Gregory	Farmer Reeves	Curtis King	Clements Saunders	Lewis Myers	Machin Tees	Gould Green*	Gibson Campbell	Rees Glover	Peacock
								4,000 travelling fans see City notch a deserved first-ever win at the Valley. Curtis upsets Addicks' manager Bob Stokoe when he clatters into Tees who collides with the trainer's hut. Stokoe calls City 'rough'. Gould finishes coolly after Gibbo's great dribble and Machin's perfect pass.												
31	H CARLISLE 25/2		29,965	1	W 6	2-1 43	1-1	Gould 44, Machin 88 McVitie 11 Ref: M Fussey	Glazier Ross !	Kearns McConnell	Bruck Caldwell	Lewis Balderstone	Curtis Passmoor	Clements Garbutt	Key* Welsh	Machin Carlin	Gould Wilson	Gibson McVitie	Rees Hartle	Farmer
								The fans' nerves are frayed again. Alan Ashman's gritty team hold out after Ross's sending off for striking Gould, until Machin's scrambled goal beats stand-in keeper McConnell. Key damages ankle ligaments and the team go to Worthing for a week's break to recharge the batteries.												

#		Date			Result		Scorers	Ref	Glazier	Bruck	Kearns	Farmer	Curtis	Clements	Lowes	Machin	Gould	Gibson	Rees	Report
32	A	11/3	NORTHAMPTON	1	D	0-0		Ref: J Carr	Glazier	Harvey	Kearns Foley	Farmer Mackin	Curtis Branston	Clements Kuria	Lowes Walden	Machin Brown	Gould Large	Gibson Moore	Rees Lines	Dave Bowen's Cobblers look doomed to another relegation. A wind-spoiled game evens the contest but City, cheered on by 8,000 fans, look the only winners. Mackin and Branston block goalbound shots and Harvey makes some good saves. City goal-less for only the second time.
			20,100	22		44				Everett										
33	H	18/3	BOLTON	1	D	1-1	Gould 40 Phillips 87	Ref: H New	Glazier Hopkinson	Bruck Hatton D	Kearns Hatton D	Farmer Rimmer	Curtis Hulme	Clements Lennard	Lowes Phillips	Machin Lee	Gould Hatton R	Gibson Bromley	Rees Hill	Sixteen games without defeat is a new club record as Match of the Day makes its first visit. Phillips' header is Bolton's first effort on target, and gains a lucky point. Rees' mazy 60-yard run sets up Gould but despite Machin's excellent display he misses four chances. Lowes struggles.
			28,674	11		45				Farrimond										
34	A	25/3	BLACKBURN	1	W	1-0	Gould 51	Ref: W Holian	Glazier Barton	Bruck Wilson	Kearns Newton	Farmer Sharples	Curtis Clayton	Clements Hole	Lowes Ferguson J	Machin Joyce	Gould Darling	Gibson Douglas	Rees Connelly	A vital win and only a second home defeat for Jack Marshall's team. Rovers have won five in a row but promotion hopes are slim. Ferguson strikes Bruck seconds before the break and walks. Gould harries Barton into dropping Rees' cross and nets. The defence soaks up the pressure.
			26,380	3		47														
35	H	28/3	NORTHAMPTON	2	W	2-0	Machin 62, Gould 83	Ref: H Davey	Glazier	Bruck Walker	Kearns Foley	Farmer Mackin	Curtis Branston	Clements Kuria	Lowes Walden	Machin Brown	Gould Large	Gibson Moore	Rees Lines	The old foe stubbornly defend but collapse after the break. In ten wild minutes a Gibbo shot hits both posts and into Harvey's arms, Harvey tips over Gould's shot and Lewis is headbutted by Branston, who is lucky to stay on. The biggest league crowd for 18 years roars the team on.
			38,566	21		49			Harvey											
36	H	1/4	DERBY	2	D	2-2	Gould 17, Machin 80 Hector 38, Thomas 60	Ref: R Farper	Glazier Boulton	Bruck Daniel	Kearns Richardson	Farmer Thomas	Curtis Saxton	Clements Waller	Lowes Hughes	Machin Hector*	Gould Buxton	Gibson Durban	Rees Cleevely Hopkinson	Several players have a bad day and Tim Ward's relaxed Rams almost end the run. They score two good but soft goals, and at 2-1 Hughes has a 'goal' ruled out. Finally Machin's header from Bruck's surging run and cross saves the day. Wolves' draw at the Den leave the rivals level.
			32,041	15		50														
37	A	8/4	CRYSTAL PALACE	2	D	1-1	Gould 69 Kember 53	Ref: P Baldwin	Glazier Jackson J	Bruck Presland	Kearns Sewell	Farmer Payne	Curtis Stephenson	Clements Bannister	Lowes Woodruff	Machin Kember	Gould Dyson*	Gibson Byrne	Rees O'Connell Long	A first-ever Saturday night match ends all-square after a titanic battle. Tempers are frayed and lots of fouls goes unpunished. City only start to play when a goal down and then pummel the home side. After close shaves galore, Gould finally scrambles in a brave header from Rees' chip.
			23,247	8		51														
38	H	15/4	HUDDERSFIELD	2	W	1-0	Gould 63	Ref: P Walters	Glazier Oldfield	Bruck Parkin	Kearns Cattlin	Farmer Nicholson	Curtis Ellam	Clements Meagan	Lowes Hellawell	Machin Clark	Gould Leighton	Gibson Dobson	Rees Hill	Seven points clear of third-placed Ipswich, City are virtually promoted. The nerve-ends show and Town look the team set for Division 1. Hill gives Kearns a roasting and Glazier twice saves City. Gould's opportunism wins the game, but the fans stay off when Ronnie Rees pulls it.
			29,683	6		53														
39	A	22/4	CARDIFF	2	D	1-1	Key 30 Brown 60	Ref: H New	Glazier Wilson	Bruck Ferguson	Kearns Coldrick	Farmer Williams	Curtis Murray	Clements Harris	Lowes Jones	Machin Brown	Gould Toshack	Gibson King	Rees* Bird Farmer	The champagne stays on ice with one point needed for promotion after a botched job at Ninian Park. A failure to capitalise on early domination and then a Toshack penalty miss on 72 minutes lets City off. Key taps in after Brian Lewis' run and shot, and Brown levels with a soft goal.
			19,592	20		54														
40	H	29/4	WOLVERHAMPTON	2	W	3-1	Machin 59, Gibson 63, Rees 85 Knowles 40	Ref: N Callender	Glazier Parkes	Bruck Thomson	Kearns Bailey	Farmer Hunt	Curtis Hawkins	Clements Holsgrove	Lowes Wharton	Machin Knowles	Gould Dougan	Gibson Burnside	Rees Wagstaffe	Both sides are up before the 'Midlands Match of the Century' starts. A record crowd with thousands locked out see a classic with City coming from behind to rip Wolves to shreds. Two friendly crowd invasions threaten to end the game, but the fans stay off when Ronnie Rees seals it.
			51,452	1		56														
41	A	6/5	IPSWICH	2	D	1-1	Gibson 27 Viljoen 83	Ref: K Walker	Glazier Hancock	Bruck Carroll	Kearns Houghton	Farmer Spearritt	Curtis Baxter	Clements Bolton	Lewis Broadfoot	Machin Hegan	Tudor Crawford	Gibson Viljoen	Rees Brogan	City let Bill McGarry's Ipswich off a drubbing after a Gibbo-inspired performance. Hancock excels, the posts intervene, and shots are cleared off the line as the Sky Blues thrill their 5,000 fans. Rees' cross is headed in by Gibson and 19-year old Viljoen looks offside for the equaliser.
			18,916	4		57														
42	H	13/5	MILLWALL	1	W	2-0	Key 9, Tudor 38, Machin 59 Neil 49	Ref: K Dagnall	Glazier Leslie	Bruck Cripps	Kearns Gilchrist	Farmer Rhodes	Curtis Kitchener	Clements Plume	Key Jacks	Machin Welsh	Tudor Neil	Gibson Hunt*	Rees Dunphy Armstrong	With Wolves losing at Palace, City clinch the title on another dramatic day. A relaxed City play flowing football which deserves more goals. Key fires in from Machin's sweet pass, Lewis sets up Tudor, and Machin and Gibbo set up a classy third. Hill leads the singing afterwards.
			32,551	8		59														
		Home Average 28,245	Away 18,996																		

LEAGUE DIVISION 2 (CUP-TIES) Manager: Jimmy Hill SEASON 1966-67

League Cup

			Att	F-A		H-T	Scorers, Times, and Referees	1	2	3	4	5	6	7	8	9	10	11	12 sub used
2	H	DERBY	7	2:1	W	1-0	Farmer 33, Clements 58	Glazier	Kearns	Burckitt	Farmer	Curtis	Bruck	Rees	Gibson	Gould	Pointer	Clements	
			14,804	22			Hodgson 85	Matthews	Richardson	Daniel	Webster	Saxton	Waller	Hughes	Thomas	Buxton	Draper	Hodgson	
							Ref: A Dimond	Derby fail to clear a Gibson cross and Farmer fires home. Reg Matthews is booed after fouling Pointer. Glazier saves well from Draper but Hodgson scores from the rebound. Kearns' long ball finds Clements, whose first is parried, but he scores from the rebound. Kearns' penalty, harshly given against Brian Hill, and saves Gould's late shot. Rees' shot is levelled when Collins' shot spins off Kearns' boot. Glazier saves Collins' penalty. Draper's late shot goes wide.												
3	A	BRIGHTON	8	1:1	D	1-0	Rees 18	Glazier	Kearns	Bruck	Hill	Curtis	Clements	Key	Tudor	Gould	Gibson	Rees	
			13,007	3:22			Collins 80	Powney	Henderson	Baxter	Collins	Gall	Turner	Wilkinson	Cassidy	Whittington	Gould		
							Ref: R Paine	After failing to kill off Archie Macauley's struggling team when they had the chances City are hanging on for dear life at the end. Glazier saves Collins' penalty, harshly given against Brian Hill, and saves Gould's late shot. Rees' shot is levelled when Collins' shot spins off Kearns' boot.												
3R	H	BRIGHTON	10	1:3	L	1:2	Gould 9	Glazier	Coop	Kearns	Roberts	Curtis	Farmer	Rees*	Machin	Gould	Pointer	Mitten	
			13,437	3:19			Livesey 16, Cassidy 44, Wilkinson 58	Powney	Henderson	Baxter	Collins	Gall	Turner	Wilkinson	Livesey	Cassidy	Whittington	Gould	
							Ref: J Mitchell	A League Cup disaster, the day after Gibson asks for a transfer, means it's crisis time. Brighton, who also hit wood twice, are deserved winners over clueless City. Rees is off with damaged ligaments and Glazier errs for the first goal. The game ends with boos and Brighton in control.												

FA Cup

			Att	F-A		H-T	Scorers, Times, and Referees	1	2	3	4	5	6	7	8	9	10	11	12 sub used
3	H	NEWCASTLE	1	3:4	L	2:3	McNamee 4 (og), Gibson 21, Rees 76	Glazier	Kearns	Bruck	Farmer	Curtis	Clements	Key	Machin	Gould	Gibson*	Rees	Morrissey
			35,748	1:21			Davies 2, 30, 75, Robson B 3	Marshall	Burton	Clark	Elliott	McNamee	McGrath	Robson B	Bennett	Davies	Iley	Hilley	
							Ref: L Callaghan	After a slow start City fight back, but out-of-touch Gould misses a sitter to grab a replay. The ruthless Davies is irrepressible and too much for Curtis. Iley runs the show, especially after the break when Gibson is injured. Gibbo's full-tilt header and Davies' first are the pick of the goals.												

	P	W	D	L	Home F	A	W	D	L	Away F	A	Pts
1 COVENTRY	42	17	3	1	46	16	6	10	5	28	27	59
2 Wolves	42	15	4	2	53	20	10	4	7	35	23	58
3 Carlisle	42	15	3	3	42	16	8	3	10	29	38	52
4 Blackburn	42	13	6	2	33	11	6	7	8	23	35	51
5 Ipswich	42	11	8	2	45	25	6	8	7	25	29	50
6 Huddersfield	42	11	3	4	36	17	6	6	9	22	29	49
7 Crys Palace	42	14	4	3	42	23	5	6	10	19	32	48
8 Millwall	42	14	5	2	33	17	4	4	13	16	41	45
9 Bolton	42	10	7	4	36	19	4	7	10	28	39	42
10 Birmingham	42	11	5	5	42	23	5	3	13	28	43	40
11 Norwich	42	10	7	4	31	21	3	7	11	18	34	40
12 Hull	42	11	5	5	46	25	5	2	14	31	47	39
13 Preston	42	14	3	4	44	23	2	4	15	21	44	39
14 Portsmouth	42	7	5	9	34	37	6	8	7	25	33	39
15 Bristol C	42	10	8	3	38	22	2	6	13	18	40	38
16 Plymouth	42	12	4	5	42	21	2	5	14	17	37	37
17 Derby	42	8	6	7	40	32	4	6	11	28	40	36
18 Rotherham	42	10	5	6	39	28	3	5	13	22	42	36
19 Charlton	42	11	4	6	34	16	2	5	14	15	37	35
20 Cardiff	42	9	7	5	43	28	3	2	16	18	59	33
21 Northampton	42	8	6	7	28	33	4	0	17	19	51	30
22 Bury	42	9	3	9	31	30	2	3	16	18	53	28
	924	253	111	98	858	503	98	111	253	503	858	924

Odds & ends

Double wins: (5) Portsmouth, Bury, Charlton, Blackburn, Wolves.
Double losses: (0).
Won from behind: (3) Preston (h), Carlisle (h), Wolves (h).
Lost from in front: (2) Huddersfield (a), Brighton LC (h).
High spots: 25-match unbeaten run – a club record.
Scenes at Highfield Road after Wolves and Millwall games.
5-0 drubbing of leaders Ipswich in December.
Gould's goalscoring feats.
Low spots: Brighton League Cup defeat.
Patchy autumn form.
Newcastle defeat in FA Cup.
Red Cards City: (0).
Red cards opponents: (4) Davidson (Hull h), Hockey (Birmingham h), Ross (Carlisle h), Ferguson (Blackburn a).
Hat-tricks: (1) Gould (Ipswich h).
Opposition hat-tricks: (1) Wyn Davies (Newcastle FAC h).
Leading scorer: (25) Bobby Gould.

Appearances and Goals

	Appearances Lge	Sub	LC	Sub	FAC	Sub	Goals Lge	LC	FAC	Tot
Bruck, Dietmar	38							2		2
Burckitt, John			1							
Clements, Dave	40		3		1		4	1		5
Coop, Mick	2	2	1							
Curtis, George	42		3		1		2			2
Farmer, Ron	32	2	2		1		2	1		3
Gibson, Ian	31		2		1		8		1	9
Glazier, Bill	41		3		1					
Glover, Benny		1								
Gould, Bobby	38	1	3		1		24	1		25
Hill, Brian	15	1	1							
Kearns, Mick	41		3		1		1			1
Key, John	21	1	1		1		6			6
Lewis, Brian	13									
Lowes, Barry	3									
Machin, Ernie	34		1		1		11			11
Mitten, John	8	2		1			1			1
Morrissey, Pat		1				1				
Pointer, Ray	7		2				2			2
Rees, Ronnie	39		3		1		3	1	1	5
Roberts, Dudley		1								
Thomas, Peter	1									
Tudor, John	16	1					8		1	8
(own-goals)									1	1
23 players used	462	11	33	1	11	1	74	4	3	81

LEAGUE DIVISION 1 — Manager: Jimmy Hill — SEASON 1967-68

No	Date		Att	Pos	Pt	F-A	H-T	Scorers, Times, and Referees	1	2	3	4	5	6	7	8	9	10	11	12 sub used
1	19/8	A BURNLEY	21,483		L 0	1-2	0-1	Merrington 81 (og) Casper 32, Irvine 62 Ref: K Howley	Glazier Thomson	Kearns Angus	Bruck Latcham	Farmer O'Neill	Curtis Merrington	Clements Todd	Key Morgan	Machin Bellamy	Tudor Irvine	Lewis Harris	Rees Casper	

7,000 City fans witness City's Division 1 debut and their first league defeat for nine months and 25 games. Manager Hill's resignation does not seem to affect the players, who appear in a strange all-white kit. Casper scores on his debut and Irvine nets when Glazier spills Morgan's shot.

| 2 | 22/8 | A NOTT'M FOREST | 44,950 | | D 1 | 3-3 | 3-2 | Gould 19, 27, Machin 38 Baker 22, Wignall 36, Moore 53p Ref: A Jones | Glazier Grummitt | Kearns Hindley | Bruck Winfield | Farmer Hennessey | Curtis* McKinley | Clements Newton | Key Lyons | Machin Chapman | Tudor Baker | Lewis Wignall | Rees Moore* | Gould Hinton |

The gates are locked. In a dramatic match with last season's runners up Curtis breaks a leg in the fourth minute in a tackle with Wignall. Bobby Gould makes his top flight bow as sub and scores twice. City lead three times but are pegged back by a deflected free-kick and a penalty.

| 3 | 26/8 | H SHEFFIELD UTD | 33,328 | 16 17 | D 2 | 2-2 | 1-1 | Key 19, Bruck 56 Reece 7, Cliff 52 Ref: M Sinclair | Glazier Hodgkinson | Kearns Badger | Bruck Shaw | Lewis Munks | Knapp Matthewson | Clements Wagstaff | Key* Cliff | Machin Fenoughty | Gould Jones | Tudor Birchenall | Rees Reece | Morrissey |

The sapping heat, a Glazier 'howler' and the Blades intention on a draw all take the edge off City's first home Division 1 game. John Key's header from a Rees corner is the best goal of the game. Dietmar Bruck saves a point with a low deceptive shot following Machin's free-kick.

| 4 | 29/8 | H NOTT'M FOREST | 41,212 | 21 2 | L 2 | 1-3 | 0-2 | Rees 81 Baker 5, 62, Moore 41 Ref: W Gow | Glazier Grummitt | Kearns Hindley | Bruck Winfield | Denton Hennessey | Coop McKinley | Clements Newton | Lewis Lyons | Machin Barnwell* | Gould Baker | Rees Wignall | Rees Moore | Hinton |

On paper, defeat is predictable. On the field a cruelly depleted City side strive with such gallantry that the score does them no justice. Kearns plays at centre-half for the injured Knapp. Glazier has a shaky game, parrying a cross to Baker for the first and missing a cross for the second.

| 5 | 2/9 | A ARSENAL | 30,404 | 19 12 | D 3 | 1-1 | 1-0 | Gould 29 Graham 79 Ref: P Walters | Glazier Furnell | Kearns Storey | Bruck McNab* | Farmer McLintock | Knapp Neill | Clements Simpson | Lewis* Johnston | Machin Addison | Gould Graham | Tudor Sammels | Rees Armstrong | Carr Court |

First ever visit to Highbury. Arsenal miss chances before Graham gives them a well deserved point after a Glazier-Clements mix-up. Gould takes a superb Machin through-ball around Furnell before slotting home. 18-year-old Willie Carr catches the eye and Glazier is back to his best.

| 6 | 5/9 | H SOUTHAMPTON | 32,986 | 15 8 | W 5 | 2-1 | 0-0 | Tudor 59, Rees 64 Chivers 49 Ref: J Warburton | Glazier Forsyth | Kearns Webb | Bruck Hollywood | Farmer Fisher | Knapp Gabriel | Clements Walker | Carr Paine | Machin Chivers | Gould Davies* | Tudor Melia | Rees* Sydenham | Morrissey Wimshurst |

The highly vaunted Davies-Chivers strikeforce is thwarted by Davies' back injury. City record their first win in a patchy, ill-tempered game with four bookings and 101 minutes played. Rees scores when the ref plays on after a bad tackle and Saints hesitate. City hang on desperately.

| 7 | 9/9 | H MANCHESTER C | 34,578 | 17 5 | L 5 | 0-3 | 0-1 | Hince 37, Summerbee 61, Bell 70 Ref: H New | Glazier Dowd | Kearns Book | Bruck Pardoe | Lewis Doyle | Knapp Heslop | Clements Oakes | Key Hince | Machin Bell | Gould Summerbee | Tudor Young | Rees* Coleman | |

The hunt for a new manager continues with Revie and Allison tipped. Mercer's men give Coventry a hiding but the resistance is puny. Colin Bell's goal is the best: he mesmerises the defence before firing home. Coventry's injury list grows longer; the stars of Division 2 are fading.

| 8 | 16/9 | A NEWCASTLE | 28,890 | 21 12 | L 5 | 2-3 | 2-2 | Rees 14, Gould 20 Davies 24, Iley 44, Bennett 72 Ref: D Laing | Glazier McFaul | Coop Craig | Bruck Guthrie | Lewis Elliott | Knapp McGrath | Clements Moncur | Carr Bennett | Machin Scott | Gould Davies | Gibson* Iley | Rees Robson | Farmer |

Ian Gibson runs the game for 20 minutes, creates two goals from corners but then is injured. City fall to pieces and superb headers from Wyn Davies, the best header of a ball in Britain, and Albert Bennett, together with a Jim Iley goal right on half-time leave them in the bottom two.

| 9 | 23/9 | H WEST BROM | 31,258 | 17 21 | W 7 | 4-2 | 2-1 | Lewis 14, Rees 43, 77, Machin 58 Astle 9, Clark 46 Ref: J Finney | Glazier Osborne | Coop Colquhoun | Bruck Williams | Lewis Collard* | Knapp Talbut | Clements Campbell | Rees Stephens | Morrissey Kaye | Gould* Astle | Machin Hope | Clements Clark | Tudor Treacy |

A convincing victory over Alan Ashman's struggling side after a run of bad results. Hill makes his Div 1 debut and shackles Kaye, Coop keeps a tight win on Clark. City win it with a gritty display in the last 20 minutes when the points are in the balance. On a sore note, Gould is injured.

| 10 | 30/9 | A CHELSEA | 29,800 | 16 19 | D 8 | 1-1 | 0-0 | Clements 64 Boyle 78 Ref: D Brady | Glazier Bonetti | Kearns Thomson | Bruck Butler | Morrissey Hollins | Knapp Waldron | Hill Harris | Rees Cooke | Machin Baldwin | Tudor Osgood | Lewis McCreadie | Clements Tambling* | Boyle |

Chelsea, with seven internationals, are going through a bad spell and don't have the stomach for a fight. But for Bonetti, City would have been easy winners before the late equaliser. Glazier saves Cooke's penalty two minutes from time after the same player is tripped by Mick Kearns.

206

Jimmy Hill's last match in charge

11	A	SHEFFIELD WED	18	L	0-4	0-3							*[Fantham 87]*
7/10		33,360	1	8			Glazier	Coop	Kearns	Morrissey	Knapp	Hill	Rees	Machin	Roberts	Lewis	Clements
							Springett	*Quinn*	*Megson*	*Mobley*	*Ellis*	*Young*	*Usher*	*Fantham*	*Ritchie*	*McCalliog**	*Eustace*
		McCalliog 2, Mobley 33, Eustace 41,															*Branfoot*
		Ref: F Nicholson															

The end of a week when veteran Ron Farmer moves to Notts County and Alan Dicks becomes Bristol City manager. Wednesday hammer City without breaking sweat. The game is over before half-time and but for Bill Glazier the scoreline could have been doubled. The Owls go top.

League Cup

2	H	ARSENAL	17	L	1-2	0-0	Machin 77	Glazier	Coop	Bruck*	Lewis	Knapp	Clements	Key	Machin	Gould	Rees
12/9		22,605	1.6				*Sammels 45, Graham 58*	*Furnell*	*Storey*	*Simpson*	*McLintock*	*Neill*	*Ure*	*Radford*	*Addison*	*Graham*	*Armstrong*	Carr
							Ref: V Batry											*Sammels*

Even with the returning Gibson and Machin, City lack the subtlety to break down a compact Arsenal. City work hard but it is uphill after Jon Sammels' superb volley. Strong City penalty claims are turned down before Machin squeezes in a consolation, following good work by Gibson.

List of Subscribers and Favourite Players

Andrew Achenbach	Dave Clements	Clive Lennox	Ronnie Rees
Phil Aston	George Hudson	Martin Lenton	George Hudson
David Austin	George Hudson	Trevor Lloyd	George Curtis
Paul Baker	Bill Glazier	Dave Long	Bill Glazier
Mark Barnes	George Curtis	Alan Ludford	George Curtis
Paul Barton	Bill Glazier	Terry McCauley	Bill Glazier
Philip Beauchamp		R McDonough	George Curtis
Clive Beevers	Bobby Gould	Paul McFarland	George Curtis
David Beidas		John McGinnity	George Hudson
Steve Berry	George Curtis	Jim McIlwaine	George Hudson
Christopher P Bevan	Bill Glazier	Paul McKevlie	George Curtis
Richard Bullard	George Hudson	Michael May	George Hudson
Brendan Burke	Dietmar Bruck	Robert Marlow	George Hudson
Jack Clarke	Clarrie Bourton	Alan Miller	George Curtis
John Clarke OBE	George Hudson	Joe Mohan	George Curtis
Don Chalk	George Hudson	Geoffrey Moore	Bobby Gould
Gary Clifford	George Hudson	Dean Nelson	George Curtis
Keith Clifford	George Hudson	John Oughton	George Curtis
Nicholas Cook	George Curtis	David Owen	
J Currington	George Hudson	Matthew Owen	
Ian Davidson	George Curtis	Steve Pittam	George Curtis
Mike Davies	George Curtis	Stephen Price	
Rod Dean	George Hudson	Frank Pritchard	George Hudson
John Douglas	George Hudson	Warren Purvis	
Steve Draper	Dave Clements	Leslie Raven	George Curtis
Bob Eales		Michael Riddell	George Curtis
Mr C Foulkes	Dave Clements	Kevin Ring	Willie Humphries
Ray Gee	George Curtis	Jon Rishworth	George Hudson
Mark Georgevic		Colin Roberts	Bill Glazier
Richard Goodyer	George Hudson	R M Sanders	George Curtis
Ian Greaves	George Curtis	Rev G H Sayers	George Hudson
John Grice	George Hudson	C Schoales	Bill Glazier
Martin Griffiths	George Curtis	David J Sidwell	Dave Clements
Pete Handy	George Curtis	Michael Smith	George Curtis
Ian Harris	Bobby Gould	Mick Sollis	George Curtis
Martyn Moose Harris	George Curtis	Bernie Spencer	George Hudson
Paul R Howard	George Curtis	Jonathan Strange	George Curtis
Bob Howe	George Curtis	Colin Taylor	Bill Glazier
Richard Hulbert	Ian Gibson	Anthony Thomas	Bill Glazier
Roger Hulbert	George Curtis	Chris Tims	George Curtis
Mick Jackson	George Curtis	Brendon Twomey	Bobby Gould
Mr R Jacques	Ian Gibson	Beverly Underhill	George Curtis
Glyn John	George Curtis	Keith White	George Hudson
Dave Jones	George Hudson	Tim Wilding	Ernie Machin
John Keningale	George Hudson	Graham Williams	Bill Glazier
Tony Kiely	John Key	Richard Woodfield	Derek Henderson
P J King		Steve Woodfield	George Curtis
Chris Lamb	George Hudson	John Young	George Hudson
Chris Lambert	Ernie Machin	Mike Young	George Hudson
Graham Law	George Hudson		
T Lawlor			
Malcolm Lee	Ian Gibson		
John Leekey	George Curtis		

12 DIFFERENT NAMES RECEIVED VOTES
1ST GEORGE CURTIS
2ND GEORGE HUDSON
3RD BILL GLAZIER